THE COMPLETE IDIOT'S GUIDE® TO

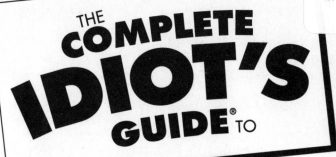

Pirates

by Gail Selinger
with W. Thomas Smith Jr.

ALPHA

A member of Penguin Group (USA) Inc.

ALPHA BOOKS

Published by the Penguin Group

Penguin Group (USA) Inc., 375 Hudson Street, New York, New York 10014, U.S.A.

Penguin Group (Canada), 10 Alcorn Avenue, Toronto, Ontario, Canada M4V 3B2 (a division of Pearson Penguin Canada Inc.)

Penguin Books Ltd., 80 Strand, London WC2R 0RL, England

Penguin Ireland, 25 St Stephen's Green, Dublin 2, Ireland (a division of Penguin Books Ltd.)

Penguin Group (Australia), 250 Camberwell Road, Camberwell, Victoria 3124, Australia (a division of Pearson Australia Group Pty. Ltd.)

Penguin Books India Pvt. Ltd., 11 Community Centre, Panchsheel Park, New Delhi—110 017, India

Penguin Group (NZ), cnr Airborne and Rosedale Roads, Albany, Auckland 1310, New Zealand (a division of Pearson New Zealand Ltd.)

Penguin Books (South Africa) (Pty.) Ltd., 24 Sturdee Avenue, Rosebank, Johannesburg 2196, South Africa

Penguin Books Ltd., Registered Offices: 80 Strand, London WC2R 0RL, England

Copyright © 2006 by Gail Selinger

International Standard Book Number: 1-59257-376-2
Library of Congress Catalog Card Number: 2005937192

08 07 06   8 7 6 5 4 3 2 1

Interpretation of the printing code: The rightmost number of the first series of numbers is the year of the book's printing; the rightmost number of the second series of numbers is the number of the book's printing. For example, a printing code of 06-1 shows that the first printing occurred in 2006.

Printed in the United States of America

Note: This publication contains the opinions and ideas of its authors. It is intended to provide helpful and informative material on the subject matter covered. It is sold with the understanding that the authors and publisher are not engaged in rendering professional services in the book. If the reader requires personal assistance or advice, a competent professional should be consulted.

The authors and publisher specifically disclaim any responsibility for any liability, loss, or risk, personal or otherwise, which is incurred as a consequence, directly or indirectly, of the use and application of any of the contents of this book.

Most Alpha books are available at special quantity discounts for bulk purchases for sales promotions, premiums, fund-raising, or educational use. Special books, or book excerpts, can also be created to fit specific needs.

For details, write: Special Markets, Alpha Books, 375 Hudson Street, New York, NY 10014.

Publisher: *Marie Butler-Knight*
Editorial Director: *Mike Sanders*
Senior Managing Editor: *Jennifer Bowles*
Senior Acquisitions Editor: *Paul Dinas*
Development Editor: *Lynn Northrup*
Senior Production Editor: *Janette Lynn*
Copy Editor: *Keith Cline*
Cartoonist: *Richard King*
Book Designer: *Trina Wurst*
Cover Designer: *Bill Thomas*
Indexer: *Heather McNeill*
Layout: *Brian Massey*
Proofreading: *Donna Martin*

Contents at a Glance

Contents

Appendixes

Foreword

Everyone has heard of pirates. We read about them in comics and adventure novels. Their swashbuckling figures stomp about our living rooms, courtesy of the television screen. Because of pirate films made by dashing actors like Errol Flynn and Johnny Depp, we can feel the terror these larger-than-life characters inspire as the skull-and-crossbones flag is raised on that nearby craft with its sleek masts. I know what it must have been like to hear the yells and derisive chants of the cutlass-wielding ruffians who are perched on the rails and in the rigging, ready to board our treasure-laden ship.

The colorful legends tell us what follows, too—how the pirates swing on ropes over the narrowing gap between the two ships, and arrive on our decks with a menacing thump of high boots. Steel clangs on steel, pistols spit flame and bullets, sailors howl defiance, bodies fall, beautiful women cower on the poop. What happens after our ship is seized is equally infamous. Casks of spirits are broken open. Rum-soaked ruffians stagger about, bedecked with stolen jewels and finery, competing to commit unthinkable atrocities.

However, while all of this occurred at certain times and in certain seas throughout history, the real story of the pirates encompasses a great deal more. Because the tales have been told and retold, and embellished and re-embellished, over the centuries the colorful figures and events have achieved the status of mere folklore, fictional characters, and conquests no longer regarded as the truth. *The Complete Idiot's Guide to Pirates* repairs this situation, by turning vague pirate lore into blood-pounding real pirate history. As the authors demonstrate, not only are the most hair-raising legends not exaggerations at all, but even more dramatic than the storybook versions to which we've grown accustomed.

In orderly fashion, this book describes the origins of pirates, privateers, corsairs, and buccaneers—their earliest records, where they came from, and what drove them to take up the bloody pursuit. Not only do we learn about the conditions onboard pirate ships and the lives that buccaneers passed ashore, but we are told about the politics of parliaments and monarchs that have, by turns, encouraged and discouraged piracy. *The Complete Idiot's Guide to Pirates* reveals such little-known facts, for instance, as that the U.S. Congress authorized a peacetime navy only because of the depredations of Barbary pirates on American shipping; that merchants in Boston, Philadelphia, and Charleston made "respectable" fortunes out of plunder bought and sold; and that the prosperity of the village of New York was founded on piratical spoils carried into port.

While we already know the romantic legend that lovely ladies were the victims of pirates, this book also discusses the small but significant number of pirates who were women themselves—women who not only defied the conventions of their sex, but the law of the sea, as well. As well as this, it puts the lie to a number of longstanding pirate myths, such as the fallacy that pirates made their victims walk the plank and that they buried their treasure instead of enjoying it while they could. Instead, we learn real historical facts that are even more fascinating.

The Complete Idiot's Guide to Pirates is an entertaining and lively overview that is dotted with villains a thousand times more gaudy than their fictional counterparts. It portrays the men—and women—as they really were, by giving their occasional gallantries their due, and unflinchingly describing their overriding nastiness. By providing the facts behind the deliciously thrilling fiction, and sieving truth from legend, the authors replace our often romantic notions with the excitement of historic truth. The result is more enthralling and enriching than even the most florid legend can be.

—Joan Druett

Joan Druett is a maritime historian and author of many books, including *She Captains* and *Shark Island*, part of the Wiki Coffin maritime mystery series.

Introduction

Pirates are a strange and fascinating breed of fighting men (sometimes women), and fighting men they were and are. Most people have a fairly accurate perception of pirates—particularly those from the Golden Age of piracy—as a complex mix of terrorist, sailor, sometimes soldier, unwashed brigand and perfumed dandy, most with a dash of Robin Hood, and each with his own colorful personality.

Piracy is global, and it has existed since man first went "down to the sea in ships." Pirates have been sighted and reported from Tortuga and the Carolinas to Malta, the Barbary Coast, down and around the dangerous Horn of Africa, and up into the Indian Ocean and the Western Pacific. They have murdered, burned, tortured, bankrupted global businesses, forced navies to alter strategy, and generally confounded world powers.

Who were these dark warriors often under black flags who sailed the oceans of the world? Here in *The Complete Idiot's Guide to Pirates*, we unmask them.

Pirates have had an enormous impact on world history—destroying entire civilizations and literally altering ethnic gene pools before the beginning of the twelfth century.

Although some pirates were thieves and murderers before they ever set foot onto a ship, many were forced into the so-called "sweet trade" both by decisions their nations' governments enacted and the religious wars that waged throughout Europe.

By the fifteenth century, after these men and women had tasted the freedom that piracy granted them over such severe governmental laws that even dictated the styles of clothes and colors they were legally allowed to wear, they had no desire to return to a lawful life. These were daring, colorful individuals who felt they had a far better chance at a good life as a criminal at sea than they had on land.

By the mid-1700s there were thousands of pirates sailing the oceans. European navies were small in comparison to the pirate fleets that sailed, and they were unable to capture any significant percentage of these cutthroats. The only solution agreed upon by many heads of state was to reduce pirate numbers by issuing pardons and hoping the majority would decide to go straight.

Piracy was not relegated to Europe, the Caribbean, and the eastern coast of North America. The pirates of Asia and Africa were as fierce and terrifying as any others.

One book cannot possibly recount the life of every known pirate or each complex reason that drove them to sea. There have been hundreds of volumes written about pirates. Some are general histories. Others are written about one individual or incident in time.

The Complete Idiot's Guide to Pirates will provide you with a solid understanding of pirates, piracy, and the issues that influenced both. So come aboard as we sail back to the beginning, when farming and trading tribes first tentatively ventured onto the waters to the fierce speedboat pirates of the twenty-first century.

What You'll Find in This Book

This book is divided into four parts:

Part 1, "Man Builds Raft, Neighbor Steals Raft," explores the fascination of pirate myths. It takes you through piracy's impact on the very beginnings of civilization itself. The impact of colonial expansion by European countries building empires through the reign of Queen Elizabeth I and the pirates that plagued them along the way.

Part 2, "The Sweet Trade," discusses how governmental policies and military codes of conduct through the years unwittingly created the first democratic society, ironically made up of pirates, why men chose to become pirates, and their life on the sea.

Part 3, "The Golden Age of Piracy," looks at how pirates operated to their greatest advantage, the chances they took with their very lives in sailing long distances for a chance at treasure. How commerce shielded them from the law and then oddly turned against them.

Part 4, "The End of Piracy? Think Again," details the actions of pirates who helped build the United States by their actions. It explores the great pirate empires in the Mediterranean and the pirate dynasties in Asia (where piracy is a constant threat even today).

You'll also find three appendixes: a glossary, for greater ease in understanding nautical terms and slang of the time; books and websites, to learn more about pirates; and information on reenactment groups, if you'd like to step back into history for a time and experience pirate life firsthand.

Charting Your Course

We've included four types of sidebars to help you sail through the narrative and add to your journey:

Pirate Yarns

Yarns are stories, and here you'll unearth the truth surrounding many a pirate myth and tall tale.

Dead Men's Tales

From beyond the grave you'll hear the adventures firsthand through letters, journals, and trial transcripts.

Knowing the Ropes

In these boxes you'll learn many definitions surrounding pirate life.

Treasure Chest

Here you'll find many gems of information waiting to be discovered.

A Thank-You Goes to Thee

This book would not have been a reality without the help of some wonderful people. To my sister Carol Sue for her remarkable moral support, countless hours of rewrites, and all-nighters—she can now recite this book by heart. To Captain Erik H. Berliner, my cheering section, love of my life, legal eagle, for his vast patience and nautical knowledge. My computer guru, Kevin Ryan, without whom I might have been forced to write on parchment with a feather quill and handmade ink. Louie Lambie, for his extreme graciousness and for trusting me with both his antiques and images. The amazing unselfish contributions of Ron Druett. William Perlis, whose photographs helped make the past come alive. Asenath Hammond for watching after me with her humor, genius, creativity, and generosity. My knowledgeable pirate fact checkers: Maria Blumberg, Christine Markel Lampe, and Michael Lampe. If you find a wrong fact in this book, the duel is with me. Kate Lennon Walker, librarian and collections manager, U.S.S. *Constitution* Museum, for digging up those little known facts. Lynn Northrup, for taking me through the proper steps; W. Thomas Smith Jr. for the lessons; and Paul Dinas for the opportunity to tell this story. To Wood Nymph and Lollipop, "look at me!" and Denise Little for just about everything. I tip my tankard to you all!

Special Thanks to the Technical Reviewer

The Complete Idiot's Guide to Pirates was reviewed by an expert who double-checked the accuracy of what you'll learn here, to help us ensure that this book gives you everything you need to know about pirates. Special thanks are extended to Joan Druett.

Trademarks

All terms mentioned in this book that are known to be or are suspected of being trademarks or service marks have been appropriately capitalized. Alpha Books and Penguin Group (USA) Inc. cannot attest to the accuracy of this information. Use of a term in this book should not be regarded as affecting the validity of any trademark or service mark.

Part 1

Man Builds Raft, Neighbor Steals Raft

From the misty fleets of the ancient world to the birth of piracy's "Golden Age" in the late seventeenth century, rogue mariners have sailed the seven seas—and then some—on a quest for treasure and a better life. The risk was high. The rewards were great. Adventure was virtually guaranteed.

Here we take a look at post–Golden Age and contemporary culture and its influence on popular perceptions and misperceptions of pirates. We also examine the early history of pirates and piracy's threat to the Roman Empire, Vikings as pirates, Spain, England, and the fact that not all swashbucklers were men.

Chapter 1

Pirates of Popular Culture and Ancient History

In This Chapter

- ◆ Our continuing fascination with pirates
- ◆ Pirate? Buccaneer? Pirate lingo explained
- ◆ Sea raiding starts early
- ◆ Pirates terrorize the Roman Empire
- ◆ Queen Teuta declares war
- ◆ Rome fights back

Pirate! The very word brings to mind images of crashing, smoking shipboard battles beneath white sails and black flags, buried treasure, and exotic places . . . Captain Kidd, Blackbeard, and others whose names are synonymous with adventure, treasure, and daring deeds . . . or terror for those who might have been on the receiving ends of their swords and pistols.

The so-called "golden age of piracy," from 1692 to 1725, was relatively short-lived, and it only took a few years after much of the known world's piracy was quashed that people living throughout the Western world began to develop a somewhat distorted view of who these rogues really were. By the late nineteenth century, pirates had become heroes (and in some cases, heroines) or at least adventurous rapscallions who—based on the vivid imaginations of novelists and poets—were noble in their own way. Beyond that, our contemporary perception of pirates has been colored to a degree—by books, movies, and even product marketing—that their very reputations have achieved near-mythic proportions.

Interestingly, however, piracy actually began centuries before these colorful characters we now think of as "pirates" first captured our imaginations. Before we explore their beginnings, however, let's look at what's behind our continuing fascination with all things pirate.

Romantic Notions of Piracy

Author Robert Louis Stevenson was not the first novelist to publish a series of adventure stories about pirates. However, his tale for young boys, *Treasure Island* (published in 1883), almost single-handedly established European and American societies' perceptions of pirates and the world of piracy. Stevenson, a life-long student of "pirate history" and sailing, was able to infuse his stories with an immediacy and a sense of realism that few novels prior to *Treasure Island* had been able to accomplish. In fact, his work had such an impact on nineteenth- and twentieth-century popular culture that most of the general public in the twenty-first century are still convinced pirates marked maps and charts with big black X's pinpointing the exact locations of previously buried treasure.

Fiction with a Dash of Reality

J. M. Barrie's *Peter Pan and Wendy*, published in 1911, depicted a frightening pirate, Captain James Hook. The story was a grand, danger-fraught adventure, which has thrilled children for nearly 100 years (today in books, movies, and theater). Like Stevenson, Barrie had read the contemporary accounts of pirates written by the likes of Alexander Exquemelin and Charles Johnson. From those accounts, Barrie patterned Captain Hook after the notorious Captain Edward "Blackbeard" Teach, whom you'll meet in Chapter 17.

Pirates of the Silver Screen

Movies have further solidified the public perception of seventeenth- and eighteenth-century pirates and their deeds. Pirates made their first motion picture debut during the silent-film era. Filmed in 1920, *Treasure Island* starred the famous female actress Shirley Mason as young Jim Hawkins. The film's success guaranteed other films of the genre would follow. For years after *Treasure Island*, the overwhelming success of the first version of *Captain Blood* (1924) convinced Hollywood writers and directors that they had hit upon a magic formula. Actors such as Douglas Fairbanks Sr.—in the 1926 film *The Black Pirate*—further cemented the public perception of pirates as swashbuckling, roguish, Robin Hood–like characters.

Errol Flynn to Johnny Depp

Errol Flynn's first starring role in 1935 was in the remake of the film *Captain Blood*. As Fairbanks before him, Flynn became the image of all things piratical on and off screen. Between 1950 and 1953, nine pirate movies were made in North America. And women were not excluded as pirate heroines in this genre. Anne Peters portrayed Anne Bonny (see Chapter 19) in the 1951 film *Anne of the Indies*. As Spitfire Stevens in the 1952 adventure film *Against All Flags*, Maureen O'Hara portrayed a woman pirate who was tough, hardy, and independent. Women were no longer seen as simply meek and vulnerable. Decades later, *Cutthroat Island* (1997) featured Geena Davis as a female pirate who proved to be as tough as any man.

The public's fascination with pirates is not uniquely American. Pirate movies have been made in almost every country throughout the world. Pirate adventures continue to be shot as small independent films, direct to video, and children's television programs. American filmmakers still have a tremendous appreciation for the value and audience appeal of pirate movies. For example, the 2003 blockbuster movie *Pirates of the Caribbean: The Curse of the Black Pearl*, starring Johnny Depp, was so successful that two sequels are currently being filmed in the United States and the Caribbean. The first, *Pirates of the Caribbean: Dead Man's Chest*, is slated for release in the summer of 2006.

> **Treasure Chest**
>
> The addition of audio to film enhanced the realism, bringing the din of battle to thrilled audiences and, in many ways, making pirate movies of the period the model on which other adventure films would be based. It did not matter whether a pirate was cast as a villain or hero. Moviegoers simply couldn't get enough.

A Pirate Fan

Few are immune to the lure of and fascination with pirates, including first ladies of the United States. As a child, Jacqueline Bouvier Kennedy Onassis hung a pirate flag on her bedroom wall. She had a love for pirates that continued well into her adulthood. Author-journalist George Plimpton wrote about one pirate adventure with Jackie for *The New Yorker*.

Vacationing in Newport, Rhode Island, in 1965, Jackie decided to a throw a pirate party for her children and their friends. Asked to assist, Plimpton was surprised at the "childlike glee" she exhibited over the details. One feature of the party was a treasure hunt. The clues led the children to an actual buried treasure a few yards from Narragansett Bay. As the children dug for the treasure, a boatload of Jackie's friends dressed as pirates—including Senator Claiborne Pell—sailed up the bay. Intent on reclaiming their booty, a "fight" ensued. The children successfully defeated the pirates, who sailed away. As part of the event, Jackie had called the nearby Coast Guard station and persuaded the Coasties to lend her a longboat to add authenticity to the scenario. Ashore with the children, she signaled when the pirates were to attack. Even the Secret Service got into the act, one of whom Jackie persuaded to "walk the plank" into Narragansett Bay.

A Clever Marketing Tool

Liquor companies such as Seagram's also continue to perpetuate the pirate mystique and image. Their great promotional icon, representing an entire product line of the company's rum, is none other than the famous buccaneer, Captain Henry Morgan (see Chapter 8).

The Myth Versus the Reality

However exciting a pirate's life appears in rousing adventurous tales, the reality of their actions was far from noble. As you'll see, whether through social circumstances, changing political climate, or simply an individual's amoral personality, the majority of pirates were cold, bloodthirsty killers. But first, let's clarify the confusion surrounding what to call these individuals.

What's in a Name?

There is a great deal of confusion nowadays regarding the various terms people use interchangeably to describe pirates. However, for a pirate, what he was called often meant the difference between his (or her) life or death.

To understand the historical differences, here are a few simple definitions. The complex subtleties are expanded upon as you meet these men and women in future chapters:

- **Pirate.** A seafaring criminal who attacks ships of any nationality, during time of war or peace, for purposes of thievery and/or revenge.

- **Privateer.** During time of war, government officials legally commissioned "civilian" sailing men to attack enemy cities and ships. They were considered adjuncts to state navies (see Chapter 2).

- **Buccaneer.** Originally French and English game hunters of the seventeenth century living on the island of Hispaniola. Their hatred for the Spanish was so intense they actively attacked that country's ships and settlements (see Chapter 6).

- **Freebooter and filibuster.** Two different names used to describe French buccaneers.

- **Corsair.** The Anglicized French term for a privateer (see Chapter 2).

- **Barbary pirate/Barbary corsair.** Named by the French, these men sailed along the North African coast. Europeans considered them pirates. They considered themselves privateers (see Chapter 20).

 Pirate Yarns ⎯⎯⎯⎯⎯⎯⎯⎯⎯⎯⎯⎯⎯⎯⎯⎯⎯⎯⎯⎯⎯⎯⎯⎯⎯⎯⎯⎯⎯⎯

Swashbuckler is technically not an accurate term used to describe a pirate. In the sixteenth century, the term was slang for a land-based, sword-wielding bandit or brigand. Novelists in the early eighteenth century thought this a far more colorful metaphor that embodied the daring men whose tales they were recounting. Novelists and screenwriters continue to use the incorrect term. Swashbuckler has become synonymous with seafaring pirates, not highway robbers.

Let's Start from the Very Beginning

So when did seagoing piracy begin? The moment man lashed reeds together for boats to travel and trade along the waterways of the known world. Thieves and murderers have always been with us, as they always will be. And the earliest Minoan and Egyptian writings reveal tales of sea battles and land raids that were strikingly similar to the piratical actions that have continued throughout history to the present day.

Early Pirates of the Mediterranean

Mediterranean topography created an excellent environment for early piracy to flourish. The shorelines were rocky with hidden inlets and mountains that divided much of the area, forcing merchants to depend on the many rivers and inlets as trade routes. Great civilizations and empires emerged along these shorelines, which were constantly plagued by hordes of pirates. At times empires alternately banded together to fight piracy or each other for dominance of the waterways and lands.

These early pirates, despite their obvious villainy and ruthlessness, can be credited with having had a direct influence (though not for positive reasons) on many aspects of cultural advances within these civilizations from shipbuilding to weaponry and city fortification in the hopes of keeping the marauders at bay.

Where No Ship Has Gone Before

In 2000 B.C.E., the people we today refer to as Phoenicians were originally Semitic farming and trading tribes who called themselves Caananites or Sidonites for the coastal areas they settled. These areas correspond today with Lebanon, Syria, and Israel. While trading along the shorelines, the Phoenician merchants took to ships for easier and safer transport. Their major cities of commerce included Sidon, Tyre, and Berot (modern Beirut). While Phoenician traders became bolder and skilled seamen within their own territories, the Mediterranean had to deal with a new and serious threat.

Enter the "Sea People"

Between 1220 B.C.E. and 1186 B.C.E., marauders from mixed tribes known collectively as the "sea people" plagued Egypt, Syria, Cyprus, and Crete. Egyptian scribes specifically mention six of these tribes from the Adriatic and Aegean regions: the Tjeker, Weshesh, Shekelesh, Shardana, Denyen, and Peleset. They attacked merchant ships and plundered towns and cities for valuables ranging from coin to cattle, to men, women, and children for slave markets. In 1186 B.C.E., the warrior pharaoh, Ramses III, successfully quashed the activities of these early pirates. His victory is lauded in what is considered the first pictorial representation of

> **Dead Men's Tales**
>
> Lo, the northern countries, which are in their isles, are restless in their limbs; they [sea people] infest the sea routes of the harbor mouths.
>
> —Temple inscription, Thebes, Egypt, circa 1186 B.C.E.

a sea battle. This carved base relief adorns a temple near the city of Thebes (modern-day Luxor).

Between 1200 B.C.E. and 1000 B.C.E., the Greeks, beleaguered by raiders from the north, ceased their sea trading to concentrate primarily on defense. For the Phoenician seamen, this opened new options. They looked past their own shores to the vast new markets beyond their horizon. But first they needed ships that could safely transport them.

Formidable Galley Ships Sail the Seas

To better meet their countrymen's seafaring needs, Phoenician shipwrights modified the traditional one-masted oared galley sailed by Minoans and Egyptians. The design of the *gaulos*, their merchant ship, had a deeper, rounder hull than previous vessels, thus allowing for increased cargo capacity. Another innovation, the steering rudder oars placed on both sides of the ship's stern, provided quicker maneuvering.

With this formidable trading ship manned by courageous crewmembers, the Phoenicians sailed beyond the safe coastlines and known waters of the Mediterranean Sea to the great oceans in pursuit of new trade routes and goods.

Ships Built for Combat

Increased commerce led to bolder thievery. To quell these attacks, shipwrights once again modified their vessels, this time for defense. The *hippos* boasted a high curved bow and stern for ramming purposes. A section of the hull housed deadly catapults. The shallow, drafted ship allowed for swifter handling and greater speed, especially over bars and reefs. With a lifesaving feature, the medicine chest, this vessel was the state-of-the-art warship of its day. As an escort ship as well as a warship, it was regularly used to accompany merchant convoys.

The Payoff: Goods and Land

With the *gaulos* and the *hippos*, the Phoenicians became international traders, and their goods were impressive. They bought and sold wool, cloth, embroideries, wine, carved wood, ivory ornaments, Spanish silver, Baltic amber, and British tin. They smelted the tin with copper and created the strongest metal of the time, bronze.

Around 1500 B.C.E., the Phoenicians carried the shellfish murex from Mesopotamia (Iraq) which produced the purple dye used by wealthy Roman citizens and imperial royalty. By 814 B.C.E. they founded the city of Carthage in North Africa and regularly circumnavigated the African continent, an arduous three-year journey.

As pirate activity against the Phoenicians increased in their homeland, loosely banded Greek tribesmen from the northern areas came to their aid. The Greeks quickly adopted the Phoenician alphabet and way of life, and looked to better themselves at their mentors' expense. Through intermarriage, the Phoenician people and civilization were completely absorbed into the new Greek culture with the exception of those who had settled in Carthage.

Greeks: They May Wear Togas, but They're Tough

While Greek tribes slowly settled and established strong independent city-states, disputes over land and trade routes created constant friction and often resulted in military conflict. As a consequence, little help was offered to one another when pirates raided. Bands of dissatisfied Greeks began to attack the Phoenician and Greek merchant ships along the coastal waters.

The Greeks preferred sailing the *celes* (a.k.a. celox), a lightweight shallow-hulled 10-oared vessel the men could easily haul onto land. This enabled them to hide behind the many rocky crags, attack, and disappear with lightning speed.

Reprisal Strikes and the Beginnings of Privateering

Larceny became so commonplace across the Greek Empire that merchants who had been robbed by dishonest merchants from another city-state were legally allowed under Greek law to make reprisal strikes to recover the estimated value of their stolen property. Technically they were required to buy a license for this privilege, but most merchants did not do so.

In a clever misuse of this law, pirates often disguised their attacks as merchant reprisals. This is the beginning of the fine line between out-and-out piracy and sanctioned government reprisal, which would become known as privateering in the thirteenth century (see Chapter 2).

Merchant or Pirate?

As city-states became wealthier pirate attacks increased. Honest merchants and pirates alike sold all manner of goods from slaves to spices to markets in other city-states and to countries as far away as Persia (Iran), Africa, and India. It became difficult to discern who was a merchant and who was a pirate. The city-states tolerated raids for welcomed commerce as long as those pirates allied themselves with a particular city-state and did not attack their own people. In fact, ports were created to accommodate the merchandise from increased pirate activity.

Knowing the Ropes

Around the third or fourth century B.C.E., the Greeks coined the term *peirates* ("one who attacks") or *peiran* ("one who makes a hostile attempt"). Later the Romans expanded on these two terms and slightly altered the definition to the Latin *piratia* or *piraicos*, meaning "of or belonging to a pirate or robber on the sea." The Latin word *piratia* became, in the common vernacular, **pirate**.

City-States Hire Pirates to Do Their Dirty Work

Many city-states hired pirates to collect tribute, which was akin to protection money. A strong city-state or individual would force a subjugated or weaker city or individual to pay money to not be attacked. Athenian tax collectors were more often than not pirates. Their extensive knowledge of where every village and town was located became invaluable in extracting the required tributes to Athens.

Greece's Pirate Navies

When wars broke out between Greek city-states or foreign countries for dominance over the entire region, most governors found themselves in a bind. They had neither adequate finances nor a sufficient number of sailors to make up a strong naval force. These officials would turn to the more-organized pirates and "legally allowed" them into their navies with the promise of large profits.

With such carte blanche authority, pirates became even more brazen. They attacked not only villages and towns for goods and slaves, but kidnapped individuals for large ransoms. The unstated rule of not attacking those with whom you traded no longer held any credence.

Eventually, pirate attacks became so extensive and out of control that towns and villages, which had been first settled along the shores, moved farther inland and were fortified.

Pirate Yarns

The word *kielhalen* (or *keelhauling* in English) first entered modern records in 1666. The Dutch word means "to haul under keel of ship." Therefore it was wrongly assumed that this widely favored Western European naval punishment was first invented by the Dutch navy.

Putting the Pirate Genie Back in the Bottle

Local governments attempted to stem the tide of piracy, but this just escalated the wrath of these marauders. During this time, a record of further pirate brutality surfaced, that of keelhauling. This torturous death consisted of tying a person hand and foot with two long lengths of rope and then dropping the victim overboard. Pulling the ropes across the deck from bow to stern, the pirates would drag their captive underwater the entire length of the ship, repeating the process a number of times. Evidence of this cruel torture is depicted on an ancient Greek painted vase housed in the National Archeological Museum in Athens.

Alexander's Dilemma

Even Alexander the Great had to contend with fleets of pirate ships that roamed the Aegean. The pirates were either allied with the Persian Empire to weaken Alexander's military and naval power, or they were individual rogues merely bent on personal gain. Whatever the case, pirates once again, by their overwhelming presence on the waters, created a commercial crisis for Greece and the ever-expanding conquests of Alexander.

In 331 B.C.E., Alexander appointed his admiral Amphoterus to stop their activities. Pirates once again were driven from the waters, only to re-emerge upon Alexander's death.

Illyrians Terrorize the Seas

The collapse of the Greek Empire was due, in part, to the Greeks' inability to defend themselves against pirate attacks. This tipped the balance of power to the Roman Empire. While imperial Rome held an iron fist, militarily, over all the lands they had conquered, they allowed their economic water routes to go unchecked.

Meanwhile, Illyria—Albania, Serbia, and Montenegro—consisted of many powerful tribal federations. Between 233 B.C.E. and 231 B.C.E., the Illyrian King Agron led a successful campaign against his surrounding enemies. The Greek historian Polybius wrote of Agron's death. So pleased was he with the defeat of his enemy, the Aetolians, Agron overindulged for days in drink and pleasure. He ultimately caught pleurisy and died.

Agron's wife, Queen Teuta, assumed control of the kingdom and immediately declared everyone her enemy. She turned the navy into a privateering fleet. This allowed her sailors to freely attack ships and settlements along the Adriatic and Ionian Seas.

Swords in Jars

Teuta did not merely sit on her throne while money poured into her treasury from the constant raiding. Like Grace O'Malley many centuries later (see Chapter 5), Teuta personally commanded many attacks against her enemies.

In one instance, Teuta and her sailors landed near the Greek city of Epidamnos (Durres, Albania). Appearing to be unarmed, they carried large clay water jugs on their shoulders up to the city gates. There they began begging for drinking water. They cried that they were dying of thirst. Moved by their apparent plight, the gatekeepers opened the gates. At that point, the jars were broken. Teuta and her men grabbed their previously concealed swords and attacked. Taken completely by surprise, the forward-most guards were instantly killed. The city troops then rallied and were able to drive Teuta and her men away. Though thwarted at Epidamnos, the tactic of concealing weapons in clay jars proved highly successful during future raids.

Enough Is Enough!

By 230 B.C.E., the Illyrian fleet had virtually halted all honest trade. Rome was outraged. Roman citizens demanded the Senate put a stop to the plundering, murdering, and abductions. In 229 B.C.E., two brothers—Gaius and Lucius Coruncanius—met with Teuta as official envoys of Rome. The two diplomats requested that the Illyrian queen restrain her fleet. Teuta stated she could control her navy, but not a private individual from conducting criminal activities at sea. One of the Roman envoys lost his temper and threatened the queen with the military "big stick" of Rome. When the meeting was concluded, Teuta ordered the man killed.

Teuta's Enemies Become Rome's Allies

Outraged by the murder, the Senate immediately directed the Roman army and navy to suppress Teuta. To Rome it was apparent this Illyrian upstart did not understand her place within the sphere of the Roman world. That was about to change.

Roman Consul Gnaeus Fulvius sailed from Rome with 200 ships under his command. His fellow commander, Consul Aulus Postumius, led an overland attack with 20,000 infantry. Unaware of the newly launched campaign against her, Teuta continued raiding neighboring city-states. So terrorized by her privateer attacks, each city-state pledged allegiance to Rome if the Roman army would assure their protection. Rome readily agreed.

The Romans attacked in great strength, overwhelming and scattering Teuta's land and sea forces. The Illyrian queen escaped to her fortress in Rhizon (Risan on the Adriatic Sea) where she and her personal guard force were quickly besieged. In 228 B.C.E., Teuta surrendered and dispatched an envoy to Rome. Then she negotiated a treaty in which she agreed to pay annual tribute and relinquish much of her territorial holdings, including the entire Illyrian coast. She retained the right to sail only two unarmed galleys at a time. Teuta's days of wealth and glory were over.

Cilician Pirates Call the Shots

The vast majority of pirates operating in the known world now settled in Cilicia, a country in Asia Minor between Syria and Armenia. Like their Greek predecessors, Cilician pirates—along with honest merchants—provided a constant flow of ever-changing products and slaves. Roman coastal cities and islands such as Delos dotted the Aegean, freely opening their harbors to pirate ships that sailed in from all over the known world. The demand for slaves became so great that pirates banded together in small convoys and systematically sacked towns taking everything, including their entire citizenry to be sold at the various slave markets. Cilicia became a great pirate haven, its inhabitants numbered in the thousands. More men joined their ranks daily. Most of the newly recruited that joined were either poor, couldn't find honest work, or were fearful of being sold into slavery themselves.

Paying Tribute and an Early "Emancipation Proclamation"

To protect the citizenry and property, many villages and towns paid annual tribute to pirates in hopes of being spared the unfortunate circumstance of being raided.

In fact, pirates had become so proficient in their acquisition of slaves and the systematic destruction of farming communities (which provided the empire's food supply) that in 102 B.C.E., the Senate declared that free-born allies from city-states who were then slaves should be immediately set free and that all provincial governors of Rome had to ensure the decree was upheld. This decree effectively shut down the profitable pirate market in places such as Side and Delos. Furious but undaunted, the bad guys simply refocused their attention back to the waterways.

Now pirates began intercepting Roman grain ships bound for the capital. They then sold the stolen grain to other ports and countries.

Rome's Famous *Trireme*

In an attempt to curtail piracy, Rome employed her most advanced warship, the *Trireme*. This vessel was a three-level oared galley ship with a main mast and foresail. Unfortunately for the Roman navy, the triremes proved inferior to the pirates' superior seamanship and swifter galley ships.

Treasure Chest
Though documented dates vary, somewhere between 75 B.C.E. and 78 B.C.E., pirates captured 23-year-old Julius Caesar on his way to Rhodes. He was held for 6 weeks until his ransom of 50 talents was paid (a talent was approximately 25,200 grams of silver). Upon his release, young Julius fulfilled his threat to his captors. He tracked down all the pirates and had them crucified. However, being that the pirate leaders had treated him "fairly" during his captivity, Caesar ordered leniency for Spartaco, Micio, and Syrus: their throats were first slit before their bodies were nailed to the cross.

Mithridates and Athenodorus

The pirates allied themselves with King Mithridates of Pontus (an ancient city in Asia Minor on the Black Sea) and together they challenged the might of Rome. Aware that Rome was no longer the strong empire she once was, King Mithridates hoped that with the help of the pirate hordes he could assume total power and be ruler of the known world.

In a short span of time, the pirates under their leader Athenodorus attacked more than 400 towns. They brazenly sailed into Roman harbors and fired upon any ship that was in port. Trade was basically at a standstill.

Though they were eventually beaten back by Roman warships from the outlying areas of the empire, the pirates successfully blockaded the city of Rome itself.

Then in 69 B.C.E., Athenodorus's pirate fleet invaded and sacked the sacred island of Delos, where the main treasury of the Roman Empire was located.

> ### Treasure Chest
>
> The island of Delos is the legendary birthplace of the god Apollo and the goddess Artemis. It was an ancient center of religious, political, and commercial life in the Aegean. Rome in 166 B.C.E. made it a free commercial port and slave market. This was done by the Roman Senate to ensure the fall of Rhodes, both commercially and militarily. Though the Senate succeeded, with no Rhodian navy this strategy allowed the Cilician pirates unfettered access to the Mediterranean.

Rome Gains the Upper Hand

With the attack on Delos, the citizenry of Rome rose up and demanded that the Roman Peoples Assembly take action. They appointed General Pompeius Magnus (Pompey the Great) to wipe out the pirate threat plaguing the entire Mediterranean. Under great opposition by members of the Senate, he was given full gubernatorial power for three years over the entire Mediterranean area. His power reached 50 miles inland from many existing coastal areas and was concurrent with the existing governors of those regions. He was granted 25 assistants of senatorial rank.

The Assembly issued him the authority to raise as many ships and troops and as much money as needed. The historian Plutarch recorded that Pompeius was able to raise 120,000 foot soldiers (20 Roman legions) and 5,000 cavalrymen. He also commissioned 500 warships and raised 6,000 talents.

To quash fears that he was not up to the task or that he would attempt a military coup, Pompeius first deployed his men to secure the food supply to Rome. He next plotted a military campaign not only against the pirate stronghold on Cilicia Tracheia, but also against any other bands scattered throughout the Mediterranean.

Pompeius Organizes His Defenses

In 67 B.C.E., Pompeius divided the Mediterranean and Black Sea with the adjoining coastal areas into 13 commands, each controlled by a commander responsible for all coastal defense, the surrender of pirate prisoners, and the destruction of any strongholds. He brilliantly arranged the commands so that they also isolated any scattered bands of pirates operating within the areas and enlisted local governors and military to capture any fleeing marauders.

Catching Pirates

The swift attack took the marauders completely by surprise. By ordering leniency to any man who surrendered, Pompeius was able to extract information concerning all their hideouts.

The historian Appian documents that his campaign captured more than 400 pirate ships and destroyed 1,300 others. They killed 10,000 pirates who resisted, and some 20,000 others, along with their families, surrendered.

In a brilliant move, Pompeius did not imprison or execute his captives. Instead, he sent them throughout the empire to agricultural areas away from waterways to begin honest employment in the hopes the gesture would discourage any further outbreak of piracy. Within 49 days—not 3 years as originally projected—Pompeius rid the area of pirates.

Pompeius then tried to maintain a permanent naval fleet to patrol for any uprising. Because the old Greek governmental system of independent yet dependent city-states remained intact, his plan was not successful. Without the fleet, outbreaks of piracy began again, though not to their former degree. It can also be assumed that many of the pirates Pompeius had pardoned and hoped would "go straight" could not resist returning to their old ways.

Caesar, Octavian, and the Self-Proclaimed "Ruler of the Sea"

Upon becoming consul in 59 B.C.E.—and having had firsthand experience dealing with pirates—Julius Caesar was determined to completely rid the Roman territories of piracy. He actively pursued and punished pirates for the remainder of his life, and piracy in the region was dramatically reduced. Upon his death in 44 B.C.E., piracy resurfaced and began spreading as the Roman civil wars were waged for control of the empire. Pirates took advantage of the state's political upheaval and formed raiding syndicates. Piracy became epidemic.

Not all pirates who sailed the Aegean were desperate men without prospects for a better life. Paradoxically, some 20 years after Pompeius Magnus rid the seas of the great pirate scourge, his only son, Sextus Pompeius, turned to the pirate life, beginning off the shores of Spain. There he began building his own pirate fleet of former pirates and runaway slaves in an attempt to wrest control of the entire Roman Empire from Octavian, Caesar's rightful heir. From the beginning of his reign as a pirate until his defeat by Octavian's fleet, Sextus Pompeius gave himself the title "ruler of the sea" and demanded all the respect such a position should afford him.

However skilled his men were as sailors, Sextus himself was not a great strategist or tactician. He relied more on his fleet's own pirate commanders to form his battle tactics. Fortifying themselves on a base in Sicily, Sextus launched raids on passing ships and began to systematically blockade cities along the coasts.

The 26-year-old Octavian, having brilliantly defeated all of his other rivals, turned his attentions to Sicily. Through heavily taxing all the cities within the empire, he was able to build or purchase more than 370 galley warships.

In 36 B.C.E., Octavian personally sailed with his fleet to Sicily. After fierce resistance, he defeated Sextus and crushed the pirate insurgency.

After Octavian defeated his enemy on land and sea, the waterways of the Mediterranean were free of pirate attack for more than 300 years. However, after the fall of the mighty Roman Empire and the beginning of the Dark Ages, pirates reappeared from an unexpected area—the cold north.

The Least You Need to Know

- The true image of pirates has been somewhat distorted by the creators of pop culture since the end of the golden age of piracy.

- Phoenician traders took advantage of Greece's weakening economy. They actively expanded their trading routes, becoming the first merchant seamen to sail far beyond the safety of land.

- The so-called "sea people" terrorized the Mediterranean for more than 34 years. They were finally defeated by a massive sea offensive mounted by Ramses III.

- Greek pirates were so feared, city-states used them to help collect taxes. City-states lost control over pirates, creating one of the major elements that led to the empire's collapse.

- In her quest for wealth and power, Illyrian Queen Teuta inadvertently helped the Roman Empire expand its territories.

- Piracy again reared its ugly head to near-epidemic proportions after the death of Julius Caesar and in the period of Rome's focus on civil unrest. But the epidemic of piracy was eventually quashed by Octavian.

2

The Next Big Surge

In This Chapter

- ◆ Viking pirates overrun the Western world
- ◆ The establishment of Viking colonies
- ◆ The Valkyries: women warriors
- ◆ King Henry III's solution
- ◆ Pirates from the other side of the world
- ◆ Christian Crusaders clash with Muslim pirates

After the fall of the Roman Empire (fifth century C.E.), Viking raiders from the cold northern European countries of Denmark, Sweden, Finland, and Norway brought piracy once again to epidemic proportions. But these raiders from the north differed from the pirates of ancient times in their tactics and in their seemingly limitless levels of brutishness and daring.

The Viking Scourge

Viking pirates were unknown to most Europeans until one fateful day—June 8, 793 C.E.—when a sleek dragon-headed longboat landed on the island of Lindisfarne, off the northern coast of England. The raiders stormed and looted the monastery, one of the richest repositories of Church wealth in all of England. Monks were slaughtered, riches stolen, and the devil ship retreated into the mist before the alarm could be sounded. Thus began the Viking age.

When news of the Lindisfarne massacre and theft reached the English mainland, the inhabitants were horrified, fearing for their own lives and unsure of what might be in store for the next victims.

This terror was a key factor in the Vikings' control over much of the known world for the next 300 years. The Vikings swept across half the globe and changed its geographic, economic, and ethnic dynamics forever.

> **Treasure Chest**
>
> The word *berserk* is derived from *berserker*, Old Norse meaning "bear shirt" or "bearskin." It referred to the warriors who worshipped Odin, the God of war. They whipped themselves into a frenzy before and during battle, thus symbolizing Viking terror.

The Viking People

Hailing from frigid, unforgiving lands, Viking men and women lived in small farming villages near the sea. They zealously worshipped gods who represented the martial qualities of honor, pride, valor, strength, and daring. They believed if one fought fiercely and bravely, yet died in battle, he or she would earn a seat in Valhalla, their heavenly city, for all eternity.

What made this warlike race even more dangerous was the fact that the Scandinavian countries, with their many inlets and waterways, enabled Vikings to develop excellent seafaring skills. They were consummate shipbuilders and masterful sailors. Not surprising, this hearty breed looked beyond their immediate horizons for trade, treasure, and survival.

Longships

The general term used today for a Viking vessel is *longship*. Though they built and sailed warships, merchant vessels, and large ceremonial boats, Vikings are best known for the *dreki* (also pronounced *drakkar*), a warship commonly known today as the dragon ship.

A dreki was a long, narrow-decked, shallow-draft vessel at least 100 feet in length with a high curved stem and stern. The stem supported a removable carved animal head such as a dragon, horse, or curled snake. The Vikings believed these heads held the soul of the ship and guarded them from all possible dangers of the sea. (These symbolic deities would become the forerunners of decorative ship figureheads.) When they sailed for home, the carved heads were removed and stored. The Vikings did not want to frighten or offend the other spirits that guarded their homes.

The ship had a single mast positioned in the center with a large square sail. Normally the sail was brightly colored in striped or checked patterns and reinforced with ropes sewn onto the material to help secure the sail during fierce northern winds.

The prow had carved weathervanes to help plot wind directions. Depending on the status of the ship's owner, it would be carved using a number of different materials, from wood to gold.

Drekis were typically outfitted with 30 oars on each side of the hull. Because there was scant maneuvering room on the deck, the ship was rowed by warriors instead of slaves. These pirates had to be in top physical condition; they were not only expected to row the ship, but also to have enough stamina remaining to fight when encountering the enemy.

Weaponry

The weapons were as terrifying as the Vikings themselves. The broad-headed battle-axe was a common land weapon. In the hands of an experienced warrior, it could kill with a single blow. During a sea battle, a medium-size axe was preferred; it was easier to wield while boarding an enemy ship. Depending on preference, the blade was either plain or etched, and the status of the owner dictated whether the etched symbols were filled with silver.

Heavy broadswords were used in close-quarters or hand-to-hand combat. Like the axe, a Viking sword could cut through a man or shield. The broadsword and axe became so favored it was common for Vikings to attach personalities and names to them. In fact, it was not unusual for the weapon to become as notorious as its owner.

Other favored weapons were bows and arrows and spears. A battle tactic that consistently unnerved a Viking enemy involved catching a spear in midair then hurling it back at the attacker with deadly accuracy.

Pirate Yarns

Despite how they are popularly portrayed, Vikings did not wear horned helmets. If they wore a conical helmet at all, it was close-fitting and made from iron or thick leather. The horned-helmet myth became popular during the Victorian era.

Detail of Viking longship.

(From Girl's Own Paper, *September 1885)*

In addition to weapons, each man brought aboard a wooden chest of personal belongings that doubled as a rowing seat. Their individual shields of painted wood (in later years metal) were secured along the outer railing of the ship. This helped to intimidate the enemy, provided additional armament against enemy fire, and served as an efficient storage place for the shields.

Traversing Land as Easily as Oceans

The tenacity and daring of the Viking pirates did not end at the coastal boundaries of countries or continents. When they realized the wealth they could acquire and the brute advantage they possessed over populations, very little stopped their forward onslaught.

River Raiders

One technique of surprise involved sailing up river systems (the shallow draft of their ships made this possible) and attacking towns and villages along riverbanks. If they encountered impassable rapids or dams, the men would simply haul their ship onto land, cut down suitable trees from available areas (and use them as rollers), and pull their ship to the next waterway.

These Northmen or Norsemen pirates, as southern Europeans dubbed them, sailed up the Thames in England and used the same technique on the Seine to attack and burn Paris. They navigated their way as far as the Slavic Baltic and down to Baghdad (Iraq) trading in furs, amber, timber, honey, and slaves. Later, Vikings became imperial guards in the court at Constantinople (Istanbul, Turkey).

Viking Settlers

The end of Viking raids came about slowly. Chieftains realized it was more profitable to stay in the lush areas they raided and claim the lands as their own. Mounting the long voyage back to their cold countries with their treasures was no longer appealing. This began a long period of colonization.

Though a number of small pirate colonies had been established before this time—and in later years pirates would control certain islands—this is the only time in history such an enormous pirate population consciously sought to claim land, settle in diverse areas, and stop their pirating ways.

> **Treasure Chest**
>
> As greater numbers of Vikings began to settle into their cities, the Slavs identified them as *Rus*, a Slavic variation on the Finnish word *ruotsi* or "oarsman." Soon that name became the common designation for the entire Slavic population—the ancestors of the modern Russians.

Vikings as Contract Warriors

As the Greek city-states used pirates to collect taxes (see Chapter 1), so did the Slavs of Eastern Europe. They hired Viking pirates-turned-mercenaries to collect taxes and help them fight off the Turkish warriors who plagued their region. These men remained and settled in the numerous towns and cities.

Gender Not an Issue

Throughout most of history, women who did not fit into the mold of what was presumed their place in society were either ignored, ridiculed, or embraced as a singular phenomenon. Vikings were not so narrow-minded a race. The women of the north were hearty and self-reliant. They held the same legal rights and status as their men. Though most women desired to stay at home to protect family and property while their men went out raiding, quite a few took up the sword and shield and sailed off with the men. The Vikings called them *Valkyrie* (a.k.a. *Valkyria*) after the Norse goddesses who rode into battle to escort dead warriors to Valhalla.

The Tale of Alwilda

In 1837, Charles Ellms wrote *The Pirates' Own Book: Authentic Narratives of the Most Celebrated Sea Robbers*. In it, he introduced to Victorian sensibilities the flowery narrative-yarn of Alwilda (a.k.a. Alfhild, Alvild), female Goth (Germanic) of the fifth century, who, refusing to marry the Danish Prince Alf, became a pirate and sailed to help the Saxons against the savage Picts (native Scots). Alwilda became such a fierce pirate that Prince Alf set out to stop her. When the prince finally captured Alwilda after a sea battle, she saw him as a worthy mate and agreed to the marriage. Alwilda's story became one of the first tales of women pirates to be published in popular book form. However, anxious to sell his tantalizing tale, Ellms failed to focus on accuracy.

> **Dead Men's Tales**
>
> Among the Vikings was Ladgerda, a famous Valkyrie, who, though a maiden, had the courage of a man, and fought in front among the bravest with her hair loose over her shoulders. All marveled at her matchless deeds, for her locks flying down her back betrayed that she was a woman.
>
> —Saxo-Grammaticus (twelfth century)

Ellms stated that Alwilda ran away to a life at sea to avoid her arranged marriage to Prince Alf. But in Viking society, women had the right to turn down a marriage proposal. In some cases they had the liberty to choose their own husbands. In the original saga written by the twelfth-century Danish historian Saxo Grammaticus, Alwilda, the daughter of Siward, King of the Goths, lived about the middle of the ninth century. Moreover, her reasons for refusing the marriage proposal or why she "exchanged woman's for man's attire, and, no longer the most modest of maidens, began the life of a warlike rover" were never mentioned. We do know that Prince Alf did defeat Alwilda during a sea battle and carried her off as his wife. What we don't know is whether Alwilda went willingly with the prince.

Little-Known Viking Women

Other accounts of Viking women taking up the pirate trade include Ladgerda of Norway (who fought the Swedes) and the Valkyries Sela, Hetha, Wisna, and Webiorg. Queen Aud (a.k.a. Ota), wife of Olaf the White (a.k.a. Turgeis)—who proclaimed himself king of Dublin, Ireland, in 838 C.E.—fought by her husband's side.

Viking and French Bloodlines

As Vikings pressed their advantage further into Western Europe, they again set their sights on France. By 911 C.E., the pirate Rollo Ragnvald (a.k.a. Hrolf, Rolf) conquered the land along the River Seine and into the heart of Paris.

Men of the North

This large force of *Normands* or "men of the north" (as the French called them) besieged the city to near-starvation. King Charles III signed a treaty to stop the Vikings. He agreed to grant Rollo the valley of the lower Seine, naming him count of Rouen (the capital city of the area). The treaty included marriage to the king's daughter Gisla if Rollo agreed to defend France from any other invaders. Rollo agreed, thus becoming the duke of Normandy and the province of Normandy (land of the men of the north) was established.

> **Treasure Chest**
>
> Rollo Ragnvald's direct descendant six generations later was Duke William of Normandy. In 1066, William launched a cross-channel invasion of the English coast from Normandy. Once ashore, he defeated the English in the Battle of Hastings, ultimately conquering the whole of England and becoming King William I, better known as William the Conqueror.

Corsairs Fight Back

The merchant families and sailors of Brittany (a province on the northwest coast of France) refused to yield to the constant attacks from other Viking clans. Taking up arms as early as the ninth century, they continued to fight the Viking pirates until the invasions ended in the late eleventh century. By then, these hearty Frenchmen had handed down the tradition of fighting from father to son as a noble seafaring profession. Dubbed *la course* or *corsaire*—later anglicized to "corsair"—the name was derived from the Latin *cursa* or *cursus*, meaning a "voyage after plunder." They considered themselves privateers, defending France and her ships from anyone who dared attack.

King Henry III Seeks Help

By the thirteenth century, a series of naval wars between England, France, and Spain had begun to seriously drain English king Henry III's coffers. In addition to a lack of warships at Henry's disposal, heavy taxes were destroying the English economy, and the money necessary to fund the wars was greatly depleting the national treasury.

Letters of Marque

To alleviate this dilemma, Henry issued one of the first known military *letters of marque*. The Old French word *marque* means "seizure of goods." From the Latin *marcare*, meaning "seize as a pledge," the original letters of marque were employed by merchant guilds as legal documents to force the payment of debts. Henry's decree permitted all crews and ships that obtained the document to attack—with impunity—any and all ships they encountered, so long as the encountered ships were not flying the flag of England.

Knowing the Ropes

Also known as "letters of reprisal," **letters of marque** were documents that allowed merchants to impound a vessel in port until a debt was paid in full.

This document served a number of useful purposes. It quickly increased Henry's fleet and defenses without forcing him to spend government money or manpower to build new warships. Men agreeing to pay the king half of everything they obtained not only built a greater financial reserve in the country's treasury, it took the burden off the English population by enabling the king to lower taxes.

Henry issued two types of letters of marque. During England's wars with France and Spain, he had issued a *General Letter of Marque*. This allowed a lawful attack on any enemy naval ship or privately owned enemy vessel. In peacetime, if merchants lost cargo or ships to pirates, they could apply for and purchase a *Special Reprisal Letter of Marque*. This allowed the private citizen to hunt down and attack any known pirate ship (whether it was the one that attacked him or not) and attempt to recover any lost revenue. Paradoxically, the special reprisal document was similar to the special license that ancient Greek merchants were able to obtain for the exact same reason from the governments of their city-states.

Privateers: Government-Sanctioned Raids

Previously, any attack on ships flying an enemy flag or the flag of their country was considered an out-and-out act of piracy. If captured, the ship's crews were considered pirates and hung for thievery. With the creation of the letter of marque, the men were granted free reign to commit acts of piracy against any and all enemies of their country without fear of criminal prosecution from their native government. Spain and France quickly reciprocated and began issuing their own letters of marque.

Dead Men's Tales

Know ye that we have granted and given license to Adam Robernolt and William le Sauvage ... to annoy our enemies at sea or by land ... so that they shall share with us half of all their gains.

—King Henry III, 1243

This created a new breed of sailing man, the privateer. Unfortunately, the line between honest privateer and pirate became an unrecognizable blur. This blur was not only confusing, but often disastrous for all involved. Constantly established, renewed, and voided treaties—as well as wars be-tween nations—created problems in communication. News traveled slowly by ship. A privateer might attack an enemy who, unbeknownst to him, had just become his nation's ally. The attacked victim suffered, as did the privateer who was then considered a pirate and hunted down.

Meanwhile, on the Other Side of the World ...

Piracy was not relegated to Europe and its surrounding seas. Japan, China, and the islands of Southeast Asia also were subjected to their own special brand of piracy. In 400 C.E., large fleets of piratical Chinese sailed during the summer months, attacking any and all who dared come into their sights.

With the establishment of individual small native states throughout the area, there was constant pirate activity for slaves and merchandise. Like their European counterparts, Asian pirates were swift attack-and-vanish raiders.

The Crusades Begin

Many great historical events seem to go hand in hand with piracy. We see this once again in the clash of religious fervor and commercial gains meted out during what was to be called the "Crusades." Arabic Muslim pirates began their control with the conquest in 709 C.E. of the major cities along the coast of North Africa and the Middle East.

The Vatican's Expedition

In 1095 C.E., Pope Urban II ordered the fighters of Christendom to travel to the Holy Land and retake the city of Jerusalem from the heathen Muslims. His intentions included the recapture of all former Christian territories, the conquest of new areas in the name of the Holy Roman Church, and to stop the spread of Islam.

This order meant that Christian warriors of Western Europe would go head to head with Muslim pirates who had been sailing the region for centuries. These pirates sailed large oar-driven galley ships with their main bases of operations located in Algiers, Tunis, and Tripoli on the coast of North Africa. Whether sold as household slaves, galley slaves, or kidnapped for ransom, people were their prime targets and their biggest commodity. Any other merchandise captured was considered a bonus.

The Knights Templar

Some of the first Europeans to encounter Muslim pirates were the French *Knights Templar*, who dubbed their Muslim enemies *corsaires*. The Christian crusaders considered the Muslims heathen barbarians. Because the pirates hailed mainly from the fierce Berber tribes, consequently the stretch of North African shoreline controlled by the Muslim pirates became known as the Barbary Coast, and the Muslims who sailed the waters, *Barbary corsairs* (see Chapter 20).

> ### Treasure Chest
>
> Because their ruler sanctioned the activities of the Muslim sailors of the Barbary Coast, the French who first encountered these men considered them privateers. Hence the French called them *corsaires*. Therefore period enthusiasts refer to the sailors of the Barbary region as either Barbary corsairs or Barbary pirates.

The Muslims viewed Christians with equal disdain, considering the latter to be nothing more than vile infidels. Consequently, the atrocities and tortures perpetrated between Barbary corsairs and crusaders became legendary.

To Hell with Winning Hearts and Minds!

Much of the alleged Muslim atrocities were part of a propaganda war initiated by the various popes raising armies in the hopes of permanently seizing the Holy Land. Moreover, because most Europeans were convinced of the validity of the allegations leveled against those of the Islamic faith, European treatment of captured or conquered Muslims was without mercy.

By the end of the Crusades in 1291 C.E., the hatred and misunderstandings between the two cultures was so intense that by the sixteenth century when honest European merchants turned their full attention to this region of the world, the atrocities escalated.

The Europeans Cometh

When returning crusaders shared tales of the exotic, wealthy lands they visited, the motives for piracy changed. No longer would they be fueled primarily by discontent, lawless individuals or groups, but also by countries vying for control of the world's wealth, as well as the Roman Catholic popes who wanted power over the monarchs.

In Rome, the papal Church—having failed a number of times—again tried to command loyalty in the name of Christ from Western European countries. This time, Spain, Portugal, and France complied. Holland and England refused.

The ploy by the pope set the stage for greater rivalry between nations. While Portuguese merchant ships and soldiers traveled to the East and acquired a strong foothold in that area, Spain, England, and France fought for supremacy of the sea routes of Western Europe.

The Least You Need to Know

- Viking pirates invaded many countries and then colonized the areas.

- There are many accounts of Viking women taking up the pirate trade and fighting alongside men.

- During wartime, governments sanctioned piracy against their enemies.

- As early as 400 C.E., Asian pirates sailed attack fleets throughout Southeast Asia, thereby influencing the economic dynamics of the entire region.

3

The Spanish Main

In This Chapter

- ◆ Bigger and better sailing ships
- ◆ A journey of exploration changes the world forever
- ◆ Total sovereignty for Spain
- ◆ Columbus sets sail again
- ◆ Religion and greed go hand in hand
- ◆ Pirates get in on the action

At the same time the Vikings were prowling coastlines, men and women from other European territories, Asia, and the Middle East were engaging in the pursuit of *presumed* quickly and easily acquired wealth. They did so with a limitless disregard for law and authority, and, like the Vikings, their activities increased over time.

By the fifteenth century, animosity among the countries of Western Europe had reached an all-time high. Religious prejudice was not simply leveled against the Muslims who—due to the influence of the Church— were considered to be valueless and dangerous heathens. Protestants and Catholics polarized nations. Entire populations were feared and despised because of their religious beliefs and practices. This intolerance spread into newly discovered territories and created an ideal breeding ground for pirates and piracy.

As the children's ditty goes, "In fourteen hundred and ninety-two, Columbus sailed the ocean blue." For the Catholic Church and Spain, the discovery of what would be called the "New World" was a splendid expedition. It resulted in the establishment of great cities, the realization of vast wealth, and the creation of legendary personas such as the famous privateer, Sir Francis Drake, whom you'll meet in the next chapter. It also resulted in the complete destruction of native civilizations, the extermination of entire populations, brutal inquisitions, and the establishment of a huge, legal slave industry that would continue for centuries.

New Profits, New Ships

To understand the impact piracy had on the New World, one must first understand the historic events that led to such an aggressive wave of plundering.

In 1143, Portugal declared its independence from Spain.

Portugal's first major industry became shipbuilding. Soon, the nation evolved into one of the world's great maritime powers, and its leaders began setting their sights on the south and east, quietly building trading centers in Africa.

In 1295, Italian journeyman Marco Polo returned from his successful venture along the Silk Road to the Orient. He brought back exotic spices and wares never before imagined by the people of Western Europe. Spain, eager to acquire such riches, began searching for its own route to the lands of the Near, Middle, and Far East.

Meanwhile between 1255 and 1262, the Germanic seaports of Hamburg, Bremen, Danzig, and Lübeck formed the commercial Hanseatic League: a joint commercial/naval alliance that would better protect their individual fleets from German pirates attacking merchants on the Baltic (in Northern Europe) and the North Seas (between Norway and the British Isles).

Pirate Yarns

In 1395, a German pirate by the name of Störtebeker created a pirate band called *The Friends of God and Enemies of the World*. Captured in 1402 by the admiral of Hamburg, Störtebeker's ship, *The Mad Dog*, was rumored to have had a mast of solid gold. Actually, it was hollow along sections of its length with gold hidden inside.

The Sailing Cog

By the fifteenth century, the league was developing a new ship aimed at increasing their sailors' chances of avoiding pirates and surviving the heavy winds of the North Sea. The vessel, known as the cog, was not oar-driven, but propelled solely by a sail mounted on a single mast. In time, two, and later three, additional masts were added. The cog had a belly-shaped hull, and was thus known as a "round" ship. She was fitted with a permanent rudder hinged on the center-line of the stern. The cog's overall design forever changed sailing vessel development. Adaptations would be made, but shipwrights would follow the cog's basic design features until the end of the era of the great sailing ships.

A Fishing Boat with Military Applications

The caravel was first launched as a Portuguese fishing boat with only two masts and *lateen sails*. It evolved over the years, but maintained its unique and innovative design feature of "planking the ship." Utilizing one continuous length of wood plank called a "strake," the plank ran the entire length of a ship's frame and butt-jointed all the other planks together. This created a smooth surface on both sides of the ship's slender hull frame. Caulking the seams then prevented water from seeping into the ship, even in heavy seas. The smooth outer skin made the ship much easier to careen.

> **Knowing the Ropes**
>
> The triangular **lateen sail** is suspended by a long yard at a 45-degree angle to the mast. This Arab-style sail was adapted by Europeans along the Mediterranean. Another nautical word, "halyard," derives from this particular sail. The command to "haul up the yard" is the order to set a lateen.

By the seventeenth century, the caravel featured three masts and square sails, thus creating greater seaworthiness and an ability to survive lengthy voyages.

The caravel also featured a poop deck built high above the quarterdeck. The poop deck was a relatively short raised deck at the rear, or aftermost area, of a large sailing ship.

Because of its breakthrough design, caravel shipbuilding spread to all the Western European countries.

From Caravel to Carrack

Soon thereafter, the carrack was developed based on the caravel model. The carrack design (discussed in Chapter 5) allowed for mounted cannons. This portable firepower would have a tremendous impact on warfare and piracy.

The Famous Galleon

The Spanish treasure ship or galleon was developed based on the carrack design (as the carrack was based on the design of the caravel). A three-masted ship, the galleon averaged 135 feet in length and 35 feet across at the beam. She carried an average of 60 guns (cannon) on her 2 decks. The stern was built up to the height of three or four decks to accommodate cabins and galleries (balconies along the outer stern of the ship commonly ornately carved with glass windows). The yardarms (the ends of the horizontally positioned wooden spar that held the square sails) had large crescent blades attached to slit any rigging or sails if an enemy ship was close enough for boarding. All treasure was loaded into locked chests and stored in a specially built treasure room on the lower deck. The room was sealed and guarded by soldiers (marines) for the entire trip from the New World to Seville, Spain.

Spanish treasure galleon.

Christopher Columbus: Sailing into History

The travel journals Marco Polo kept spurred the imagination of Christopher Columbus, who became convinced that by sailing westward he would find a new and faster route to India and the Orient. After being refused by many nobles of Italian city-states, he presented his case to the king and queen of Spain. Arduous lobbying on the part of Columbus eventually persuaded Spanish Queen Isabella to finance his plan. The queen realized there was little for Spain to lose and much to gain if Columbus was correct in his assumptions.

Columbus was known to be an excellent navigator, and his conditions were reasonable. In addition to a one tenth percentage of all precious metals discovered, Columbus wished to be named admiral, governor, and viceroy, plus hereditary peerage of the lands he acquired for Spain. Assuring himself a coveted position in Spanish society was one of his highest priorities. For Spain it meant a chance at great wealth. Once again, commercial interests created a major turning point in piracy.

On August 3, 1492, Christopher Columbus set sail with the *Niña*, the *Pinta*, and his flagship, the *Santa María*, to find his route to the East. On October 12, 1492, an island was sighted. Columbus called it San Salvador. The natives he met were the Tainos people. Columbus named them *los Indios*, or the Indians, because he was convinced he had made landfall somewhere in the Indian Ocean.

With native guides Columbus explored more of the island chains. Next, they showed him the island he would name La Isla Española (Little Spain Island). Later renamed Hispaniola (now Haiti and the Dominican Republic), it would become home to buccaneers. On Hispaniola Columbus met the Arawak people. Almost immediately, his interest was piqued by the gold jewelry that adorned their bodies. The discovery that gold nuggets flowed down the mountainous rivers convinced Columbus he had stumbled upon easy wealth. He loaded his ships with gold, exotic fruits, parrots, and unwilling natives chained in shackles. He could not wait to return to Spain with proof of his discoveries and get the recognition he felt he deserved.

> **Treasure Chest**
>
> In 1476, Columbus himself fell victim to pirates. Sailing with a Genoese convoy bound for England, pirates sunk his ship off Portugal. Able to swim ashore, he took refuge in Lisbon. There he took up residence with his brother, a cartographer, and resumed his seafaring career. Examining his brother's charts, Columbus became convinced that Asia could be reached by a westerly route.

Treasure Chest

On the island of Cuba, Columbus was introduced to tobacco by observing the native people inhaling lit rolled brown leaves.

Upon his return to Spain in 1493, word quickly spread throughout Europe of his great discovery. Rumors abounded of gold flowing abundantly down rivers of this new land. Honest citizens along with pirates and privateers were intrigued by this sensational news. The Spanish court agreed to mount another expedition that very same year. But first they decided to hedge their bets before other nations tried to claim the area first.

Catholic Spain Is Granted Total Sovereignty

As preparations were underway to outfit another voyage, the king of Spain petitioned Pope Alexander VI for a blessed edict. The pope in 1493 conferred on Spain the right of total sovereignty of all the new lands that Columbus would explore and claim. This edict encompassed the entire known and future lands 100 leagues (approximately 320 miles) west of Cape Verde Island, off the west coast of Africa.

The Pope Gets His Cut

The pope was more than pleased to grant Spain's wishes. King Ferdinand and Queen Isabella agreed that Spanish explorers would Christianize all "heathen peoples" they encountered. With Protestant countries such as England openly defying all that he and the Church stood for, Pope Alexander VI envisioned a huge influx of devoted Christians who would be subject to Vatican edicts. Additionally with the Church's tithe system in force, a percentage of all the riches of the explored lands would find their way into the coffers of the Church.

Portugal, France, and England Yell "Foul"

The papal edict enraged the rest of Western Europe. Catholic Portugal was furious and protested directly to the pope. They believed that as a devout Catholic country the pope should rightfully issue them an identical holy edit. In 1494, after many heated discussions and by mutual consent with Spain, the Treaty of Tordesillas was signed. In effect, it moved the invisible line of Spain's land claim 270 leagues farther west of the Cape Verde Islands. This enabled Portugal to eventually claim the entire country of Brazil under their sovereignty without fear of outright reprisals from Spain.

King Francis I of France felt that he and his countrymen had every right to claim whatever land or riches they could find in the territories. His protest was officially sent to the pope, and he vowed that the issue would not end there. Determined to stake his claim for France in the New World, the king commissioned his privateering corsairs to set sail for the Caribbean.

Dead Men's Tales

The sun shines for me as for others. I should like to see the clause in Adam's will that excludes me from a share in the world.

—King Francis I, 1494

King Henry VII of England, having just signed a peace treaty with France two years before, needed to continue rebuilding his treasury and navy. Though outwardly less verbal over the pope's edict, he continued to issue letters of marque and waited to see if the rumors of great wealth in those New Worlds were true.

Columbus Tries Again (and Again)

On Columbus's second voyage, the fleet consisted largely of farmers and supplies for establishing colonies. Priests boarded with their religious paraphernalia. Men of diverse professions also volunteered, eager to be some of the first to acquire new lands and riches.

Discovering Jamaica

Convinced he still would find a route to India, China, and Japan, Columbus landed the settlers on Hispaniola and again embarked on a search of his sea route. He came upon a large island the natives called Jamaica. This island would become another notorious haven for pirates and buccaneers (see Chapter 15). What he didn't find was his trade route. Returning to Hispaniola, he discovered the Spaniards were more interested in hunting for gold than establishing farms and settlements.

Disillusioned, Columbus sailed back to Spain to organize another expedition and report the fact that Portugal was colonizing areas.

When news began circulating along the Spanish seaports that Columbus was attempting to mount yet another expedition to leave in 1498, few people signed on. By then it was believed that there was little gold to be found in the New World.

Convict Crews

If it weren't for the fact the Spanish monarchy would have lost face, the expedition would not have been outfitted at all. This time, to acquire a full complement of sailors and settlers, jails were emptied and the convicts given a second opportunity for freedom if they sailed with Columbus.

Dead Men's Tales

None of the settlers came save in the belief that gold and spices could be gathered in by the shovel full, and they did not reflect that, though there was gold, it would be buried in mines, and the spices would be on the treetops, and that the gold would have to be mined and the spices harvested and cured.

—Christopher Columbus to the Spanish monarchs, May 1499

Columbus sent three ships to Hispaniola with settlers. With his three remaining ships, he attempted to find the lands earlier navigators thought lay beyond the equator before the Portuguese discovered them. Columbus landed on Trinidad to a hostile reception. The natives had heard of the cruelty the Spaniards had been inflicting on the people of the other islands.

Continental Discovery

As Columbus and his men fled from the attacking natives, he noticed a large mountainous area to the north. Once safely aboard his ship, he sailed to the shoreline that was to be named Venezuela.

Columbus explored what would be known as South America for five months before returning to Hispaniola.

Though Christopher Columbus did not succeed in his quest to find a sea route to India, his daring and tenacity changed the map of the known world and opened an entirely new region for pirate attacks.

Spanish Cruelty and Abuses

The arrival of the Spanish to the islands became a nightmare for the natives. With the exception of the warlike Carib Indians, most of the natives Spain encountered were peaceful people who lived off the land.

The Spaniards immediately deemed these men, women, and children heathens. They had no written languages, walked around half-clothed, and were dark-skinned like the pictures of the devil in Bibles and church murals. The Spanish felt it was their moral obligation to instantly convert them to Christianity. Because the natives refused (most likely they didn't even understand what was being asked of them), the Spaniards believed it their legal right to enslave these devil-worshippers. The natives were considered on a level with any beast of burden and therefore could be dealt with harshly as examples to others. Thus the subjugation, torture, and eventual extermination of entire races began.

It began in earnest on Hispaniola. There, in 1502, Governor Don Nicolás de Ovando set up permanent settlements. Using the natives as beasts of burden, the settlers opened and dug gold and silver mines. They turned the once-wild sugarcane fields into commercial plantations. Ovando also started tobacco plantations with the plants brought over from Cuba. The young Spanish dons who sailed to the Spanish Main deemed manual labor far below their place in society and used the Indians for all sorts of work. Unfortunately for the natives, they were not hearty enough to survive the rigors of plantation work and perished quickly.

Within 40 years of first meeting Columbus, the Tainos and Arawak people were nearly extinct. This was due to slavery and diseases brought from Europe.

The Black Gold Trade and the Beginnings of American Slavery

To remedy the situation the Spaniards contracted with Portuguese traders at their centers in West Africa to purchase black slaves. In 1512, the Portuguese imported the first slaves to Hispaniola. The blacks of West Africa were able to withstand the island heat and the grueling physical labor. Not to be denied the opportunity to make money, Dutch and British traders approached the plantation owners, offering to sell them slaves. This would enable the Spaniards to save the 30 ducats (a ducat was the approximate equivalent of $60) per head tax normally paid the Spanish Governmental Trading House with every Portuguese purchase. So the lucrative *black gold trade* began. When pirates got wind of this successful commerce, they set their sights on slave ships en route from Africa.

Knowing the Ropes

The **black gold trade** was the term used to describe the African slave trade. Because slavers could make a fortune selling slaves, blacks were viewed in terms of gold value. Another term used for these slaves was black ivory.

By now disenfranchised men (sailors, convicts, debtors) from all nations, including runaway slaves, settled on some of the smaller uninhabited islands. Using rowboats and fishing vessels, they mounted quick raids on ships in the area. Soon their numbers swelled, and Spain felt the first sting of pirate attacks in the Caribbean.

More Conquests, More Enslavement

In 1519, Hernán Cortés conquered the Aztec Indians of Mexico. Taking Emperor Mactezuma hostage, the Spanish sacked the temples and palaces of gold and jewels. By sheer numbers and firepower, they enslaved the natives to work in the gold and silver mines. Aztecs were tortured until they revealed their method of smelting metals. If any slaves tried to escape, their hands were cut off or they were burned alive as examples to others.

By 1529 Francisco Pizarro dealt with the native population in a similar manner. Starting from the coast of Ecuador, his troops marched inland to Peru. Any opposition they met was dealt with by enslavement or slaughter. He did not stop until he reached the heart of the Peruvian Inca Empire. Here, too, slave labor was enforced upon the natives in gold and silver mines. In Colombia the Spaniards couldn't believe the number of emerald mines dotting the mountain regions, and while exploring the island of Cuba, they discovered and began mining copper.

Instead of protesting the harsh treatment of these people, the Catholic priests used their own brutal methods. They employed the techniques of the Inquisition in Spain to convince the natives to convert to Christianity. If they (man or woman) survived the tortures without converting, they were burned alive. The priests believed that was the only option to saving their souls. Ironically in the coming years, the Spanish and Portuguese would get a taste of their own inhumanity from the most unlikely quarter—pirates.

The Territorial Area of the Spanish Main

By the end of their territorial conquest in 1530, Spain laid claim to an area larger than Europe called the *Spanish Main*. It stretched across the islands bordering the Caribbean Sea and the Gulf of Mexico (Trinidad to Cuba and the Straits of Florida) and consisted of Mexico and Central and South America. Such a large area proved too much for the Spanish to successfully patrol and secure, and pirates became well aware of that fact.

Originally named *Tierra Firma*, the area known as the Spanish Main only described the first large land mass encountered (South America) by Columbus. The English called it the "Spanish Mainland," and then shortened it to "Spanish Main." The term came to include the islands and waters off the coast.

The Spanish Main.

Stealing Spanish Treasure

Though individual ships had previously sailed to Spain with cargo holds filled with gold and silver, it wasn't until 1521 that a treasure fleet was dispatched to Seville. The first shipment of Aztec wealth was loaded onto three ships. They were so packed and heavy they rode low in the water and maneuvered slowly.

King Francis I had announced he had every right to riches from the area. Thus, Captain Avila, in charge of this Spanish treasure fleet, was concerned about the threat of French corsairs. He had every reason to worry.

As Avila sailed past the Azores (islands in the mid-Atlantic with the same latitude as Portugal), six swift ships were sighted bearing down on his fleet. Realizing they were French corsairs, he ordered his men to battle stations. Unfortunately, his ships were only armed with a few cannon, and the sailors aboard were not experienced combatants.

One Man's "Champion," Another Man's Pirate

With Jean Fleury (a.k.a. Jean Florin) commanding from his flagship, *Salamander*, the French vessels maneuvered swiftly between the three lumbering treasure ships. They fired continual broadsides until one ship lost a main mast and another took on water from a hole in the hull. The third Spanish ship managed to escape. The corsairs grappled and boarded the Spanish ships, transferred the treasure to their own vessels, and sailed home.

As Fleury eased into the northern French seaport of Dieppe, the city was abuzz with news of his victory and rumors of the amount of seized treasure. The treasure reality proved to be as exciting as the rumors to the citizens of Dieppe. A partial inventory of the manifest read as follows:

- 680 pounds of pearls

- 500 pounds of gold dust

- 150,000 ducats

- 3 cases of gold ingots

- 5 cases of silver ingots

- Feathered cloaks

- Chests of jewels, gold masks, and figurines

- Exotic birds and animals

The king of France had finally received a bulk of wealth from the Spanish Main.

Jean Ango, the viscount of Dieppe, a nobleman with close ties to the court of Francis I, had financed the mission. Fleury, the daring leader of the attack, would earn a reputation as a champion of France. (His seizure of the treasure galleons is depicted in stained glass in the church nave at Villequier, Normandy.) The raid would be the first of many Fleury would launch against the Spanish. In fact, he would continue to attack Spanish shipping until 1527, when he was captured, turned over to the Spanish, tried as a pirate, and hanged.

All approaches to Europe, especially the coasts of Portugal and Spain, became prime pirate hunting grounds. Pirates and privateers of every nation simply waited to attack the Spanish treasure fleets as they made their way home. Outraged, King Carlos I (now king of Spain and proclaimed Holy Roman Emperor Charles V) demanded his navy immediately implement greater measures to ensure that attacks such as Fleury's never happened again. Of course, it was an impossible task.

Sixteenth-Century Convoys

By 1543, all treasure fleets (or flotillas) had warships (the man-of-war or man-o'-war) accompanying them on scheduled convoys to guard against attacks. Every spring, a convoy of ships loaded with supplies, such as wine, clothing, books, and olive oil, for Spanish settlers sailed to Vera Cruz (Mexico) where the Mexican treasure hordes were stored waiting to be shipped to Seville. In autumn, the second fleet left Spain hoping to miss the hurricane season and made a number of stops to offload supplies and load treasure from Cartagena to the thriving city of Nombre de Dios in Panama that housed the great Inca treasures to the island of Jamaica, the Yucatan (Mexico), and finally Havana (Cuba).

In February, the two convoys would converge in Havana to load the last of the treasure and exotic products of the area and set sail together for Spain. This convoy could number up to 100 ships.

The Spanish convoys became so predictable that pirates and privateers who had settled on Caribbean islands or sailed the Atlantic Ocean into the Caribbean Sea need simply wait along these established routes to attack and plunder them. (In their arrogance and believing no one would dare attack their convoys, a number of Spanish naval officers grew indolent. Their belief made the plundering of their own treasure ships convenient prey.)

The Least You Need to Know

- The design of the famous Spanish galleon was based on that of the carrack, which was based on that of the caravel.

- Christopher Columbus made several voyages looking for a western route to the Orient.

- The pope attempted to control the ownership of the New World. He awarded the area to Catholic Spain and Portugal, excluding the other European countries and thought they would abide by his edict.

- Spanish and Portuguese cruelty would foreshadow how pirates would treat their own captives.

- By 1543, Spanish treasure routes were so predictable that pirates and privateers knew exactly where to launch an attack.

Chapter 4

England Adds Her Two Pence

In This Chapter

- A shrewd queen rules England
- France and Spain at odds
- John Hawkins sails the Main as a slave trader
- Francis Drake's world tour
- English "sea dogs" continue the attack
- Sea beggars: pirates, patriots, and colonists

By the mid-sixteenth century, Spain had established and was maintaining a firm commercial/naval monopoly along the Spanish Main. To stave off pirate attacks, a number of Spanish cities were fortified and others were established along harbors where harsh winds and dangerous currents served as a natural deterrence.

In 1554, England's Queen Mary I, Elizabeth's Catholic half-sister (not to be confused with Mary Queen of Scots), married Philip, Spain's heir to the throne. The marriage was not based on love, but on hopes of achieving political and religious (Catholic) solidarity between the two nations. After Mary's death in 1558, Elizabeth I, who was to become both patron and scourge of pirates and privateers, ascended the throne of England.

Elizabeth I Throws Down the Gauntlet

With Mary's death, good relations with Spain were, at best, tenuous. Mary's will stated that Philip *should* become king, but the English council refused to acknowledge her dying request. Believing he had been cheated of the crown, Philip's second bid for the English throne was also thwarted when Elizabeth I refused his marriage proposal. Philip hated Elizabeth for her refusal and her diplomatic strategies, and he mistrusted her because of her strong Protestant beliefs.

Ascending the throne, Elizabeth was confronted with a depleted national treasury and weakened military forces. She knew she had to strengthen her country's defenses because Spain might move against England. But the politically clever Elizabeth was able to use diplomacy to buy time, thus avoiding war between the two countries, until the situation came to a head in 1588.

Decrees Banning Trade

Spanish royal decrees were sent out to all Spanish subjects stating that trading rights with any other country were strictly forbidden. Anyone who approached them for trade would be considered pirates. The government made it clear that any violation of the decrees would be dealt with harshly.

Until Elizabeth was confident enough she could openly win a confrontation with Spain, she attempted to establish legal trade rights within the Spanish Main. Therefore, her royal counselor, Sir William Cecil, approached the Spanish ambassador with the queen's formal request. The request was refused; however, Sir Cecil let it be known to the ambassador that the answer received would not necessarily be honored.

Dead Men's Tales

Secretary Cecil ... sent to ask me to furnish them with a memorandum of the places where it is forbidden to trade without your majesty's license. I sent it to him saying that the places were all the West Indies, continent and islands ... he [Sir Cecil] sent to say that the [English] council do not agree.

—Don Diego Guzman de Silva, Spanish ambassador to England, 1566

An Opportunity for Piracy

Not that English pirates hadn't been plaguing "the Main" (sailors in the time of Elizabeth shortened the term from Spanish Main) for years prior to this formal request. But Sir Cecil's reply was fair warning that England was going to acquire whatever benefits it could from the Main, with or without Spain's approval.

The French Distract Spain

England wasn't Spain's only problem. France and Spain were also at odds over religion and territorial conquest. And while Elizabeth and Philip danced around each other, France and Spain were openly at war. The infamous French corsairs, based largely in the city of Dieppe and on the islet of St. Malo, increased their raids not only on Spanish shipping in the Atlantic, but also at the very heart of Spain's wealth, the cities of the New World.

The Raid of La Barburata

In 1553, the corsairs launched a daring raid on the city of La Barburata (on the coast of Venezuela) that encompassed the famous pearl fisheries of South America. Fearing for their lives, the entire city's inhabitants evacuated, leaving everything to the successful marauders. The corsairs gladly moved in. For many years thereafter, La Barburata was a corsair settlement plus a thriving trading center for all types of contraband goods.

Spanish settlers from other areas traded in the city. Otherwise "honest," these men were willing to break the law, because Spanish tax regulations on goods bought or sold through legal channels cut too deeply into the settlers' profits. Flush from the victory over La Barburata, the corsairs took over the islands of Trinidad, Cuacoa, and La Margarita.

The Man with the Wooden Leg

But corsairs did not always settle the cities they raided. In 1556, the notorious François le Clerc (a.k.a. Jambe de Bois, French for "leg of wood")—better known to the Spanish as Pie de Palo or Pegleg—and his lieutenants Jacque de Sores and Robert Blondel sailed their fleet to Havana. They captured, looted, and then burnt the city to the ground. In retaliation for the Catholic persecution of French Protestants who were attempting to settle in the New World, they desecrated the cathedral and tortured its priests before sailing triumphantly away.

These raids on cities and islands, as well as the depletion of tax monies coming from the area, drastically reduced the Spanish national treasury and diverted Spain's attention numerous times from the English. This made it easier for English pirates and privateers to trade with and plunder the entire Spanish Main.

England's Wealth Built on Slave Profits

Sir John Hawkins (Hawkyns) (1532–1595), born into a British shipping family, learned his sailing skills traveling with his father and in later years fighting the French in the English Channel. Over many pints of ale and stories from successful merchant friends, he became convinced that large profits could be made in the Spanish Main as long as he was able to steer clear of large cities and Spanish warships. Now he needed to figure out what merchandise would yield him the greatest profit. He had heard of plantation owners living along the lesser-patrolled sailing routes who would pay handsomely for African slaves.

So, at age 30, Hawkins solicited backers for his first slave-trading expedition. They weren't difficult to find. Some of his London backers were prominent men of the time: Sir William Wynter, the surveyor of the Queen's ships, and Benjamin Gonson, treasurer of the Queen's navy, who also happened to be his father-in-law. This guaranteed Hawkins three reliable ships for the long and dangerous voyage he was proposing.

With this fleet, Hawkins set sail in 1562 for Sierra Leone on the coast of Guinea, Africa. From Portuguese and African slavers, he purchased and jammed 300 slaves into the ships' tight cargo spaces and sailed for the plantations on Hispaniola.

Hawkins was cautious upon landing, wary of the kind of reception he might receive as an Englishman illegally trading on Spanish territory. He didn't need to worry. The thrilled plantation owners not only bought his entire cargo of slaves but clamored for more. Hawkins's fleet sailed back to England loaded with gold, silver, hides, and sugar.

Slaver to Privateer

Elated by his success and the relatively easy voyage, Hawkins—upon landing in England in September 1564—immediately began to organize a second expedition. For this trip his major investor would be none other than Queen Elizabeth I. Having heard from her counselors of his great profits, she offered Hawkins not only a royal ship, the *Jesus of Lubeck* (for a percentage of his profits) as his flagship, but also the right to fly her personal banner on its mainmast. Hawkins graciously accepted her support (not that he could refuse and keep his head). Hawkins was no longer simply a slave trader (a profession frowned upon, in many circles, even in sixteenth century), but a royally commissioned privateer. And while his new ship was being refurbished, he outfitted and stocked two of his own vessels.

Spain Infuriated

Upon learning of Hawkins's commission and forthcoming expedition, the Spanish ambassador sent a formal protest to the queen in hopes of stopping the venture. His request was denied. Frustrated, the ambassador sent warning dispatches throughout the Main. Now the Spanish governors would be waiting for Hawkins as he sailed throughout the islands. On this trip (October 18, 1564 to September 20, 1565), it became increasingly difficult for his ships to dodge the Spanish authorities. Only through the use of tactical diplomacy and armed threat was Hawkins able to sell his slave cargo at a profit.

> **Treasure Chest**
>
> John Hawkins's flagship, the *Jesus of Lubeck,* was built by the Hanseatic League in the city of Lubeck. It was purchased by Elizabeth's father, King Henry VIII, in 1544, and at the time was one of the oldest and largest ships in England's fleet.

Elizabeth was thrilled at his success. Not only did it vex Philip further that she had dared send Englishmen into his territory to trade, it relieved the heavy tax burden off her subjects. Her share of the profits was great enough to begin building naval ships at the docks of Plymouth.

Unfortunately, Elizabeth paid no mind to the fact her profits were derived from human suffering. In fact, to denote his successful occupation as a slave trader, she presented Hawkins with a coat-of-arms on which the top design displayed the image of a bound African male. She, like most Europeans, did not consider Africans human beings. As such, Africans were considered to be valuable merchandise. Nothing more.

A Betrayal of Honor That Spurred Revenge

A third expedition was mounted. This voyage would become a pivotal turning point in political relations between England and Spain. It also shaped the fate of Hawkins's 22-year-old cousin, Francis Drake.

Once again Elizabeth was the prime investor. The crown supplied two ships, *Jesus of Lubeck* and *Minion.* For the journey, Hawkins outfitted his own ships, *William and John* (named for his older brother and himself), *Swallow, Angel,* and the *Judith.* He appointed Drake captain of the *Judith.* Four hundred and eight men signed on to sail aboard the six ships.

Slaves or Gold?

In an attempt to fool the Spanish, Hawkins insisted his voyage to Africa was exclusively in search of gold. Ambassador Don de Silva did not believe him. He met with the queen to plead the Spanish cause. Elizabeth lied to him. Aware of their duplicity, the ambassador could do nothing except warn the Spanish authorities that once again Hawkins was sailing. To them Hawkins was nothing more than a *pirate* working with the blessings of his queen.

However, this expedition, launched October 2, 1567, was doomed from the start. Inclement weather pounded the convoy the entire journey. Once on the African continent, the European slavers refused to sell to them. The Portuguese wanted to strengthen their own monopoly in the slave-trade markets of Africa.

A Hippopotamus and a Hurricane

Hawkins obtained two more ships and began capturing or buying slaves from rival native chiefs. Disease and native attacks plagued them as they sailed up rivers. Worse, while attempting to capture slaves, one of the ships collided with a hippopotamus and sank (many of the ship's crew were then killed by the massive animal). So when the quota of slaves was finally met, they sailed to the Caribbean. Compared to what had transpired in Africa, the trip to the Spanish Main was uneventful.

During his second voyage, Hawkins encountered difficulty selling his slave cargo. In 1564, a royal edict prohibiting any interaction with rival countries had finally reached the colonies, consequently some of the more cautious Spanish settlers refused to trade with him. By the third voyage, Spanish officials were following the edict to the letter and prosecuting all violators.

Hawkins was barely able to cajole and barter enough sales from the settlers throughout the Spanish territory to make the trip worthwhile.

On the return trip to England, the ships ran headlong into a hurricane in the Gulf of Mexico. The *William and John* became separated from the convoy but somehow managed to sail back to England. The storm severely crippled the *Jesus of Lubeck*. Having little choice, the fleet sailed to the nearest harbor on the island of San Juan de Uluá (15 miles south of Vera Cruz, Mexico) for repairs. Hawkins's ships didn't receive a warm welcome. Insisting he was there only to repair his battered vessels and not to steal the treasure stockpiled on the island, Hawkins managed to negotiate an armistice with the governor.

Spanish Ships Attack the English Fleet

As fate would have it, before the repairs were completed a Spanish flotilla with the new viceroy of Mexico, Don Martin Enriquez, arrived. Though he had been personally tasked by King Philip to rid the area of all foreigners, Don Enriquez publicly permitted the truce to continue, but his written guarantee was a mere charade. On the morning of September 23, 1568, the Spanish attacked the English fleet. After a fierce battle the only ships to survive were the *Minion* and the *Judith*. By the time they sailed into Portsmouth on January 25, 1569, only 65 men remained from the original 6 manifests.

Stories of the horrible fate of the captured crewmen at the hands of the Spanish (torture, slavery, being burned alive) reached England and incensed the populace. The blatant disregard for the armistice fueled Francis Drake's hatred for the Spanish.

Drake's Motives for Action

Prior to this incident, Francis Drake (1540?–1596) had good reason to dislike the Spanish. His family, devout Protestants, was forced to flee their home in Devon during the religious persecutions of Queen Mary I and live in an abandoned ship in Kent by the sea. Love of sailing and a hatred for Catholicism shaped Drake's future. Although not a vindictive man (Drake always treated his captives and enemies with courtesy), after the bitter betrayal at the island of San Juan de Uluá, a degree of revenge against Catholic Spain became one of his motivating forces.

Drake was a brilliant strategist and navigator. And despite his anger, he was not a hot-headed skipper. He was always regarded as being a well-tempered leader: thoughtful in planning and cool under fire.

Drake's 1570 Expedition

Determined to deprive King Philip of as much treasure as possible while also disrupting Spanish trade, Drake, with a privateer's commission granted by Elizabeth, set sail in 1570 on his first of many reconnaissance and attack-planning trips to the Caribbean. His cousin, the newly knighted Sir John Hawkins, privately funded these expeditions.

Drake was able to sail to South America with little attention drawn to his activities by sailing in the *Swan*, a small ship with few weapons aboard. Finding a secluded harbor at the Gulf of Darien (east coast of the Isthmus of Panama), Drake set up a secret base smack in the middle of King Philip's territory. Port Pheasant, named for the abundant birds in the area, was ideal for reconnoitering the coast and mounting successful surprise attacks on passing ships.

The secret to Drake's success was twofold: a number of prefabricated pinnaces (shallow-hulled oar and sail vessels) were brought over in the hull of the *Swan* that were easily assembled and used for lightning-fast raids. He also befriended the local Indians and escaped African slaves (Cimarrons), whose hatred of the Spanish was beyond his own distaste for the same. The locals and the Cimarrons provided valuable information concerning the treasure and troop movements of the Spanish.

A Grand Scheme

Drake realized that Panama was the weak link in the Spanish Main. All goods and riches were carried by long mule trains across Panama and shipped from the unfortified city of Nombre de Dios (the Spanish thought no one would dare attack a well-armed city in the middle of Spanish territory), where the annual treasure fleet annually sailed to Spain.

Drake devised a grand albeit ill-fated scheme. His men, along with the Indians and Cimarrons, sailed the pinnaces at night and successfully attacked the city. Drake, struck in the leg by a musket ball, collapsed from loss of blood. His loyal men abandoned the raid on the full treasure house and carried him to safety.

Drake's next target was the mule train itself. But that required a waiting period of four months until the rainy season ended in January. In the meantime, while his leg healed, he terrorized shipping in the area and acquired the name *El Draque* ("The Dragon"). Drake's identity was now known. He was considered by the Spanish government a pirate to be caught and sent to the Inquisition to be tried and killed. But first they'd have to catch him.

Finally the day came when Drake received news that the treasure fleet was anchored at Nombre de Dios waiting for the mule train. He took 30 Cimarrons and 18 Englishmen, marched for days inland into the jungle, and simply hid in the thick foliage for the treasure to come to him.

Unfortunately, one of Drake's men—a nervous and drunken crewman by the name of Robert Pike—failed to wait for the ambush signal. Pike leapt from his concealed position too early, spooking the mule train, which wisely turned back and thus avoided a nasty fate at the hands of Drake's bushwhackers. Drake was not deterred by his failed plan. He, in fact, became more determined than ever to attack the trains.

As luck would have it, Drake met and teamed up with the French corsair Guillaume Le Testu and his crew. This time Drake's plan was to attack the treasure train just as it was leaving the jungle. He hoped the tired guards would drop their vigil as they were safely in sight of the city. Together the combined crews waited for the next mule train filled with treasure to begin its journey. This time the plan worked. The pirates overwhelmed the guards and found themselves face to face with 200 mules carrying hundreds of pounds worth of silver and gold apiece. There was so much treasure the men couldn't carry it all in one trip. However, Testu was badly wounded in the attack. It was decided he would stay in the jungle with two loyal crewmen and the now buried silver. Drake and the others would take the gold first and come back for the men and the silver. Upon their return to the jungle, the pirates discovered the men and silver gone, both most likely retrieved by the Spanish.

> **Treasure Chest**
>
> During his march inland, at the summit of the mountains that bisects the Isthmus of Panama, the Cimarron chief pointed out the Pacific Ocean to Drake. It was 25 miles south of the Atlantic Ocean and a completely different color. Drake prayed that one day he'd be able to sail its waters. His prayer would be answered.

Drake divided up the gold between the English and French crews and at the request of the Cimarrons disassembled the ships they no longer needed and gave them the iron fittings and nails. Drake, now with enough gold to make him a millionaire, sailed for England. But first he defiantly sailed past Cartegena (the capital of the Spanish Main) with the red and white cross of St. George (the English flag at the time) whipping boldly from the mainmast of his ship.

Return to England

On Sunday, August 8, 1573, Drake eased his ship into Plymouth Harbor. Churchgoers, hearing all the commotion, deserted their pews—leaving the preachers speechless—and raced down to the harbor. Drake instantly became a hero and celebrity to the people of England. But he had put his queen in a precarious political situation.

Elizabeth was still attempting to avoid open war with Spain. Philip was feeling the staggering economic depletion of his treasury from the English as well as French and Dutch pirate raids. Finally the Spanish king was ready to listen to his advisors and loosen his death grip of a trade embargo along the entire Spanish Main.

The day Francis Drake sailed into Plymouth, England and Spain were in the midst of serious negotiations to resume peaceful and normal economic trade relations. Drake quickly realized that his return to England with a ship loaded with stolen Spanish treasure would be a huge political embarrassment to the crown. He also feared the queen would be pressured into arresting him on charges of blatant piracy and his hard-earned treasure confiscated. Elizabeth, pleased with his success and desirous of removing him from London, sent Drake with the earl of Essex to quell an uprising in Ireland, having him return to England only when tensions at court eased. Political events soon turned in his favor and his greatest adventure would begin.

A Journey Around the World

When relations with Spain again deteriorated, Drake went to his friend Sir Christopher Hatton with a proposal for the grandest expedition he had ever mounted. Intrigued by the plans and knowing the character of his friend, Hatton not only agreed to invest a large sum of his own money into the pirating adventure, but persuaded Elizabeth to grant Drake a private audience.

Obviously, Drake's vision of a voyage to attack the city of Panama itself and anything and everything Spanish in between piqued Elizabeth's interest. To prevent the voyage from appearing officially sanctioned, Elizabeth wisely invested her private—nongovernmental—funds.

Drake's Five Fingers

A fleet of five ships—his flagship the *Pelican*, as well as the *Elizabeth, Marigold, Swan,* and *Christopher*—left Plymouth on November 15, 1577, and sailed first toward Africa. (En route to Africa, Drake renamed the *Pelican* the *Golden Hind.* This was to honor his friend and benefactor Sir Christopher Hatton. On the top of Hatton's coat of arms rested the image of a golden hind.) Off the coast of Africa, Drake seized a Portuguese ship and captured its navigator, Nuño de Silva, to aid in the navigation of his own ships safely across the South Atlantic and through the South American coastal areas unknown to him. With the loss of crew, Drake had to abandon the *Swan* and *Christopher* along the coast of South America. By September 1578, the remaining ships managed to cross the Straits of Magellan only to get caught for two months in horrific storms. The *Marigold* went down with all hands, and the *Elizabeth* got caught up in the straits but managed to sail back to England. Drake took the *Golden Hind* and journeyed around the Pacific.

Unimagined Treasure and the California Coastline

Drake again employed pinnaces to successfully plunder cities and ships as he circumvented the globe. He attacked where his ships were least expected. He captured sea charts, Chinese silks, taffeta, and porcelains, coin, and gem-encrusted jewelry. His greatest prize this trip was the capture of the galleon *Nuestra Señora de la Concepcion*, commonly called the *Cacafuego* (the Spitfire). She was a Peruvian treasure ship that had just sailed from Panama. The haul was so tremendous it took two days to transfer and inventory their prize. It consisted of 13 chests of silver coins, 80 pounds of gold, and 26 tons of silver bars. The silver bars alone were so abundant Drake threw their common ballast (any heavy material used in the hold to improve a ship's stability) from the hold overboard and replaced it with the silver.

> **Dead Men's Tales**
>
> In some parts of the Pacific Northwest, the argument over where exactly Drake landed dwarfs the argument over who wrote Shakespeare's plays.
>
> —Oliver Seeler, *Francis Drake in Nova Albion—the Mystery Resolved* (2001)

Drake realized his dream when he reached the Pacific Ocean and sailed past Mexico and up the west coast of North America as far as the state of Washington. Turning southward, he anchored off northern California before continuing home to England. (A controversy still rages over the exact location of the harbor he named Nova Albion.) There, Drake landed, rested, and claimed the harbor off northern California for Queen Elizabeth I.

Around the World and Back Again

Using captured sea charts and a captive navigator, Drake continued his journey, successfully circumnavigating the globe. The *Golden Hind* sailed into Plymouth on September 26, 1580. Unsure of the political climate and his reception, Drake was prepared to disappear. That proved unnecessary. Elizabeth, undaunted by the outrage of the Spanish government, publicly boarded Drake's ship. Before a huge crowd, she knighted Drake, calling him "the master pirate of the known world."

Drake's Right Arm

Drake's sea artist (navigator) was considered one of the most important people aboard his ship (see Chapter 10). The navigator's sea charts, along with his knowledge, enabled his captain, Drake, to safely fulfill his ambition. But it wasn't just Drake and his men who benefited from the increasing accuracy of sea charts in the post-Columbus world. Accurate charts enabled all sailors, privateers, and pirates to venture to points around the world previously unimagined, and then—barring any unforeseen enemy vessels or shipwrecking weather conditions—return safely and expeditiously home.

The charts most sought-after became those aboard the Spanish treasure galleons of the early 1500s. Pirates and privateers were ruthless in their pursuit of these charts. In fact, the first items searched for when a captured prize was boarded were the charts. If a vessel was captured, the captain or navigator would attempt to destroy their charts rather than let them fall into the hands of pirates or their nation's enemies.

> ### Treasure Chest
>
> In 1584, Dutch pilot and cartographer Lucas Janszoon Wagenaer (a.k.a. Waghenaer) published his compilation of nautical charts that span the Zuider Zee (North Sea inlet in the Netherlands) to Cadiz (seaport in Spain). The atlas became known as a Waggoner or Wagner. Since then it has become the general term for all volumes or atlases of sea charts. In 1588, Howard of Effingham, lord high admiral of England, commissioned Anthony Ashley to prepare his own atlas of sea charts. Simply re-engraving Wagenaer's charts, Ashley titled the volume *The Mariner's Mirrour*. It was widely used by English sailors for centuries.

The Book Men Cried Over

Sea charts proved to be the most valuable finds aboard any ship for centuries to come. In fact, sea charts were so important that in 1682 (more than a century after Drake's world voyage), during Captain Bartholomew Sharp's (see Chapter 14) trial on charges of piracy, England's High Court of the Admiralty acquitted Sharp of all charges. The previous year, Sharp had boarded the Spanish ship *El Santo Rosario* and brought back to King Charles II an atlas of extreme importance. It not only detailed the entire Pacific coastline of South America, it instructed a pilot how to safely sail into any harbor from Acapulco to Cape Horn. Instead of the gallows, Captain Sharp was given command of an English warship. Spain was naturally outraged. (Spain and England had a tenuous peace at the time.)

> ### Dead Men's Tales
>
> I took a Spanish manuscript of prodigious value—it describes all the ports, roads, harbours, bays, sands, rocks and risings of the land, and instructions how to work a ship into any port or harbour. The Spaniards cried when I got the book.
>
> —English pirate-captain Bartholomew Sharp, 1681

In 1685, William Hack finished the English translation of Sharp's stolen atlas and named it *The Waggoner of the South Seas.*

Sea Dogs Nip at Spain's Heel

In the late 1500s, Spain attempted to conquer England covertly by fomenting insurrection in Ireland and Scotland. Finally, Queen Elizabeth's patience wore thin. She understood war with Spain was inevitable. Against her counselor's advice, she ordered the building of warships. While her armaments were stockpiling, she needed a diversion and—with it—private financing. She knew right where to turn.

Elizabeth appealed to Sir Walter Raleigh for assistance. He agreed to help finance her privateers for a percentage of all confiscated treasure.

Elizabeth then commissioned her most loyal subjects: Sir Francis Drake, Sir Martin Frobisher, Sir Richard Grenville, Sir John Hawkins, Thomas Cavendish, and all English sailors (popularly called *sea dogs*). Issuing letters of marque, the orders were to harass the Spanish wherever encountered and degrade their sea forces.

Knowing the Ropes

The term **sea dogs** has a number of definitions. In England, for years, it was derogatory slang used to describe a seasoned sailor as an unsavory character. Queen Elizabeth took the phrase and flipped it to mean sailors who bravely defended England.

Thus, the famous Elizabethan sea dogs sailed. These men were more than happy to comply with the queen's orders. Each man knew they would be considered pirates by the Spanish, and if captured they would be killed. This knowledge did not stop them, and many sailors signed on to the English crews.

Drake Sails Again

Sir Francis Drake again set sail for the Main to continue his personal war against Spain. In 1586, his ships—alone—captured the cities of Santo Domingo (Hispániola), the capital city of Cartagena (Colombia), and the Spanish city fortress of St. Augustine, Florida. He returned to England to fight the war (1588) with the Spanish Armada. After the English navy routed the Spanish fleet, Drake persuaded the queen to let him sail again to the Caribbean. Drake continued his personal attacks of reprisal.

On January 28, 1596, at the age of 55, Drake died. The captain's log stated he passed from fever and "the bludie flix" (dysentery). He was buried at sea with full naval honors just miles offshore from Nombre de Dios, the city he first raided 23 years earlier.

Capturing Treasure While Trying to Circumnavigate the Globe

If Drake was gracious to his captives, Thomas Cavendish (1560–1592) was a bloodthirsty fiend—fitting all the negative stereotypes of a pirate—and was so toward his enemies as well as his crew. He was also obsessed with circumnavigating the globe.

In 1586, like Drake and the other sea dog commanders, Cavendish was commissioned to sail. His orders? Seek treasure. That he did, attacking the Spanish at every opportunity, and acquiring prize ships for a larger fleet along the way.

Treasure Chest

Control over the spice trade led to wars and territorial disputes. When Portugal banned Spain from using the sea lanes around Africa, the Spanish had to devise their own route to Asia. The first ships left Mexico in 1565. The Manila galleon route was sailed continuously from Mexico to Manila for 250 years. The average speed was a mere three miles per hour. Currents, winds, and storms determined the length of each journey. It took three months to sail from Mexico to Manila and eight months for the return voyage. Sickness, scurvy, pirate attacks, and storms were the ever-present enemy. In all those years, Englishmen captured only four ships.

Hawkins Builds the Fleet

War with Spain now inevitable, Elizabeth appointed John Hawkins treasurer of her navy. Her council had misgivings over his appointment. Hawkins, however, turned his full attention to outfitting and building the best navy possible. The defeat of the Spanish Armada proved him correct. Elizabeth knighted him for bravery in battle. Now in his late 60s, he sailed with Drake to continue intercepting treasure fleets. In 1595, Sir John Hawkins died from a raging fever off the coast of Puerto Rico. His strong belief that the riches of the area belonged to any and all men brave enough to seize them inspired many of his fellow sea dogs to continue raiding the Spanish Main.

Cavendish Seizes the *Santa Ana*

The Spanish were more concerned with potential pirate attacks on the city of Acapulco. The year before, the city authorities removed the cannon off the treasure galleon *Santa Ana*. When Cavendish's fleet cornered the treasure ship, she had a mere 50 soldiers aboard with muskets. With his ship's hold already filled with treasure, what Cavendish couldn't take with him he burned along with the *Santa Ana* just outside the harbor of Cabo San Lucas. Cavendish hanged a shipboard priest from the mainmast yard and tortured many of the sailors. In addition to chinaware, carved religious icons, silks, perfumes, and spices, the value of the pearls and gold aboard was estimated at 122,000 pesos ($3,660,000). His crew, having enough of the man's brutishness, demanded he share out on the spot. After all the spoils were accounted for, Cavendish sailed his ship *Desire* east, abandoning his other remaining ship.

The attack was a crushing financial blow to the Spanish treasury—this being the first Manila galleon lost to an enemy, which revealed the wealth the ship carried. Manila galleons thereafter became a magnet to raiders from all countries.

Cavendish Returns Home

Triumphantly, Cavendish, now a millionaire, returned to England in 1588 and learned he missed the Armada's defeat by mere months. Squandering all his money by 1591, he gathered together another fleet of ships and again attempted to circumnavigate the globe. This voyage proved disastrous. Severe weather, differing personalities, impatience, and flaring tempers all played a part in the ill-fated expedition. Cavendish believed his officers and crew were incompetent and plotting against him. Moreover, storms near the Straits of Magellan made the passage impossible.

Characteristically, Cavendish abandoned his fleet and sailed his flagship to Brazil, attacking ports along the way.

Cavendish died at age 32 while at sea, accusing his men of being insolent, mutinous mariners. Only 15 sailors out of his fleet of 75 crewmen managed to return to England.

Frobisher the Rogue

Sir Martin Frobisher (1535?–1594) was Elizabeth's rogue sea dog. Rarely did he follow orders, even when issued by his queen. He spent years sailing with Drake, pirating along the Spanish Main. He was knighted for his bravery during the battle of the

Armada. Then, once again, he joined Drake raiding along the Main. He died at age 59 from botched surgery from battle wounds incurred near Brittany, France.

Grenville's Revenge

Sir Richard Grenville (1542?–1591) was originally more interested in the navigation and colonization of North America than seeking treasure, though he wouldn't pass up the opportunity to attack a Spanish ship if it presented itself. However, after his colony on Roanoke Island (off the coast of Virginia) was attacked and brutalized by Spaniards, his hatred for the Spanish was without bounds. He sailed to the Azores, a Spanish-held archipelago off Portugal. There, out of revenge, he pillaged and burned Spanish towns and brutalized his prisoners.

At the head of a squadron of Elizabeth's ships, Grenville sailed in 1591 with Lord Thomas Howard back to the Azores to intercept Spanish treasure galleons. King Philip's spies in the English court warned of their departure. A squadron of warships was lying in wait. Outnumbered, the English were forced to retreat. But Grenville's ship, the *Revenge* (Drake's former flagship), was surrounded. Putting up a fierce resistance for 14 hours, the lone ship managed to damage 15 Spanish warships. Eventually, Grenville, mortally wounded, ordered his men to abandon ship and blow her up. His men surrendered instead. After his death a sudden cyclone ripped through the harbor at Flores sinking the *Revenge* and many of the Spanish ships. Grenville was 50 when he died of his wounds.

> **Treasure Chest**
>
> In 1878, English poet Alfred Tennyson immortalized Sir Grenville in his poem "The Revenge—A Ballad of the Fleet."

The Fighting's Not Over Yet

With the great Armada defeated in 1588, people had hopes that the wars between England and Spain had finally ended. Unfortunately, it wasn't going to be that easy. Philip II refused to give up his dream of conquering England. Elizabeth I refused to entertain the notion of his winning. For the next 16 years, the Armada would be launched three more times against England. Elizabeth's sea dogs, privateers, and the severe unpredictable channel winds were all the luck England needed for her resounding success.

"We Almost Died—and for What?"

After the Spanish defeat, hundreds of ships anchored at harbors in England intent on unloading thousands of men. Unfortunately, that is not what happened.

Typhus and fatal dysentery had spread like wildfire throughout the fleet during the three weeks of intensive fighting. The men's food and water rations were depleted. Government officials found themselves without sufficient facilities in cities to tend to the seriously ill. Sailors were forced to remain onboard for weeks. The overcrowding and filth caused the diseases to spread more rapidly. The numbers of dead and dying soared. When the few surviving crewmen were finally allowed to go ashore, there was nowhere for them to bunk.

There was yet another concern. Veterans came home to a country that didn't have enough money in the national treasury to pay their wages. Whether Queen Elizabeth had sufficient funds in her private accounts to pay everyone is unknown. There are only state records indicating the treasury was out of cash.

The lord high admiral, Charles Howard of Effingham (Elizabeth's first cousin), was appalled by this obvious effrontery to his men—the heroes who had successfully sailed against the dreaded Armada. He dipped into his own private funds and paid off as many sailors as his bank accounts could allow. Lord Howard's was a noble gesture. But there remained hundreds of penniless, starving, and ill sailors wandering the port towns and dropping dead in the streets.

Spain's Appreciation a Bit Better

The same conditions aboard the English ships held true for the Spanish. The difference was how their country's government took action. King Phillip's reaction was in drastic contrast to the English. Pensions were set up for orphans and widows. Makeshift hospitals were quickly opened to treat the ailing sailors. Though gracious and swift in his handling of his military, Philip's treasury was strained. Pirates from Holland, France, and England were still raiding the treasure fleets. Though the Spanish government was slow in paying sailors their wages, they had more opportunities for employment waiting for them in Spain and along the Spanish Main.

Pirate or Privateer? Make Up Your Mind Already!

In 16 years of sporadic fighting, the line blurred between enemy and ally. After months at sea, if a friendly ship didn't cross one's bow with recent news, one never knew what was going on between states. An attack on an enemy could suddenly become an attack on an ally. If that were the case, letters of marque were no longer valid. Thus, whether one was a pirate or privateer became a very fine line.

A crew could chance sailing out of port a privateer with everyone rooting for them only to return as a dreaded pirate (in which case they would be arrested, sent to jail, tried, and eventually hanged). This occurred frequently. In fact, this is what happened to the famous Captain Kidd many years later; some now think he was not a pirate at all, but a very unlucky and naively trusting privateer. You'll read his tale in Chapter 14, and then you can judge for yourself.

Peace Between Sworn Enemies

England and Spain finally came to their senses and signed the Treaty of Westminster in 1604. The peace treaty was not signed by those archrivals Queen Elizabeth I and King Philip II, but by their successors, King James I of England and King Philip III of Spain. Warships sailed to their home ports. Western Europe thought that peace was finally accomplished. Little did anyone surmise that wars and skirmishes would continue to crop up again and again.

"Thanks, Veterans, Now Go Away"

Large numbers of English naval ship fleets disbanded after the peace. Men were discharged. They dispersed through harbor cities and towns by the thousands. If a veteran happened to live where his ship docked, he had the easy choice of returning home. Without their back pay, many men discovered they hadn't saved enough money to travel home. Fewer naval ships needed crews. Sailors tried to sign on to merchant ships. However, most commercial ships needed no recruits. Desperate sailors turned their attention to trade shops.

What was the reaction to these men seeking jobs on land? Mothers locked their daughters in their homes. Job markets closed. To those who lived on land, sailors were so alien in looks with their tanned leathery faces and strange sea jargon, they might as well have dropped from the moon.

Men with money in their pockets might have chosen to return home. After years at sea, they had no idea if parents, siblings, wives, or children still lived or even remembered them. For those originally raised in farming areas and having their fill of the sea, the idea of returning to farm life was tantalizing.

Enduring Much, and Nothing to Show for It

For a great number of unemployed, and who were often cheated out of months of rightful pay, the prospect of going home with nothing rankled them to their cores. They had every right to complain. Probably not a one had escaped service without a series of lash marks on their backs.

Such conditions created an ever-larger group of men who felt they deserved the freedom to have a say about how they lived their lives. If they couldn't get their wages from the backbreaking work they had done, they would acquire wealth the exact same way they saw their governments obtaining it: they'd pirate their wealth and settle some scores of revenge along the way.

Not every man who decided to turn to piracy had been an honest man turned bad by circumstance. As in any society, there were psychopaths, murderers, thieves, and rogues out for what they thought would be a fast and easy way to enormous wealth and luxury. Those men who had never sailed before and joined a pirate ship were in for an even greater surprise than their intended victims.

Sea Beggars

After many years and lost lives during Spain's invasion and occupation of the Netherlands (Holland, Utrecht, Noord-Brabant, Gelderland), a truce in 1609 was finally declared. The hatred their citizenry held for Spain could not be easily forgiven. The Inquisition's famed cruelty during those years of occupation touched most families. The *sea beggars* of the Netherlands first sailed in the sixteenth century as pirates in the Spanish Main. The majority of them returned home to fight the Spanish invasion as a maritime resistance group.

Now that a truce was signed, the sea beggars immediately sailed back to settle the smaller islands in the Caribbean overlooked by the Spanish. They successfully turned the Leeward and Windward Islands of St. Martin, St. Eustatius, Saba, and Curaçao into pirate havens and smuggling stops firmly held by the Netherlands. Not to be greedy among their brotherhood of pirates, they shared the island of St. Croix with their English cohorts.

> **Knowing the Ropes**
>
> The pirates of the Netherlands were called **sea beggars** (or freebooters). The Anglicized names come from the Dutch term *watergeuzan* and *vrijbuiter* meaning "free booty" or "plunderer."

Better yet, they resumed their attacks on Spanish shipping and towns along the Main. A group of veteran sea beggars with private monetary backing formed the Dutch West India Company. Charted in 1621, their purpose was not only legitimate trade around the world, but also plundering the wealth and goods of all their sworn enemies. This clearly meant Catholic Spain and Portugal. Through trading with willing Spanish colonists and mining the salt beds on the island of Curaçao, off Venezuela, to supply their fish industries, they fluctuated between out-and-out piracy and privateering.

These men were expert sailors as well as astute businessmen. As with other countries that watched with envy as the treasure fleets sailed to Seville, the Dutch set their sights on capturing a Spanish treasure fleet.

A Pirate's Sweet Revenge

One of the most renowned and successful Dutch admirals (the Spanish and the Portuguese considered him to be a pirate) was Piet Heyn (1577–1629), who sailed for the Dutch West Indies Company.

In 1628, Heyn captured a Spanish flotilla off Cuba. Heyn was more than familiar with the route the ships had taken. He knew that they had initially loaded treasure in Panama. Then they sailed to Mexico. There they joined the galleons that had gathered the wealth from all over Mexico. Heyn waited with his own fleet of 31 swift caravels off the northern shore of Cuba.

Heyn fully intended to capture this particular flotilla or die trying. From his spies, he learned that the commander of the Spanish flotilla was none other than Juan de Benavides, a famous Spanish admiral, who had captured Heyn years earlier and enslaved him, albeit temporarily, on a galley. Heyn had a score to settle with Benavides, and this time he was going to be the victor.

Trapping Benavides

When the flotilla was sighted, Heyn divided his force, dispatching half his ships eastward to cut off any escape on the part of the Spanish. In so doing, Heyn was able to prevent the flotilla from entering the safety of the harbor of Havana. The flotilla turned east and sailed 10 miles to the Bay of Matanza hoping to escape. All Benavides managed to do was ground his fleet in the shallows.

As Heyn's men approached the galleons, they were puzzled why no defending shots were fired. The answer was simple. The ships were so filled with silver and gold ingots along with stacks of chests, the cargo actually blocked the canon gun ports.

To Heyn's great disappointment, Benavides could not be found aboard his flagship. Nevertheless, the treasure Heyn confiscated was one of the most spectacular hauls ever, worth twelve million guilders, roughly $192,000,000.

Heyn sailed his fleet along with 15 captured Spanish ships (to help haul the booty) to Amsterdam. Hailed a hero by the Dutch and a vile pirate by the Spanish court, Heyn finally got his personal revenge. But what of Admiral Benavides? He had vanished, all right: at the first sign of the approaching Dutch vessels, Benavides secured a rowboat and sailed to what he was hoping would be the safety of the harbor. Arrested by his own countrymen, he was tried for cowardice and desertion of his post during a time of battle. Found guilty, he was beheaded. Heyn was killed during a battle in 1629.

Dead Men's Tales

The cargos ... consisted of 177,357 pounds of silver, 135 pounds of gold, 2,270 chests of indigo (cloth), 735 chests of cochineal, 37,375 hides, logwood, 235 chests of sugar ... with spices, pearls, and personal treasures ... of the Spanish aboard. A triumph not to be repeated for thirty years.

—Jennifer Marx, *Pirates and Privateers of the Caribbean* (1992)

The Least You Need to Know

♦ Queen Elizabeth I was a master politician, able to prevent open conflict with Spain while building a strong navy.

♦ France and Spain fought over religious ideology and territory.

♦ Much of England's wealth was acquired through piracy and trafficking of slaves.

♦ English privateers such as John Hawkins and Francis Drake depleted Spain's treasury.

♦ English sea dogs were famous for their loyalty, sailing abilities, combat prowess, and nerve.

♦ During Spain's occupation of the Netherlands, the sea beggars abandoned their pirating ways to fight for their country's freedom. Later they returned to the Caribbean as colonists.

Chapter 5

Lady Pirates in the British Isles

In This Chapter

- ◆ England not immune to pirate raids
- ◆ Lady Mary Killigrew's wild night of reckoning
- ◆ The notorious exploits of Grace O'Malley
- ◆ A meeting between two powerful women

Piracy increased during the reign of King Henry VIII (1509–1547), and England's coastal dwellers increasingly found themselves either directly involved in piracy or victimized by the practice. Many fishermen and sailors became pirates as a temporary means of supplementing their meager incomes. Other men found piracy too lucrative to bother with other professions. They continually attacked ships in the English Channel while England's navy was preoccupied with the urgent matters of imperial survival.

When Elizabeth I ascended the throne, an established and thriving network of piracy was firmly in place. Large syndicates worked from Land's End (the tip of England) to the Irish coast. The drastic weather change in 1560 ruined harvests and forced even greater numbers of people into the trade. Though Elizabeth tried to control these activities along her home shores, she had no better success than the Spanish did against her own privateers. England found itself in the same predicament as the ships attacked by her pirates and privateers operating along the Spanish Main. While Hawkins, Drake, and others were pillaging their enemies, Elizabeth's own countrymen—and women—were raiding their own homeland for booty.

Piracy In and Around the British Isles

Instead of transporting goods throughout England by overland routes, it was far more economical to do so via merchant ship. This provided constant opportunity and temptation for pirates plying the waters off England. One method of attack and storage of stolen goods was from the use of many well-hidden coves along the shores. Some pirates rented the privilege of cove use from the landed gentry or distinguished business families. These landowners would turn a blind eye to the goings-on along the waters edge. For a percentage of the take or a monthly fee when necessary, they assisted in the various nefarious endeavors. Some families were involved for generations, piracy being just one offshoot of their many business endeavors.

Lady Mary Killigrew: Genteel Hostess or Accessory to Crime?

One such family was the family Killigrew of Cornwall. Sir John Killigrew was vice-admiral of Cornwall and hereditary royal governor of Pendennis Castle. His home, Arwenack Manor, by the mouth of Falmouth Harbor, just happened to be a major clearinghouse for pirate activity in and around the area. His wife, Lady Mary Killigrew, was the daughter of a gentleman pirate from Suffolk, England, Philip Wolverston. Mary's son John and her daughter-in-law Elizabeth were also heavily involved in the traditional family business of piracy. Beyond these limited facts, nothing else at this time is known concerning Mary's life.

Although Sir John never engaged in actual hands-on acts of piracy, he was not above bribing officials and naval officers to turn a blind eye when necessary.

> ### Knowing the Ropes
>
> A **carrack** was a large heavily built ship for travel and cargo with a castlelike superstructure at the bow and stern. It was a popular vessel of the time with two to four masts for square-rigged sails with a lateen sail on the mizzenmast to help steer.

Lady Mary managed the handling of confiscated items brought ashore. She kept accounts and distributed the pirated goods throughout their large syndicate, operating as far as Ireland. She was known to be a gracious hostess and entertained the more gentlemanly and respectable pirates in her home.

Lady Mary Killigrew's reckoning came about on New Year's Day in 1582. The *carrack Maria* sought refuge from a severe storm within Falmouth Harbor. Once docked, the vessel's owners, Philip de Orozo and Juan de Charis, paid no mind to their ship's safety. After all, England and Spain were not at war, and they were docked right in front of the vice-admiral's manor house. What danger could there be? Leaving a watch crew, the two owners went into town to wait out the weather.

A carrack.

(Artist: Ron Druett)

Lady Killigrew's Descent into Piracy

The *Maria* was rumored to be carrying barrels of coins along with abundant exotic merchandise. This merchant ship—within sight of her own home—proved to be too much of a temptation. On the evening of January 7, Lady Killigrew, with two personal servants, Kendal and Hawkins, boarded the *Maria*.

Now, here is where the story's variations come into play. One account states Kendal, Hawkins, and Mary slaughtered the ship's crew, dumping the bodies overboard before taking the goods. Mary then instructed her husband's piratical cohorts to sail the ship to Ireland as a prize. The other version suggests there were only two crew members aboard, whom Lady Killigrew personally killed, again dumping the bodies overboard and stealing the ship. Whichever version one wishes to believe, men were killed and the ship indeed disappeared from Falmouth Harbor along with its cargo.

Enraged, the ship's owners, Orozo and Charis, made an official complaint to the appointed commissioner of piracy. This commission had been set up by the English government to monitor piratical activity in Cornwall. Ironically, according to the historical commission papers of that time, the commissioner was none other than John Killigrew, Lady Killigrew's son. He ruled that because there were no eyewitnesses to the event, the only facts known were the ship with its crew and cargo no longer resided in Falmouth Harbor.

Killigrew Jailed

Not satisfied with the runaround they received in Cornwall, Orozo and Charis traveled to London and demanded an audience with the earl of Bedford of the queen's privy council (a judicial and political group of men selected by the queen). Bedford's impartial inquiries into the incident found the culprits guilty. Hawkins, Kendal, and Lady Killigrew were jailed with death sentences on their heads.

Sir John could do nothing to save the two servants from hanging, but he managed to get his mother's sentence reduced to time in prison. Some say he bribed the court to lessen the charges. Others believe Queen Elizabeth favored Lady Killigrew and did not wish her executed. Here again there is no concrete evidence aside from the fact that Lady Killigrew languished in jail for quite a while before being freed. It can be assumed that upon release she left the pirating to her more experienced crews because she was no longer mentioned in any other legal piratical documents.

Grace O'Malley: Gutsy Pirate and Matriarch of Clans

Few facing charges of piracy had as easy an escape from prison and death as did Lady Killigrew or Anne Bonny (see Chapter 19). Some had only their brains and courage to squirm out of a tight situation. Grace O'Malley tops that list.

History knows her by many names: Granuaile, Grania ni Mhaille, Graine Mhaol, Grainne, Grace of the Cropped Hair, or simply Grace O'Malley. Whatever name one wishes to call her, the records indicate she was born in Ireland (circa 1530) during turbulent times of continual clan wars and the beginning of the English occupation. Grace was the daughter of Owen (Dudara or Black Oak) O'Malley, a powerful Irish chieftain. Their territory located on the remote western coast of Ireland boasted a huge cattle herd from which hides and tallow were traded. Their other legitimate business included a large fishing fleet that traded salt fish with France and Spain. They were a proud seafaring warrior clan, and Grace was no exception.

Grace's early life ran its expected course. At about 16 she entered into a political marriage to Donal O'Flaherty (Donal-an-Cogahaid or Donal of the Battles), heir to the powerful O'Flaherty clan. She gave birth to three children while assuming her duties as mistress to her husband's castles of Bunowen and Ballinahinch. After that, nothing in her life remained normal. Her husband, a reckless leader, brought his clan to the brink of starvation. It fell upon Grace to lead her new clan out of crippling poverty. During O'Flaherty's absence battling other clans, Grace superseded her husband's authority assisting his clan members. It was at this time she began her career in piracy with O'Flaherty men willingly crewing her ships.

> **Treasure Chest**
>
> The O'Malley motto, *Terra Marique Potens* ("powerful by both land and sea"), dates back centuries and fits the clan perfectly. Not many Irishmen sailed beyond Ireland's shores as the O'Malleys did, making them not only wealthy, but a powerful adversary.

Clan Warfare

In revenge for O'Flaherty's seizure of a disputed island fortress on Lough Corrib, the Joyce clan killed Donal O'Flaherty. (One of O'Flaherty's many pseudonyms was Donal-an-Cullagh or Donal, "the cock.") For his courage in the battle for this island, the castle was renamed "Cock Castle." With O'Flaherty's death, the Joyces assumed the castle would again be theirs. They didn't know Grace. With a crew of O'Flaherty warriors, Grace sailed to avenge her husband's death and defend the castle. Her heroism and skill in keeping the castle from Joyce hands earned her the courageous title, "the hen." To this day, the castle is still called Caislean-an-Circa or "Hen's Castle."

The city of Galway at the time was a major trade center not only for Ireland, but for all of England. For years many city charters and by-laws had been enacted prohibiting any trade within the city limits by the Gaelic clans or other nonresidents of Galway. This restriction obviously prohibited many from earning a living, but not Grace. Enraged by the imposed restrictions, Grace considered all areas outside the harbor fair game and embarked upon a career of piracy.

A Growing Thorn in the English Crown

Wisely, Grace didn't have her men board and indiscriminately plunder the ships they seized. She first negotiated with the captain concerning a fair fee to ensure safe passage to Galway. Depending on the outcome of those talks, her men would then one way or another confiscate their share. Though the Irish and English councils were outraged by these blatant acts of piracy, they didn't have sufficient knowledge of the shoreline or swift enough ships to apprehend Grace.

Grace at no time gave up her legitimate merchant trading. With a fleet of oared galley ships and loyal men of the O'Flaherty clan, she frequently sailed to the continent, returning with products as varied as fabrics, wine, Spanish steel, and Portuguese cargo ships for sale.

According to ancient Irish law, women were able to fight beside their husbands, but not inherit their title or lands. With the eventual death of Donal O'Flaherty, Grace had no more claim to his property. She had no choice but to return to the O'Malley homestead. Records show that 200 O'Flaherty men pledged their loyalty to her and insisted on accompanying their leader. Grace cleverly chose Clare Island in Clew Bay, county Mayo, as her base to continue her legitimate and illegitimate operations. The highest point on the island provided a commanding view of the surrounding horizon, yet was hard to spot from a distance.

The political winds blowing along Ireland did not favor the Gaelic people. The English feared Spain would conquer Ireland and have a back door to invade England. The English military presence in Ireland grew. Their orders were to suppress any attempt at overthrowing English authority. Grace and her pirate raids frustrated the English governors. The harder they tried to capture her, the more pirate raids she mounted.

A Marriage of Strategic Convenience

Needing a safer place for her fleet to operate, Grace in 1566 arranged to marry Richard-in-Iron Burke (Richard-in-Chainmail or Richard-an-Iarainn Bourke), heir to the MacWilliams and Burke clans. They pledged marriage for a year and a day (typical vows of the time). Grace moved with her fleet into Rockfleet Castle (a.k.a. Carrickahowley or Carraig-an-Cabhlaigh), deeper in the protective northern shores of Clew Bay.

Neither marriage nor the birth of her favorite son in 1567 ceased her pirating; it simply added to the legend that surrounds Grace. As stated in the official Annals and

State Papers of that year, she named her son Tibbot-na-Long (or Theobald of the Ships, or Toby of the Ships). The story passed down through the centuries tells of a battle aboard her galley ship the day after Toby's birth.

Returning from a trade mission, Grace's fleet was attacked by Turkish corsairs. Her captain went below to inform Grace while she was nursing that the battle was going poorly. He suggested her presence on deck would help the men. Furious, she stormed on deck with a pair of loaded blunderbusses (flintlock pistol with a broad muzzle) and yelled to her crew in Gaelic "May you be 7 times worse this day 12 months, who cannot do without me for one day." She then proceeded to fire her weapons straight at the Turkish leaders howling, "Take this from unconsecrated hands!" Managing to fight off the Turks, she went back to nursing her son. Her fleet continued to Clew Bay.

Surviving the English Power Struggle

Grace was no man's fool. She watched the power of the English crown wield greater influence and grind away the authority of the old Gaelic chieftains. As more of the clans agreed to the submission of fealty to England and her laws, Grace realized submission was the only option for survival. In 1577, she went with her husband, now chief of the MacWilliam's clan, to met Sir Henry Sidney, English lord deputy of Galway, to willingly agree to the MacWilliam submission.

Dead Men's Tales

There came to me also a most famous feminine sea captain called Grany Imallye, and offered her services unto me, wheresoever I would command her, with three galleys and 200 fighting men, either in Scotland or Ireland; she brought with her her [sic] husband for she was as well by sea as by land well more than Mrs. Mate with him … This was a notorious woman in all the coasts of Ireland.

—Sir Henry Sidney, 1583

Governor Bingham's Personal Vendetta

Although caught and jailed a number of times for piracy, history does not record how Grace managed her escapes or release from such ominous prisons as Dublin Castle. Whether she agreed to relinquish her career if set free, Grace always returned to her pirating ways.

Richard Bingham in 1584 became governor of Connacht (the northwest province of Ireland). His main mission was to bring all the Irish chieftains into sworn fealty to Queen Elizabeth and uphold the laws of England to the letter. His personal target was Grace O'Malley. Bingham proceeded to strip the clan Burke of its wealth and in doing so reduce the hold Grace had over the region. In 1586, Richard Bingham managed to personally capture Grace, built new gallows, and prepared to hang her.

Her son-in-law, Richard Devil's Hook Gurke, approached Governor Bingham and petitioned, as was the custom of the time, for the release of Grace O'Malley by offering himself as hostage. Bingham agreed to the exchange. Richard Devil's Hook languished in prison for years. To break Grace's spirit, Bingham had his men murder her eldest son, Owen O'Flaherty, while confiscating her herds of horses and cattle. By 1592, Bingham's troops raided Clew Bay and impounded Grace's fleet. She managed to flee to Ulster in time.

Bested by a Woman—and an O'Malley to Boot!

Grace O'Malley was now in her 60s. Most of the men in her family were imprisoned or dead, and her livelihood gone. She was well aware of the fact that Governor Bingham reveled in his victory. He intended on seeing her and her multiple family clans destroyed. However, Bingham truly didn't understand the kind of woman he was fighting. Shrewdly, Grace realized she had only one chance. To survive and restore her family rights Grace petitioned aid from none other than Elizabeth I, Queen of England. Grace traveled to London in May 1593 to accomplish her goal.

State papers record that Grace's letter to Elizabeth arrived in July 1593. She humbly requested that her imprisoned family be freed, and that her two surviving sons be granted the legal right under English law to keep their lands. Grace went on to request monetary assistance for her old age and pledged to fight England's enemies.

Pawns and Letters

Governor Bingham heard of Grace's correspondence with the queen. Bingham quickly dispatched his own letters to Lord Burghley and the queen. He warned them of Grace's duplicity and in great detail justified his actions in carrying out the queen's orders concerning the Irish. In an attempt to further stop Grace, Bingham imprisoned her son Tibbott-na-Long on charges of treason. This only spurred Grace to quicker action.

The queen had to have been intrigued by this woman. Official dispatches from Ireland had mentioned her for more than 40 years. Elizabeth, through her personal secretary, Lord Burghley, sent Grace a questionnaire with 18 articles of interrogatory for her to answer. Grace's replies (also recorded in state papers) were guarded, yet diplomatic.

Because the official date for all governmental petitions had ended by the time her son was arrested, Grace took another gamble. She traveled to Greenwich Palace from London City on the slim chance of securing a direct audience with the queen. The ramifications of her possible arrest as a known pirate did not deter her.

> **Dead Men's Tales**
>
> In tender consideration … in regard of her great age, she most humbly beseeches your majesty … to grant her some reasonable maintenance for the little time she has left … to grant free liberty … to invade with sword and fire all your highness enemies … without any interruption of any person.
>
> —Grace O'Malley, in her petition to Queen Elizabeth (July 1593)

Women Warriors, Face to Face

In September of that year, Grace O'Malley, Lady Burke, was granted an audience with Elizabeth. It was a meeting now steeped in legend. No details have been uncovered, if indeed any records were taken. As far as anyone can tell, it was an unprecedented rare private conversation between two remarkable women.

Suffice to say, Elizabeth granted all her requests. Elizabeth wrote to Governor Bingham on September 6, 1593. The letter ordered him to release all of Grace's family he had imprisoned. Elizabeth also granted her a governmental pension deducted from her son's land taxes, and the release of her impounded fleet.

Revenge Works Both Ways

Queen Elizabeth, by granting Grace's request, for all intents and purposes, handed her a privateering license. Governor Bingham felt this was a grave oversight on the queen's part. Who's to say? Perhaps Elizabeth knew exactly what privileges she handed Grace. Unless documents are uncovered to the contrary, this will remain a mystery, just like their private conversation.

Enraged, Bingham feared that Grace would go back to her pirating ways. He ordered a detachment of English soldiers to billet on Clare Island. Every one of her galleys sailed with a soldier aboard to guarantee her expeditions were honest. Bingham actively withheld the monies Elizabeth had granted her. Grace petitioned the royal treasurer and the privy council. However, with the rebellions and military skirmishes in Ireland heating up, her correspondence went unanswered.

Things began to look up for Grace toward the end of 1595 when Governor Richard Bingham was recalled to England in disgrace. Grace O'Malley had survived every obstacle he had thrown in her way. Now a matter of sheer survival, Grace needed to rebuild the wealth she and her clans once possessed. At the age of 66, Grace boarded one of her ships and ordered her fleet to go pirating once again.

Can't Keep a Good Woman Down

Grace increased her activities along the Irish coast. She refused to take sides in the war for control of Ireland. Changing her tactics somewhat, she now boarded any and all ships not for their cargo, but for extortion. For a fee, Grace would guarantee safe passage along the Irish coast. Her pirating continued well into her seventieth year. When an English military warship captured one of her galleys in 1601, Grace wisely decided she was no longer physically able to continue.

Ironically, in 1603, both Grace O'Malley and Elizabeth I died. It was also the year her son Tibbott-na-Long was knighted Sir Theobald Burke for aiding the English monarchy in Ireland.

The Least You Need to Know

- ◆ England's coastline was plagued by unchecked pirate attacks for years.
- ◆ Lady Mary Killigrew not only handled the monetary accounts from pirating ventures but also the distribution of goods. When the mood struck her, she pirated ships.
- ◆ Grace O'Malley was a shrewd businesswoman, pirate, and protector of her clan.
- ◆ The private meeting between Queen Elizabeth I and Grace O'Malley was a great, albeit little-known, historic occasion.

Part 2

The Sweet Trade

Piracy was indeed a "sweet trade," often characterized by an unpredictable life on the rolling sea, no home, no bounds, no law, and few rules save for those that the crew agreed on. Beyond that, the life of a pirate offered far more opportunities for a common man (and occasionally, a woman) than he might find in corrupt, overcrowded, and diseased cities.

Though ruthless in their behavior toward their victims, pirates followed a somewhat-gentlemanly code of conduct among themselves. After all, they were brothers in arms, figuratively and in some cases substantively. Not all men volunteered to be pirates, but once tasting fresh air, salt spray, and freedom, many stayed on, mastering both the sailing craft and weapons skills: they had to if they hoped to live beyond the next horizon.

6

Buccaneers: How It All Began

In This Chapter

- ◆ Breeding ground on Hispaniola
- ◆ "Undesirables" meet the Arawaks
- ◆ Child buccaneers
- ◆ An edict to evict
- ◆ Le Grand's daring raid
- ◆ Buccaneer-turned-author Alexander Oliver Exquemelin

No one historian can point to any one specific individual and say without equivocation that he was the very first buccaneer. But by the 1600s, the presence of buccaneers was well known throughout the Antilles Islands of the Caribbean.

Buccaneers were a different breed of pirate than those pirates and privateers who lived in Western Europe and prowled the Spanish Main. Most Western European pirates and privateers, if they survived, returned home to their country of origin after a raid. Buccaneers, on the other hand, made their homes in the Caribbean.

As first mentioned in Chapter 1, buccaneers began as game (land animals and fowl) hunters wanting only the freedom to live as they chose. But from that hunting breed, the Spanish authorities inadvertently created a special breed of pirate that would plague Spain for many years.

The Breeding Ground

The Spanish were convinced of their God-given right to own and control as much of the Western Hemisphere as they could conquer. Naively, they failed to consider the manpower and financial cost required to maintain such a significant hold over so wide a region.

Hispaniola—Home of the Arawak Indians

In the Greater Antilles chain, Columbus found and claimed an island for Spain in 1492. He named it *Española*, or "Little Spain." The name was later corrupted into the English version, Hispaniola. It is a large island 400 miles long and 150 miles wide at its broadest point. Today the island is divided into the countries of Haiti and the Dominican Republic. The peaceful Arawak Indians occupied Hispaniola before Spain's cruel occupation all but annihilated their civilization.

Originally, Spain intended the island to become a large agriculture-producing asset. But farming the rugged landscape proved difficult for European settlers. Consequently, the majority of settlers drifted to the southern city of Santo Domingo or the Banda del Norte, the three northern coastal settlements. The farmers left their livestock to run free and allowed the forests to reseed and vegetation grow wild.

Though multinational privateers—consisting of Dutch, English, Portuguese, French, and even Spanish sailing men—plundered the Main, Spain decided to concentrate its inadequate defenses on the most vital cities and islands that maintained the flow of gold and other treasures to the coffers in Seville. This led to the abandonment or, at best, neglect of her other settlements.

By the mid 1500s, Spain had colonized—then abandoned—many islands throughout the West Indies. Island cities such as Santo Domingo, Havana, Santiago, and San Juan continued to flourish. Other towns and villages on the same islands were virtually ignored. High prices and heavy taxes were levied on products shipped into those areas, financially strapping small farmers and plantation owners.

With Spain's own gold rush occurring on the South American continent, many settlers who were unable to afford living on the Greater and Lesser Antilles islands moved to Mexico and Peru in search of their own fortunes. Onto these abandoned islands settled the men later known as *buccaneers*.

The Early Buccaneers of Hispaniola

Thieves, naval deserters, cutthroats, runaway slaves, convicts, and religious and political refugees (as well as the occasional shipwreck survivor) all found their way to the isolated areas of this lush island. But they were by no means the only ones who gravitated there for freedom. Before the African slave trade became such a booming enterprise, European indentured servants or bondsmen furnished the bulk of the manual labor for the Spanish colonies. These individuals were classified into categories:

- For their free passage to the West Indies, "freewillers" sold themselves as indentured servants for five to seven years to a plantation owner. Under this contract they acquired their freedom and financial compensation.

- "Redemptioners" signed contracts with ships' captains, who allowed them free indentured passage to the West Indies. Once landed, they had a set number of days (each contract varied) to find a "redeemer," a planter who would buy their passage paper. More often than not, unscrupulous captains forcibly detained redemptioners until the contract lapsed. By law, captains could sell the duped individuals at auction for a far greater profit.

- "Transportees" were undesirables such as convicts, vagrants, political enemies, and prostitutes. Their indentured contracts were sold at auction by their own governments. Once free, if they returned to their native country, they would be jailed for life.

Punishment was harsh for anyone who escaped during his or her term and was later caught. Moreover, abuse by masters was the norm. The consensus among most planters was the men were indentured—they reasoned, why overwork a slave who was owned for life?

Expecting financial compensation when their servitude expired, many were cheated out of their rightful pay. With no job or money, they flocked to the freedom of Hispaniola, settling in the more uninhabited areas. Unbeknownst to the Spanish citizenry on the island, they set up their own nomadic settlements.

Going Native

By the middle of the seventeenth century, this motley group of "undesirables," indentured servants, and runaway slaves befriended the surviving Arawaks and were taught a variety of survival skills by the Indians. The Arawaks taught them how to determine which fruits and plants were edible and which were poisonous. They also learned to track animals and kill wild goats, pigs, and cattle, and how to clean hides.

How the Buccaneers Earned Their Name

One of the most profitable skills the natives taught was preserving meat. The boucan or buccan was a drying smokehouse. It consisted of a three-sided hut with a widely spaced thatched roof and a green-wood rack grill. Strips of beef and pork were slowly cured for hours until dried, producing what we today call beef jerky.

Pirate Yarns

It's a fallacy that all buccaneers were those colorful Englishmen who sailed during the late seventeenth century. The majority of early buccaneers were French. In fact, the term *buccaneer* comes from the French word *boucaniers,* meaning "smokers of meat."

The men thrived, hunting and providing hides, tallow, and meat to passing ships. When a ship was spotted, a group of men took a rowboat or sailed a small pinnace out of the harbor and traded. French, English, and Dutch privateers bartered canvas, linen, iron axes and awls, needles, ready-made shirts, swords, daggers, liquor, and the most valuable of items: rifles, gunpowder, and shot. Because they constantly reeked of the smoky meats, privateers began calling them *boucaniers* after the smokehouse. Later the name became corrupted and anglicized to buccaneer.

Hunting Buccaneers

With this new life came the tradition of stripping themselves completely of their past. One would take on a new identity or have a nickname decided by others.

Each buccaneer lived with a partner. They watched each other's back, and took care of one another. It was understood if one should perish, his partner inherited his possessions. Hunting in groups of six or eight, they slept on the ground or in lean-tos. They slept close to their boucan, which were scattered throughout the island's hunting areas. They discovered that the boucan's smoke would drive away mosquitoes and other insects.

The men dressed in rough linen long-shirts. The fibers of their shirts were soaked with blood, grease, and the guts of butchered animals, so much so the men constantly stank. Uncured hide breeches and boots protected them from sharp brush and charging animals. Round leather caps protected their scalps from the harsh sun and provided an easy place to stash a set of dice. Their axes, butcher knives, and swords were carried around their waists on wide leather belts.

> **Treasure Chest**
>
> The English word *freebooter* means a man freely roaming the seas in search of booty. It was a term applied to buccaneers. The French term is *Flibustier*, while the Dutch adopted the word *vrijbuter*.

A hunting buccaneer.

(Courtesy of the Library of Congress)

After slaughtering and skinning the animals, they'd begin the curing process. They ate raw marrow from the bones and gambled while the meats cured. Post-camp bathing was never a priority, liquor was.

Underaged Buccaneers

Not all buccaneers were adults. Children, usually boys, also found their way to the safety of these islands. Their journey to the Caribbean was not usually of their own accord. One of the more infamous suppliers of indentured servants was the "spiriters." They specialized in kidnapping and trafficking stolen children of either sex. The easiest for them to nab were the numerous orphans and street urchins. However, if they saw an opportunity to snatch any unescorted child, they did not hesitate to do so. Originally stealing children as young as 6 years old, spiriters discovered to their disgust those children were too weak to survive the harsh conditions of transit. So they targeted children 8 years or older. One French spiriter claimed to have sold more than 500 children in a year's time.

These boys were welcomed into the close-knit community of hunters, and they were taught to survive. This knowledge and freedom empowered them to fight for their new way of life.

> **Dead Men's Tales**
>
> You would say that these (men) are the butcher's vilest servants who have been eight days in the slaughterhouse without washing themselves.
>
> —Abbé Jean Baptiste du Tertec (an abbot who freely ministered throughout the Caribbean Islands), 1670

Human life was considered a cheap commodity in those days. Governmental authorities had even less sympathy for a child. When 16-year-old Alice Deakins managed to escape her kidnapper, she pressed charges. Her kidnapper was tried in a London court. Found guilty, he was fined a mere shilling (12 pennies) and released. On the other hand, had he stolen goods from a store or vendor worth more than 12 shillings, the man would have been hanged as a felon.

The Spanish Get Wind of Buccaneer Operations

It took a while, but it eventually dawned on the Spanish government that their profits from selling and taxing hides had plummeted. They came to discover the buccaneers and their smuggling operations.

In 1603, the Council of the Indies sent an edict to Governor Antonio Osorio of Hispaniola. He was ordered to evacuate the three isolated settlements of the Banda del Norte. Their entire populations were to relocate nearer Santo Domingo to better check the flow of smuggling. Needless to say, Governor Osorio and his military faced heavy opposition to their orders. Eventually, the soldiers burned the settlements and forced the colonists south. As soon as the northern harbors were deserted, bands of buccaneers moved into the area, and their operations increased. This gave the men the added luxury of safe harbors. For added revenue, small expeditions of buccaneers sailed periodically from the Banda del Norte after small unsuspecting ships.

Tobacco Was Also an Issue

When Christopher Columbus introduced tobacco to Europe, it quickly became all the rage. Tobacco plantations were economic gold for Spanish growers. It became a major imported product throughout the Netherlands and England, and across the entire European continent.

Why, one might ask, did King Philip III of Spain in 1606 dispatch a royal edict to the prosperous tobacco plantations in Caracas, Venezuela, and on the islands of Margarita and Cumaná to immediately stop planting, harvesting, or curing tobacco?

Philip came to his decision upon being informed by his council that hundreds of thousands of pounds of tobacco leaf were being smuggled to Europe. Spain was not receiving a peso for the crop. Philip truly believed if he shut down the tobacco industry the foreigners would be driven away for good. He was correct on one point: they sailed away, straight to the other Spanish tobacco plantations on smaller islands such as Trinidad. Philip could not seem to grasp the determination of these men to acquire as much profit as possible from the area.

With this edict Philip further depleted the monies going to his treasury. Without caring how his decision would affect his colonists, Philip drove legitimate growers out of business. This decree created an enormous influx of unemployed men who eventually made their way to Hispaniola and other islands.

English Tobacco Growers Take Their Shot

Tobacco smugglers not only traded with smaller planters, they started to settle into the area themselves. One such Englishman was Thomas Warner. He noticed a small island in the northernmost section of the Lesser Antilles chain the Spanish had never settled.

Years earlier, Spanish explorers believed there to be nothing exceptional about the island. Therefore, it couldn't possibly be profitable for anyone else. It was also home to the fierce and cannibalistic Carib Indians. The Spanish were convinced no one would be willing to battle the Caribs.

But scouting the island, Warner decided it was perfect for cultivating tobacco. Almost immediately, he sailed home and found willing backers for his enterprise. Returning to the West Indies in 1624, he established St. Christopher Island, or as we know it today, St. Kitts. It would be the first legitimate non-Spanish settlement. When a French privateer, Pierre Belain, sailed his damaged vessel into the harbor, he formed a bond with Warner. Banding together, both groups routed the remaining Caribs and claimed the entire island. Warner and Belain agreed to equally divide it into territories claimed for both England and France. The groups would share in all production and profits. And they produced a huge volume of products.

By 1628, they and other settlers on the island were exporting large quantities of cacao, sugar, ginger, cotton, indigo, and tobacco. When Spain discovered the presence of these heathen upstarts, the Spaniards were livid that others dared settle and profit in their territory.

The government decided to set an example for all interlopers. The annual supply fleet of 1629 along with its regular stop to Cartagena and Veracruz had additional orders. Accompanying the supply ships were 35 heavily armed galleons and 7,500 soldiers. Their orders were quite simple. Wipe out the settlements on St. Kitt. The commander of the attack fleet, Vice Admiral Don Fadrique de Toledo, obeyed his orders to the letter. Killing scores of men and capturing more than 700 French and Englishmen, his men destroyed everything in their wake. Those few who escaped fled to Hispaniola, Cuba, and Jamaica. Their hatred for the Spanish was at an all-time high.

A Move Across the Channel

Despite the buccaneers' live-and-let-live policy, the governor of Hispaniola considered their presence intolerable. The Audiencia de Santo Domingo ordered 500 troops deep into the northwest to flush the buccaneers out and hunt them down. It was far easier said than done. Though the soldiers killed a number of men, many more fled deep inland or across the channel while the soldiers struggled through the rugged terrain.

Undaunted, the Audiencia hired Spanish and *Mestizo* hunters to exterminate all the feral animals on the island. The government reasoned that by depriving the men of their livelihood they would leave and become someone else's problem. Part of their strategy proved correct.

After killing off all the animals, there was nothing left for the hunters to barter. And yes, in 1630 the remaining buccaneers did leave the island. However, they settled on an island a short distance off Hispaniola—the island of Tortuga del Mar, or Turtle Island, so named for its turtlelike shape. The island boasted fresh water, defendable harbors, easy anchorage, and high mountains. Better yet, it was situated along the Windward Passage, the route taken by the treasure fleets to sail back to Spain. The buccaneers' livelihood and purpose had now changed: revenge and thievery became the order of the day. They set out to attack Spanish ships and settlements.

Upon their arrival on Tortuga, the buccaneers rooted out all Spaniards and forced them off. It was now their home. Using rowboats or pinnaces, the buccaneers sailed the waters plundering small villages or ships. Soon thereafter, a French captain would launch a bold attack that would fire the imaginations and resolve of other buccaneers and spread fear throughout the Caribbean.

> **Knowing the Ropes**
>
> A **Mestizo** is a child of European and Amerindian parents who has a 50-50 ratio of mixed heritage. During this era, other terms were employed for individuals with varying degrees of racially mixed ancestry.

A French Raid Becomes a Model, and the Spanish Respond

In 1635, French buccaneer Pierre Le Grand and his 28-man crew sighted a Spanish treasure galleon off the coast of Hispaniola. What happened next would become a model for buccaneers operating against Spanish vessels in the region.

With sails up and rowing their pinnace hard, Le Grand's men managed to near the galleon by dusk. According to one narrative published many years later, Le Grand and his crew had been sailing for weeks with no luck of plunder or renewed supplies. Near starvation, they maneuvered under the bow of the great ship ready to attack.

Succeed or Die!

Le Grand suggested to his men they should sink their own vessel. By this act, no man could lose his resolve. There would be no turning back. They would successfully board and capture the vessel or die in the process. With his crew's hearty approval, Le Grand bore holes in her hull and sank the craft.

His men grappled onto the galleon's fore chain. Silently, they pulled themselves up and climbed over the galleon's rail. Part of his crew went straight for the weapons room and seized pistols. Taking the crew and officers by complete surprise, Le Grand demanded the captain surrender. The captain, with a pistol at his heart and shocked at their audacity, had no alternative. One of his officers reportedly asked if Le Grand's men "were devils." Le Grand offered the galleon's crew the opportunity to sail with him. The captured crew that refused was set ashore on Hispaniola. Le Grand and his men now commanded a treasure-laden galleon.

They sailed back to Dieppe to live out a rich comfortable life and never sailed again. Whether the narrative is accurate or not, the truth of the matter is that Le Grand and his men did capture a Spanish galleon and he never sailed the Caribbean again. His brazen act convinced others that treasure galleons were easier targets then originally assumed.

Spain Launches a Preemptive Attack

Spain—unnerved by Le Grand's audacious attack and concerned Tortuga would eventually be claimed by the government of France—mounted a preemptive assault against the island. They slaughtered everyone they found and reclaimed Tortuga for Spain. Those who were able to escape sailed back to Hispaniola. Most of the buccaneers who were out at sea sought safety in Jamaica. The Spaniards occupied Tortuga for some time before the military was ordered to pull out, leaving no garrison of soldiers behind.

The only explanation one can surmise from this military blunder is that some high-ranking officer in his arrogance and sheer stupidity felt this assault was brutal enough to terrorize the buccaneers from ever returning. Once again, this action had the opposite effect.

The buccaneers waited for a time in case the maneuver was a trap. Upon realizing the soldiers were off the island for good, they simply moved back to Tortuga. Now their ranks swelled to far greater numbers and with an even greater hunger for revenge.

> **Dead Men's Tales**
>
> The planters and hunters of the isle of Tortuga had no sooner understood this happy event, and the rich prize those pirates had obtained, but they resolved to follow their example. Hereupon many of them left their ordinary exercises and common employment, and used what means they could to get either boats or small vessels wherein to exercise piracy.
>
> —Alexander O. Exquemelin, *Bucaniers of America*, 1684

Skills for Hunting Now Skills for War

With Le Grand's success as an example, buccaneer attacks on the Spanish grew bolder. When danger presented itself on Tortuga, the men merely shuttled back and forth to Hispaniola.

Alexander Oliver Exquemelin: Indentured Servant, Buccaneer, and Writer

Alexander Oliver Exquemelin (a.k.a. John Esquemeling) of Honfleur, France—an indentured servant destined to become a buccaneer—sailed aboard the *St. John*, owned by the French West India Company, to the island of Tortuga. There he endured life in indentured servitude under an extremely cruel and abusive master. After falling deathly ill, Exquemelin's indentured papers were sold to a second master, a kindly surgeon who not only nursed him back to health, but taught the young man the skills of a surgeon and barber. When Exquemelin's contracted servitude was completed, Exquemelin's master gave him money and presented him with a set of surgical tools so that the newly freed man might have a good start on a new life.

Exquemelin soon found work as a surgeon and barber aboard various buccaneer vessels. And wherever he sailed with the buccaneer crews, he kept extensive journals on the flora and fauna he observed, as well as the people he encountered.

Exquemelin served alongside the infamous Captain Henry Morgan (yes, the smiling Morgan you've seen on the rum label) when Morgan sacked the city of Panama in 1671 (see Chapter 8). But soon after, having his fill of the buccaneering life, Exquemelin settled in Amsterdam and began preparing his journals for publication. They were first released in the Dutch language in 1678.

A listing in the Amsterdam Surgeon's Guild Book of 1597–1734 states that one "A. Exquemelin of Honfleur" passed his state exams and became an official surgeon in 1679, one year after his book was first published. Exquemelin's book, *Bucaniers of America: or, a true account of the most remarkable assaults committed of late years upon the coasts of the West-Indies, by Bucaniers of Jamaica and Tortuga, Both English and French*, became one of the most widely read and quoted books of that period.

An instant success, the book was translated into Spanish in 1681, and English in 1684. The English edition sold out within three months. A second edition was soon released, and Exquemelin's book is still published today.

As Exquemelin observed, the relationships they forged while hunters on Hispaniola seemed to mirror the relationships forged at sea. But the buccaneers who sailed starting in 1630 on would be a different class of men than those who sailed for riches in later years. These buccaneers were at war with the Spanish and only the Spanish. And in that mutual hatred a new camaraderie was born.

The Least You Need to Know

- The original buccaneers, mostly French, were hunters and smugglers who lived and worked in the Caribbean.

- On Hispaniola, early buccaneers were taught survival skills by the Arawak Indians.

- Kidnapped children found their way into the buccaneer community.

- After being forced off of Hispaniola, buccaneers simply moved across the channel to the island of Tortuga.

- Pierre Le Grand's capture of a Spanish galleon served as a model for future captures and emboldened the buccaneers.

- From his humble beginnings as an indentured servant, Alexander Oliver Exquemelin went on to become an important writer of his time.

7

Brethren of the Coast

In This Chapter

- ◆ A famous fort chiseled in rock
- ◆ The brotherhood of buccaneers
- ◆ Democracy for all: ship's articles
- ◆ The original workmen's compensation
- ◆ Pirate justice
- ◆ The tale of Alexander Selkirk

Though the English called them buccaneers—the former "meat smokers" and sworn enemies of the Spanish who had destroyed their livelihoods and homes—they had another name for themselves. They were the *brethren*, or more formally, the *brethren of the coast, the brotherhood of the coast*, or simply *the brotherhood*. These buccaneers lived by a code unheard of before in Western civilization. The brotherhood of the buccaneer was considered by some historians to be the first *true* democracy (not a representative democracy or a republic) among a group of men and women. In reality, it was a loose confederation of groups of buccaneers who belonged to the brotherhood in varying degrees.

Instead of thwarting the buccaneers' activities as they had hoped, Spain had caused them to scatter throughout the Caribbean, where they simply regrouped. Though some small groups continued to hunt and trade, the majority congregated into larger groups. At sea, they formed rules by which they all agreed to abide. Their unifying factor, no matter what their original nationality, was their common hatred of the Spanish.

Le Vasseur's Island

His religious beliefs drove Jean Le Vasseur, a French Huguenot, from his home to the Caribbean and piracy. Originally settling in Jamaica in 1640, he traveled to Tortuga two years later.

A former military engineer, Le Vasseur wasted no time in surveying Tortuga. He quickly realized the island's natural military potential, and determined to relocate there and design and build a formidable island fortress.

Looming over Basse-Terre, the main harbor of Tortuga, was a high flat mountaintop. It boasted a sheer 30-foot outcropping of solid rock, a natural spring, and a densely packed forest and underbrush. There, Le Vasseur carved out a fortress—*Le Fort de Rocher* or "Fort of Rock"—armed with 24 cannon and accessible only from the harbor side. Le Vasseur's fort was deemed impregnable. It was estimated by buccaneer and author Alexander Oliver Exquemelin (whom you met in Chapter 6) that 800 men could easily withstand a siege. Until Le Vasseur's assassination in 1653 by his chosen heirs, the fort was never overrun.

In January 1654, five Spanish warships and accompanying transports sailed into the harbor. While the invaders kept most of the buccaneers facing them occupied, hundreds of slaves hacked out a cannon road and dragged the heavy armaments up to the rear of the fort. The ensuing artillery barrage forced the defenders to call it quits. Those lucky enough to escape sailed again to English-controlled Jamaica and the isolated areas of Hispaniola. It would be the only time in history that Le Vasseur's fort would fall to an invading force.

The revolving invasion of Tortuga by Spanish, French, English, and Dutch for control over the tiny island continued for years. Depending on whose flag flew on the island, when governments changed, buccaneers simply shuttled back and forth to Tortuga.

Birth of the Brotherhood

By 1640, the term and true society of *brethren of the coast* or *brotherhood of the coast* (both titles seem to be interchangeable) came into the buccaneer lexicon. Principally, it denoted the strong bond these men had for each other and their united purpose. The partnership and camaraderie first forged as hunters of hides and meat easily transitioned into their lives at sea.

It was an unusually democratic bond. The men felt it high time they took control of their own lives. Unless mutually agreed upon, no one man had say over another's actions. They believed the old seafaring superstition to hold true. All had at one time or another crossed the tropic of Cancer, and during that crossing, their former identities had drowned. New customs and rules formed. Now each man was free to be whatever or whomever he chose to be. Considering the rigid social order of the time in which they lived, this was considered by almost all Western European society to be nothing less than radical and bordering on anarchy. For many a buccaneer, the first change was the acquisition of a new name or a nickname. It mentally freed the individual from his past and the hope that his past would no longer follow him.

> **Pirate Yarns** _____
>
> From fishermen to seamen to pirates, sailing men had an entire culture built around superstitions, some so powerful they could prevent a ship from setting sail. For example, it was considered bad luck to sail on a Friday. Ships could leave port at 11:59 P.M. on Thursday or 12:00 A.M. on Saturday, but you couldn't get a ship off wharf between those hours.

Commandments, Not Guidelines: Ship's Articles

Members of the brotherhood understood that for any system of democracy—including buccaneer democracy—to be effective, rules and regulations had to govern their conduct. Thus, the buccaneers wrote, approved, and signed (or placed their individual marks on) what were known as *ship's articles* or *articles of agreement.*

At no time was the formation of rules of conduct more prevalent than prior to a group setting out to sea. The crew would assemble before departure to determine their destination. More important, each man had equal input concerning the content of the ship's articles. When all agreed, everyone swore an oath—to observe and uphold the articles—over a boarding axe or Bible. With the proper pomp and a swig of rum mixed with gunpowder, one would set his signature or mark upon the written document. Typically, in a further display of equality, all of the men, including the captain, signed along the borders of the parchment, not under the last written line. This denoted that no one individual held greater authority over another.

By the mid-eighteenth century, during the height of the golden age of piracy, some captains were writing their own ship's articles. A man interested in joining such a ship had the option of signing or not sailing. He had no input in the rules of that vessel. In his book, *The General History of the Robberies and Murders of the Most Notorious Pyrates*, Captain Charles Johnson listed three ships' articles that have survived the centuries intact. They are interesting to compare for their differences and similarities.

It is noteworthy that these articles were all written in the mid-1720s. Unlike earlier buccaneer articles, these were not strictly adhered to, as the history of ships and crews can attest.

Knowing the Ropes

Ship's articles or **articles of agreement** were detailed obligations that each crewmember promised to observe while at sea. Ship's articles were established soon after the buccaneers began sailing and pirating in the mid-seventeenth century.

The articles listed in Johnson's book are those of the ships *Revenge*, under Captain John Phillips (see Chapter 10); the *Delivery*, under Captain George Lowther (see Chapter 19); and the *Royal Fortune*, under Captain Bartholomew Roberts (see Chapter 18). These are the only three sets of ships' articles believed to have survived to the present day.

Articles Aboard the *Revenge*

Captain John Phillips signed the following articles in 1723 with his crew. All swore their oath upon an axe, because no bible was available. In April 1724, off the coast of Newfoundland, his mutinous men bound Phillips and threw him overboard.

  I Every Man shall obey civil Command; the Captain shall have one full Share and a half of all Prizes; the Master, Carpenter, Boatswain and Gunner shall have one Share and (a) quarter.

 II If any Man shall offer to run away, or keep any Secret from the Company, he shall be maroon'd, with one Bottle of Powder, one Bottle of Water, one small Arm and Shot.

III If any Man shall steal any Thing in the Company, or game to the Value of a Piece of Eight, he shall be maroon'd or shot.

IV If at any Time we should meet another Marooner (that is, Pyrate) that Man that shall sign his Articles without the Consent of our Company, shall suffer such Punishment as the Captain and Company shall think fit.

 V That Man that shall strike another whilst these Articles are in force, shall receive Moses's Law (that is, 40 Stripes lacking one) on the bare back.

VI That Man that shall snap his Arms, or smoak Tobacco in the Hold, without a Cap to his Pipe, or carry a Candle lighted without a Lanthorn, shall suffer the same Punishment as in the former Article.

VII That Man that shall not keep his Arms clean, fit for an Engagement, or neglect his Business, shall be cut off from his Share, and suffer such other Punishment as the Captain and the Company shall think fit.

VIII If any Man shall lose a Joint in Time of Engagement, he shall have 400 pieces of Eight, if a Limb, 800.

IX If at any Time we meet with a prudent Woman, that Man that offers to meddle with her, without her Consent, shall suffer present Death.

Articles Aboard the *Delivery*

Swearing on a ship's bible, Captain Lowther in 1720 signed the following articles with his crew. In 1723, the crewmen were careening their ship on the Isle of Blanco in the West Indies. Surprised by agents of the South Sea Company, and with their ship grounded, the men were forced to surrender. Lowther with a dozen men and boys jumped through the cabin window and fled deep into the island. Rather then risk capture and hanging, Lowther committed suicide.

 I The Captain is to have two full Shares; the Master is to have one Share and a half; the Doctor, Mate, Gunner, and Boatswain, one Share and a quarter.

 II He that shall be found guilty of taking up any unlawful Weapon on board the Privateer, or any Prize, by us taken, so as to strike or abuse one another, in any regard, shall suffer what Punishment the Captain and the Majority of the Company shall think fit.

III He that shall be found Guilty of Cowardice, in the Time of Engagement, shall suffer what Punishment the Captain and Majority shall think fit.

IV If any Gold, Jewels, Silver, & c. be found on board of any Prize or Prizes, to the value of a Piece of Eight, and the Finder do not deliver it to the Quarter-Master, in the Space of 24 Hours, (he) shall suffer what Punishment the Captain and Majority shall think fit.

V He that is found Guilty of Gaming, or Defrauding another to the Value of a Shilling, shall suffer what Punishment the Captain and Majority of the Company shall think fit.

VI He that shall have Misfortune to lose a Limb, in Time of Engagement, shall have the Sum of one hundred and fifty pounds Sterling, and remain with the Company as long as he shall think fit.

VII Good Quarters to be given when call'd for.

VIII He that sees a Sail first, shall have the best Pistol, or Small-Arm on board her.

Articles Aboard the *Royal Fortune*

Written at some point around 1720, each man swore his oath on Captain Roberts's personal bible. Though all his men signed the document, Roberts found it difficult to enforce the articles concerning gambling and drinking aboard his ship. He was killed in 1722 during a battle with the H.M.S. *Swallow*, a naval ship. Roberts's crew was too intoxicated to put up a good fight.

If not specified in the articles, it was assumed all boys under the age of 15 received one half share of the booty. Slaves received nothing.

I Every Man has a Vote in Affairs of Moment; has equal Title to the fresh Provisions, or strong Liquors, at any Time seized, and may use them at Pleasure, unless a Scarcity make it necessary, for the Good of all, to vote a Retrenchment.

II Every Man to be called fairly in Turn, by List, on board of prizes, because, (over and above their proper Share) they were on these Occasions allowed a Shift of Cloaths: But if they defrauded the Company to the Value of a Dollar, in Plate, Jewels, or Money, Marooning was their punishment. If the Robbery was only betwixt one another, they contented themselves with slitting the Ears and Nose of him that was Guilty, and set him on Shore, not in an inhabited Place, but somewhere, where he was sure to encounter Hardships.

III No Person to Game at Cards or Dice for Money.

IV The Lights and Candles to be put out at eight a-Clock at Night: If any of the Crew, after that Hour, still remained enclined for Drinking, they were to do it on the open Deck.

V To keep their Piece, Pistols and Cutlash clean, and fit for Service.

VI No Boy or Woman to be allowed amongst them. If any Man were found seducing any of the latter Sex, and carry'd her to Sea, disguised, he was to suffer Death.

VII To Desert the Ship, or their Quarters in Battle, was punished with Death or Marooning.

VIII No striking one another on board, but every Man's Quarrels to be ended on Shore, at Sword and Pistol, thus; The Quarter-Master of the Ship, when the Parties will not come to any Reconciliation, accompanies them on Shore with what Assistance he thinks proper, and turns the Disputants Back to Back, at so many Paces Distance: At the Word of Command, they turn and fire immediately or else the Piece is knock'd out of their Hands; If both miss, they come to the Cutlashes, and then he is declared Victor who draws the first blood.

IX No Man to talk of breaking up their Way of Living, till each had shared a 1000£. If in order to this, any Man shall lose a Limb, or become a Cripple in their Service, he was to have 800 pieces of eight, out of the publick Stock, and for lesser Hurts, proportionably.

X The Captain and Quarter-Master to receive two Shares of a Prize; the Master, Boatswain, and Gunner, one Share and a half, and other Officers one and a Quarter.

XI The Musicians to have Rest on the Sabbath Day, but the other six Days and Nights, none without special Favor.

> **Treasure Chest**
>
> According to captured crewmen, the original articles of the *Royal Fortune* were thrown overboard before the ship was captured. Charles Johnson speculated that to be so unceremoniously discarded, there were probably extremely cruel or incriminating articles in the original.

A Buccaneer's Form of Workmen's Comp

Another unique tradition among the buccaneer brethren was the fact that they took care of their wounded. This financial compensation continued until the end of the golden age of piracy, around 1725.

Pirate Yarns

It was uncommon for men who lost a hand to replace the appendage with a hook, which was expensive and frequently ill-fitting. Captain Henry Johnson (circa 1720), alias Henriques the Englishman, reportedly an expert shot, was known for aiming his pistol by resting the barrel on his stump.

Ship's articles also stipulated a monetary recompense for individual body parts. An average compensation would be written as a matter-of-fact statement: a loss of a right arm was 600 pieces-of-eight or 6 slaves; a left arm, 500 pieces-of-eight or 5 slaves; a right leg, 500 pieces-of-eight or 5 slaves; a left leg, 400 pieces-of-eight or 4 slaves; for an eye, 100 pieces-of-eight or 1 slave; and for a finger on either hand, 100 pieces-of-eight or 1 slave. A slave was considered either a captive whom one could personally ransom and keep the entire payment or a person kept as personal property.

It is interesting to note that buccaneers and later pirates put a greater value on the loss of their right leg and arm than their left. And apparently, the loss of either eye or a digit on either hand was not considered much of a handicap.

Their Own Form of Justice

As specific as their division of treasure and conduct aboard ship, buccaneers and later pirates wrote laws governing those who disregarded the articles. Although a man might be forgiven for breaking one of the minor articles, if he thought he could get away with a major infraction, he was in for a big surprise.

Aware of the disastrous effect arguments could have on a crew, captains paid particular attention to how and how much punishment was meted out. Of course, pirate punishment was harsh, but it was far more reasonable—and in many instances, equitable—than that which was meted out aboard state naval or merchant vessels (see Chapter 9).

Heated disagreements aboard ship were not allowed to escalate into an actual fight for fear the entire crew would end up participating. Disputes were settled on land according to ship's articles. The choice of pistol or sword seemed to be at the discretion of the quartermaster and captain. A fight to the death or first blood drawn was decided by articles or captain before the altercation began.

Crime and Punishment

Most infractions were clear-cut: stealing from the common stock (shared treasure), wagering one's entire share of booty (prohibited for fear of immediate and deadly retribution), and cheating while gambling. All these were punishable by having the guilty party's ears cut off or his nose split in two.

In the early days of the buccaneer brotherhood, men had the option to disembark a ship whenever they chose. A man's decision could have him put ashore on an inhabited or an uninhabited area.

However, by the 1720s (a time when the previously listed articles were drawn), it became increasingly common to have a ship of cutthroats crewed by a large majority of forced men. This explains the rule on Captain Ned Low's vessel, the *Fancy*. It states that any man who even mentioned leaving the ship mid-voyage for any reason would be shot.

The Most-Feared Penalty

Marooning was the ultimate punishment, reserved for such serious offenses as murdering a shipmate in cold blood or stealing from a shipmate. One would be forced onto an island that was little more than a sandbar at low tide. There he'd wait to meet his fate. He'd be provided a single jug of water, a pistol with one charge of gunpowder and ball, and perhaps a piece of hardtack. Helpless, he could only watch as his former mates sailed away. If his mates were generous, they'd allow him to keep his clothes. This provided some scant protection against the brutal sun. Everyone knew what awaited him: dehydration, starvation, blistering sunburn, heat stroke, insanity if he survived long enough, and always death.

> **Dead Men's Tales**
>
> A ship's boat landed on one of these sandpit islands and found they were not the first. There on the sands lay a bleached skeleton with a shattered skull, and beside it an empty bottle and an equally empty and rusted pistol.
>
> —George Woodbury, *The Great Days of Piracy in the West Indies*, 1951

Selkirk's Choice

So began the harrowing tale of one Alexander Selkirk (a.k.a. Selcraig). A hotheaded Scotsman, Selkirk was sailing aboard the 16-gun privateer *Cinque Ports*. His ship's captain, Thomas Stradling, held a letter of marque from Prince George of Denmark to pursue Spanish vessels. A fellow mate on the expedition's sister ship, *St. George*, was William Dampier, a renowned navigator, explorer, and writer.

Captain Stradling's attacks against the Spanish led only to overall failure and damage to their own ship. Selkirk could not help but notice his captain's stubborn refusal to properly repair the vessel. Fearing the ship would sink if not tended to immediately, Selkirk argued with his captain to no avail. Wanting no part of Stradling and his perceived incompetence—and convinced he would be spotted and picked up by another passing ship if marooned—Selkirk willingly chose to be marooned on Más a Tierra, an island in the Juan Fernandez chain some 400 miles west of Valparaiso, Chile.

Selkirk was put ashore in October 1704 with his personal possessions, a supply of provisions, powder and shot. Because the island was the perfect place for careening a ship, Selkirk believed he soon would be rescued by another ship. So he settled in to wait. Unfortunately, the passing vessel he was so sure would sail by did not.

Meanwhile, back in England, 29-year-old privateer Woodes Rogers received a letter of marque from the admiralty granting him permission to attack Spanish and French vessels. In early 1709—with two ships, the *Duke* and *Duchess*—Rogers successfully rounded Cape Horn and anchored off Más a Tierra. There he was surprised to spot a signal fire lit on the island and sent men to investigate. On February 2, 1709, the marooned Selkirk came face to face with another human being.

Treasure Chest

It is speculated that Selkirk became Daniel Defoe's model for Robinson Crusoe. Defoe published his famous novel in 1719, its original title being *The Life and Strange Surprising Adventures of Robinson Crusoe, of York, Mariner: Who Lived Eight and Twenty Years all alone in an un-inhabited Island on the Coast of America, near the Mouth of the Great River of Oroonoque; having been cast on shore by Shipwreck, where-in all the Men perished but Himself. With An Account how he was at last strangely deliver'd by Pyrates.* Today the book is simply titled *The Adventures of Robinson Crusoe.*

Remarkably, William Dampier was Captain Rogers's navigator. After Selkirk bathed and changed into clothes, Dampier was shocked to recognize the man Captain Stradling had marooned four years and four months earlier. As fate would have it, the *Cinque Ports* did prove unseaworthy. She sank off the coast of Peru. Stradling and 70 survivors were languishing in a Peruvian jail at the time Selkirk was rescued.

The Least You Need to Know

- *Le Fort de Rocher* on Tortuga, built by Jean Le Vasseur, was designed to protect up to 800 pirates against a military siege.

- Rebelling against the harsh laws of their former countries, buccaneers set up their own democratic code.

- Breaking the rules they agreed to live by was dealt with by severe punishment. They were as hard on themselves as on those they attacked.

- Buccaneers and pirates were committed to caring for their disabled comrades. They set up a system of monetary compensation.

- Alexander Selkirk chose to be marooned on an uninhabited island rather than sail with a captain he could not trust.

Chapter 8

Bloody Buccaneers and Daring Opportunists

In This Chapter

- ◆ "Flail of the Spaniards": Francis L'Ollonais
- ◆ Jekyll and Hyde: Rock Brasilliano
- ◆ Escape artist: Bartholomew the Portuguese
- ◆ Pirate with a conscience: Red Legs Greaves
- ◆ Infamous exploits: Sir Henry Morgan

In the minds of most people, the image of the meat-smoker-turned-pirate is more closely related to the polite and courtly Hollywood version of a dashing buccaneer than the truly roguish seafaring soul he was. As we know, most buccaneers came from dubious or grim circumstances. In time, most were forgotten. Some became mere historical footnotes. A few became world famous.

One of the latter was Sir Henry Morgan. He was then—and is today—famous for his audacity, charisma, and tactical fighting ability. He was also *infamous* among many of his contemporaries for his alleged deceit and cruelty.

But there were many others besides Morgan. We'll take a look at some of these colorful characters first, and then tell you what made Morgan so famous.

The Brutal Exploits of Francis L'Ollonais

Jacques Jean-David Nau spent the years 1650 through 1653 as an indentured servant in the Caribbean on Spanish plantations. He endured his time with nothing to show for his years of hardship and drifted to Hispaniola as many before him had done. Changing his name to Francis Lolonois (a.k.a. François L'Ollonais, after his birthplace of Sables d'Ollonne in Brittany), he joined other buccaneers raiding Spanish ships in 1653.

Resettling on Tortuga, L'Ollonais's daring exploits caught the attention of Monsieur de la Place, the island's French governor. La Place also appreciated L'Ollonais's fierce hatred of the Spanish, and, in 1660, the governor awarded L'Ollonais a captaincy and his own ship. Thus began the successful and barbarous career of the man Alexander Exquemelin (see Chapter 6) thought a psychopath and whom the Spanish dubbed Fléau des Espagnols, or "Flail of the Spaniards."

Francis L'Ollonais.

(From Bucaniers of America, *Alexander Exquemelin, 1684)*

FRANCIS   LOLONOIS.

L'Ollonais attacked Spanish ships with an unsurpassed vengeance. He was known to either decapitate captured crews or hack them to pieces. Each time an unfortunate enemy crew fell into his hands, he killed all but one or two to ensure news of his black deeds would spread throughout the Caribbean. His reputation for torture was in fact so terrifying the Spanish preferred to die fighting or jump overboard rather than be captured.

Along the streets of Tortuga, men chose to ignore and avoid L'Ollonais and his cruelty. They cared nothing for him, but were mightily impressed with the enormous wealth seen flashing from his bejeweled men each time his expeditions docked.

Though L'Ollonais needed no excuse to raid towns along the Main, when another war erupted between France and Spain in 1667, he saw it as a fresh opportunity for piracy.

> **Dead Men's Tales**
>
> L'Ollonais grew outrageously passionate; insomuch that he drew his cutlass, and with it cut open the breast of one of those poor Spaniards, and, pulling out his heart with his sacrilegious hands, began to bite and gnaw it with his teeth like a ravenous wolf.
>
> —*Bucaniers of America*, Alexander Exquemelin (1684)

To Maracaibo

With more than 1,000 men, L'Ollonais sailed a fleet to the treasure city of Maracaibo. A fort guarded the narrow channel to the city. This did not deter the buccaneers. After a three-hour barrage of fire, the fort fell. The city was theirs to plunder.

Many of the citizens—who earlier had fled to perceived safety in the woods—were hunted down like animals by L'Ollonais and his men. He then tortured the women and children to make them reveal where any treasure might be hidden.

After spending weeks in Maracaibo, L'Ollonais turned his attention to Gibraltar. In a wicked piece of master strategy, he sacked the great rock, then waited. He believed not all the treasure of Maracaibo had been revealed to him. To the shock of its citizenry, his fleet returned. L'Ollonais's intuition served him well. The fleet docked at Tortuga laden with more than 100,000 pieces-of-eight worth of silks and fine linens, and 260,000 pieces-of-eight to divide among the crews.

The Flail's Ill-Fated Nicaraguan Raid

Flush with success and shamelessly enamored of himself, L'Ollonais mounted another expedition to raid the renowned silver caches in Nicaragua.

In 1668—with 6 ships and more than 700 men—he landed, trekked inland, and raided the mines. The raiders were ambushed at the mouth of Lake Nicaragua by a warrior band of Darien Indians. The Indians were very familiar with L'Ollonais and his methods. He had, after all, not limited his torture to the Spanish.

According to the few lucky buccaneers who managed to escape, L'Ollonais died as he had killed many others. While still alive, the Indians took care to slowly cut him into pieces and throw his body parts into a raging fire. Two conflicting story endings to his life suggest that either his cooked body was then eaten or his ashes were thrown into the air.

The Dr. Jekyll and Mr. Hyde of Buccaneers

Rock Brasilliano (a.k.a. Roche Braziliano) was one of the many Dutchmen who originally settled in Brazil through the West India Company of Amsterdam. When the Portuguese, by edict of the pope, seized Brazil in 1654 as their territory, Brasilliano sailed to the English-held island of Jamaica and settled in Port Royal. A strong, stocky man, he soon acquired his infamous nickname—Rock.

Rock Brasilliano.

(From Bucaniers of America, *Alexander Exquemelin, 1684)*

ROCK . BRASILIANO

When sober, Brasilliano was level-headed, friendly, and courteous to all. He was elected captain many times. However, when drunk, a completely different person emerged. He became so violent even his closest friends went out of their way to avoid him. Anyone he came across became a target of his vicious attacks. It was widely known throughout Port Royal that if caught in Brasilliano's clutches during one of his drunken rages, it was far better not to resist. That way, one might be lucky enough to come away with all his extremities or his life. In fact, he was so feared by everyone that in 1667 the governor of Jamaica moved his official residence out of Port Royal and into Spanish Town.

When in a socially agreeable mood—and not wanting to drink alone—Brasilliano would purchase an entire pipe (a huge barrel) of wine. Rolling it outside the tavern, he'd jovially invite any passers-by to share in his drink. None refused, because the offer usually came with a pistol pointed at their heads.

One Frightened and Gullible Governor

Brasilliano's claim to fame is an interesting tale indeed. He and his crew preferred to raid along the Yucatán Peninsula. In one instance, he and his men were captured and thrown into the dungeons of Campeche. There, they awaited hanging.

Brasilliano was not about to let that happen. Mysteriously, he was able to get a letter delivered to the governor. The premise of the ruse was intriguing. Theoretically, the missive was sent from a pirate fleet just off the coast sailing toward the city. Its captain threatened total destruction and death if the prisoners were harmed. Because the governor had been through a number of pirate raids, he, in a panic, stayed their execution. The governor then had the pirates loaded onto a ship for Spain and used as galley slaves. During the journey, Brasilliano escaped and returned to Port Royal.

> **Pirate Yarns**
>
> Pirates seldom buried treasure to be dug up at a later date. A few might hide booty for a short period, but maps to the location were not drawn for fear that the map and ultimately the treasure would fall into someone else's hands.

The Rock Cracks

Not one to learn from close calls, Brasilliano acquired another ship and sailed the Gulf of Mexico back to the Yucatán. His ship captured, he found himself once again in the dungeon of Campeche. This time the governor handed him over to the dreaded

Inquisition headquartered in town. After horrific torture, Brasilliano admitted to burying a portion of his treasure on the Isle of Pines, a small island south of Cuba. Spanish soldiers sent to the island recovered 100,000 pieces-of-eight. That was the last time anyone ever heard of Rock Brasilliano.

Bartholomew the Portuguese

During 1655, Bartholomew the Portuguese (a.k.a. Portuguese Bartolomeo) arrived at Port Royal. His unfortunate destiny was that he would never hold on to captured treasure long enough to enjoy it. But unlike Rock Brasilliano, Bartholomew seemed to have a guardian angel. Time and again, he would capture a great prize only to lose it in a storm or have it seized by the Spanish. Yet he always managed to escape.

Bartholomew the Portuguese.

(From Bucaniers of America, *Alexander Exquemelin, 1684)*

BARTOLOMEW PORTUGUES

Jailed at Campeche

Once, after capturing a rich vessel only to have it fall back into the hands of the Spanish, Bartholomew and his men were transported to Campeche. Upon docking, his mates were immediately seized and transferred to the dungeons. The magistrate, however, recognized Bartholomew as one who had terrorized the city on numerous occasions yet managed to escape the dungeon as many times. To prevent that from happening again, Bartholomew was held aboard ship awaiting execution.

An Ingenious Escape

During the night, Bartholomew killed his jailer with a stolen knife and prepared to flee. Like most individuals, he did not know how to swim, but that didn't stop him. He plugged two large, empty earthenware jars, and quietly climbed overboard. Once in the water, he used the jars as flotation devices. By the time his escape was discovered, he was far away. He then hiked 126 miles to the friendly haven of El Golfo Triste (Sad Gulf) on the eastern tip of the peninsula. There, he hitched a ride home to

Knowing the Ropes

Going **on the account** meant a voyage was being mounted where no money was paid to a pirate until treasure was captured. The expression "No Prey, No Pay" relates to this arrangement.

Port Royal on a buccaneer vessel. Undeterred, Bartholomew went *on the account* numerous times after that, only to have his bad luck continue until his dying day.

The Buccaneer with Scruples

Captain Red Legs Greaves sailed the Caribbean in the years between 1670 and 1680. He knew the area intimately as he had been born into slavery to Scottish political prisoners shipped to Barbados during the English Civil War. Escaping captivity in his teens, he stowed away on the only vessel anchored in the harbor—a pirate ship. Their captain, a native of Barbados by the name of Hawkins, had the reputation of giving no quarter and reveling in torture. His success at acquiring rich prizes was the main reason men signed on. Forcing Greaves at gunpoint to sign the ship's articles (see Chapter 7), the teen found himself sailing his home waters as a pirate.

Having experienced untold cruelty firsthand, Greaves had no intention of dealing it out to others. He would kill only in self-defense and he refused to participate in the torture of others. It wasn't long before the two opposing philosophies of these men literally came to blows. Greaves killed Hawkins and was elected Captain. He quickly earned a reputation for humanity, a rare thing among pirates.

Pearls, Every Man's Dream

After many small successful raids, Greaves turned his attention to the pearl fisheries of Margarita. Catching a Spanish treasure galleon off-guard, his crew captured the vessel. Turning the Spanish guns on their own fort, Greaves captured the garrison. He and his men then departed with a huge haul of pearls and silver, which had been stored in the fort waiting for the annual treasure fleet from Spain.

Early Retirement Is Not Always the Safe Play

After "sharing out" with his crew, Greaves retired. Buying a sugar plantation on the island of Nevis he intended to spend his remaining years in obscurity. Unfortunately, he was recognized as a pirate with a reward for his capture. Taken to Jamestown in 1680, he was tried, convicted, and jailed while his gallows were being constructed. As if it were divine intervention, a devastating earthquake and subsequent tidal wave hit the island. The entire city of Jamestown was consumed by the sea. Narrowly escaping the fate of most, Greaves clung to life on bits of wreckage.

> **Treasure Chest**
>
> Red Legs Greaves got his name because of his Scots heritage, fair skin, and habit of going around barelegged. The unforgiving Caribbean sun never tanned his skin, but burned it "red."

A passing whaling ship rescued Greaves. In gratitude and needing to technically remain "dead," Greaves joined the crew. Some time later, he assisted in capturing a gang of pirates attacking commercial whaling fleets. As a reward for his bravery, he received an official pardon for his past crimes. Now free, Greaves retired to the islands and died an old man.

The Man Behind the Myth

Sir Henry Morgan was a highly intelligent, complex, and resourceful man. He also was very dangerous. Though the specifics of his origins are somewhat debatable, they were indeed loftier than Alexander Exquemelin's published remarks that Morgan was born of a yeoman farmer and indentured in the West Indies.

What is known of Morgan is that he was born in Wales in 1635 (about the same time the Caribbean buccaneers were coming into their own as pirates). One of Morgan's uncles was a major general. Another was a colonel. In those days, it would have been virtually impossible for those born into families of low social standing—as Exquemelin suggested Morgan had been—to achieve the high military rank Morgan's uncles had.

Countering Exquemelin

Morgan, of course, objected to Exquemelin's derogatory and defamatory comments about his beginnings. And when the buccaneer-turned-author accused Morgan of being a pirate, the latter sued the book's publisher for slander and libel in the London high court. The court favored Morgan. He was awarded the sum of 200 pounds sterling and a guarantee that all future English book editions would be revised. Those, apparently, are not the editions in wide circulation today.

In his own writings, Morgan never mentions his early years beyond comments that he performed better at military matters than he did schoolwork. We know that in 1654—when he was only 19—Morgan sailed with a British expeditionary force to the Caribbean. The British were hoping to capture Hispaniola from Spain, but the expedition failed for a variety of reasons. So, as a consolation prize, the British decided to snatch lesser-defended Jamaica. That they did in 1655.

Post-Service Pirating

Having had a taste of combat—and liking it—the young Morgan remained in the Caribbean as a buccaneer when he cashed out of the king's service. He then became one of many seafaring souls who defended the English-held islands from Spain's various attempts to drive them out.

Under the tutelage of Commodore Sir Christopher Myngs (a.k.a. Mings), Morgan—who proved to be a quick learner—studied and absorbed the particulars of combat maneuvers at sea. Morgan was savvy. Unlike most buccaneers, he chose not to squander all his prize money on immediate gratification only to die impoverished. Before each of his drinking and gambling escapades, he made sure he put aside some *blunt*.

By 1661, Morgan had purchased and was commanding his own ship. His vessel became one of the ten commissioned to sail with Commodore Myngs's expedition against the city of Santiago, Cuba.

> **Knowing the Ropes**
>
> **Blunt** was a slang word for money or cash. Its origin is obscure, but is thought to refer to the rounded edges of minted coins.

Like his predecessor Queen Elizabeth I, King Charles II was walking a fine line between the necessity of maintaining a deployable armed force for his Caribbean holdings (Jamaica, in fact, became a strong base of operations for English and Colonial American privateers operating in South American waters) and achieving a lasting peace with Spain. To that end, Charles recalled his warships from the region.

An Edict of Emasculation and a Bought Commission

In 1663, the king sent a royal edict to Governor Sir Thomas Modyford of Jamaica forbidding buccaneers from any acts of violence against Spain. Aware that this would leave Jamaica defenseless, Modyford—for a fee and a percentage—began issuing his own letters of marque to any and all who would keep the Spanish at bay and preoccupied. With Myngs and the rest of the navy recalled to England, Captain Edward Mansfield became the elected leader of the brethren.

Purchasing their own commissions, Morgan—with four other captains and some 200 eager buccaneers—mounted an expedition. Morgan quickly surfaced as the expedition leader, and his strategy was to attack towns along treasure routes that had been ignored by marauders for long periods of time.

Paying close attention to tales passed along by veteran buccaneers, he learned of the Spanish propensity for lax garrison security due to lengthy stretches of military inactivity. This intelligence combined with a strategy of employing inland attacks against coastal defenses enabled Morgan's fleet to raid numerous cities and towns with great success. But before sailing back to Jamaica with their booty, Morgan and his men focused their attentions on one more city the buccaneer captain was determined to plunder.

Morgan's Obsession Makes Him Rich

Like many others, Morgan had heard stories of Gran Granada. Over the years, legends had abounded of an ancient city on the original site of a great Indian treasure with a rich silver operation. It was a city the Spanish now supposedly occupied. Morgan and his mates knew only scant bits of information: the city lay somewhere deep in the perilous jungles of Nicaragua, over steep mountains, and next to a beautiful lake.

As usual, it was easy for the persuasive Morgan to find and employ Indian guides. Now he turned his charm on the fleet to convince the others. Prevailing, he had his men paddle Indian canoes up the northern fork of the San Juan River. One hundred and eleven miles later, an estuary on which they were traveling spilled into Lake Nicaragua. To their astonishment, a bustling city, larger then Portsmouth, England, stretched out before them.

They attacked the unsuspecting city in broad daylight and quickly seized and secured the armory. They spent the remainder of the day loading treasure into the canoes. To make pursuit impossible, they sank their enemies' boats along the lakeside. When the expedition returned to Jamaica in 1665, Morgan was hailed a hero.

Instead of wasting time celebrating and basking in the glory of his successful expedition, Morgan focused his attention on the news that his uncle, Colonel Edward Morgan, had become lieutenant governor. Edward acquired the position in 1665 through his acquaintance with George Monck, duke of Albemarle, a close friend and ally of Charles II. Governor Modyford, the duke of Albemarle's cousin, and Edward became fast friends.

Morgan, whether for love or political and social advantage, married his first cousin Mary Elizabeth. When Edward died, Modyford—impressed with Morgan's intelligence and leadership ability—appointed him to his uncle's former position as commander of the militia in Port Royal.

Sir Henry Morgan.

(From Bucaniers of America, *Alexander Exquemelin, 1684)*

News of Captain Mansfield's death at the hands of the Spanish, three years later, left the position of admiral of the buccaneers vacant. Morgan's reputation enabled him to be easily elected by the brethren on Jamaica. At 30, he had it all: wealth, property, and power.

Ever the Optimist

The on-again off-again wars between Spain and England gave political maneuverability to the buccaneers acquiring commissions.

When informed war was again raging, Morgan sat down and gleefully penned out his wish list of cities to plunder. It was impressive: Havana, Portobelo, Veracruz, Puerto Principe, Cartagena, Maracaibo, and Panama. With his letter of marque, he let it be known he was going on the account. Seven hundred men and a dozen ships gathered for the expedition. During the council of captains, it was decided Morgan's dream of attacking Havana was impractical. The city was too heavily fortified. Instead, the hide-trading center of Puerto Principe became their first target. Employing Morgan's inland attack strategy, they captured the city. Having been forewarned, the citizens fled with their valuables.

Pick a City, Any City

Undaunted, Morgan checked his list of cities. He decided the next target would be Portobelo (a.k.a. Portobello). Not a rash man, he had firsthand knowledge from an escaped Indian slave of the city's true condition well before his fleet sailed. But he worried the buccaneers would refuse to attack what was rumored to be a highly fortified city.

With its two castles and a fort encircling the city, Morgan realized it sounded like a suicide mission. Consequently, as his mates eagerly signed on and inquired as to their target, Morgan told them it was secret. Aware that there were Spanish spies everywhere, the men accepted his explanation. Four hundred and sixty veteran buccaneers sailed. Canoes, having proven to be effective during the raid on Gran Granada, were Morgan's choice of assault platforms. He loaded 23 onto 9 ships.

When the crews realized their destination, it took everything Morgan had as a leader to convince them the fortifications were more imposing than practical.

An Amphibious Assault

Once again dropping anchor a great distance from their intended target, they manned the canoes. Morgan hoped for another surprise land attack as the maneuver had proven successful in the past. Unfortunately, his men were spotted.

Hurrying, the buccaneers landed three miles from the city. Taking the lookout sentry prisoner, they were relieved to learn the call to arms had not been sounded. Marching to the city's blockhouse, the privateers demanded the soldiers' surrender. Though outnumbered, the Spaniards fought. The ensuing gunshots alerted the city and the surrounding castles of Santiago and San Phelipe. The buccaneers easily captured all but the castle, Santiago. Not willing to risk any more of his men or waste any more time, Morgan issued a ruthless order: his men were to use their prisoners—nuns, friars, the town mayor, women, and the elderly—as human shields. The buccaneers advanced with lit torches and axes behind the townsfolk to the main gate. Though reluctant to fight and afraid of killing one of their own, the soldiers were threatened by their commanders. One cannon filled with chain shot was fired, wounding two friars and a few buccaneers. As Morgan hoped, his opponent's on-scene commanders had been overly cautious and slow to respond.

An old rusted cannon was fired and jumped from its carriage. With the ensuing mayhem atop the castle parapets, the buccaneers burst through the main gate. A second wave of buccaneers successfully scaled the walls. Waiting on the hillside in reserve, the remaining buccaneers received the signal to advance. Within a few short hours, Portobelo fell.

Loot, Pillage, But Don't Burn

Morgan let his men run free in the city with the stipulation they refrain from torching the town. The buccaneer captain had special plans for Portobelo. Don Agustin de Bracamonte, the interim president of Panama, had sent dispatches requesting military assistance when he learned of the fall of Portobelo. In haste he rode out with an inadequate force hoping to retake the city. Sergeant Major Antonio de Lara, who carried a ransom letter, intercepted him. The missive demanded 350,000 pesos. If not paid, Morgan threatened to strip the town of all its artillery and then burn it to the ground.

Almost as an afterthought, Morgan threatened to take the entire population to Jamaica to be treated as kindly as English prisoners had been treated by Spain. Bracamonte was incensed: not so much that Morgan had captured Portobelo, but that during a time of peace a mere pirate had dared address him as an equal. He immediately sent the sergeant major back with his reply: "I take you to be a corsair and I reply that the vassals of the king of Spain do not make treaties with inferior persons."

Morgan was amused and unimpressed. He sent a second letter, this time daring Bracamonte to come out and fight. But the Spaniard could do nothing without additional help. Wisely, he entered into negotiations with Morgan and waited for reinforcements. They never arrived. After weeks of parlay, all Bracamonte could do was pay the ransom.

When Broke, It's Time to Plunder

A wealthy Morgan was eager to settle down and enjoy married life on his Jamaican estates. But being admiral of the brethren of Port Royal compelled him to postpone his life of leisure. After his men wasted all their swag in the taverns and brothels, they demanded their leader go on the account once more.

This time Morgan chose Maracaibo. A French corsair who had sailed with L'Ollonais assured Morgan he could guide him straight to the center of the city. With 650 men and 8 ships, they set out from Jamaica. As they sailed into the Gulf of Venezuela, they were stunned. The Spanish had built a fort along the narrow channel to the town. Their presence was spotted and an alarm sounded. By the time the men reached the city, it was deserted. Determined to go home with treasure, the buccaneers spent the next two months in the region. They tracked down fleeing townsmen and tortured them for their valuables.

Eventually, Morgan's men set sail for the city of Gibraltar, plundering along the way.

Not This Time, You Don't!

Admiral Don Alonzo de Campos y Espinosa of the Spanish West Indian fleet had heard rumors of a possible buccaneer attack. His primary orders were to escort the annual silver treasure fleet in Vera Cruz to Havana and then safely to Spain. Espinosa calculated he had enough time to sail to Isla Vaca, on the northern section of Hispaniola, where it was rumored the pirates were assembled and destroy them. He set sail with three men-of-war: his flagship *Magdalena*, *Nuestra Señora de Soledad*, and *San Luis*. From information gleaned from a Dutch *sloop*, he learned the pirates' true destination. By the time he arrived at the lagoon near Maracaibo, Morgan's fleet had left the city.

Thrilled to discover no pirates manned the fort, Espinosa sent soldiers and supplies to see what might be salvaged. They were able to repair six cannon. In a daring move, he took a chance and maneuvered his deep-draft ships into the narrow shallow channel. He managed to block Morgan's escape route. Now he waited for their return from Gibraltar.

> **Knowing the Ropes** _____
>
> **Sloops** originally were small, single-masted ships with only a fore and main sail. Variations were created from the simple design to suit the requirements of trade and war. From the late-seventeenth century, England's Royal Navy modified the ship to carry up to 16 guns on a single deck. With the addition of numerous yards for additional sails, it became a speedy pirate chaser. Pirates coveted this fast vessel and frequently attacked a trading sloop, then modified the ship to fit their own needs.

"We'll Meet You in Battle"

Arriving back in Maracaibo, Morgan was surprised to see the warships. The only way out of the channel would be a fight, and the odds were against him. A letter demanding complete surrender was soon delivered to the buccaneer captain. Aware that he could not make this decision alone, Morgan assembled the crews.

Solemnly, he read the demand in English and French asking his mates for their decision: surrender or fight. Morgan sent back his men's answer: "We'll meet you in battle."

The buccaneers spent the next few days preparing their ships. Spies reported they were outfitting a captured Cuban merchant ship into Morgan's flagship. Guns were being mounted on her and carpenters were working on her hull to make her battle ready. They also reported that a sloop was being rigged as a *fire-ship*. Espinosa took nothing for granted. He prepared all three ships with push booms and buckets of water, and he drilled squads for fire fighting duty. He was ready.

> **Knowing the Ropes**
>
> A **fire-ship** was a vessel that was filled with explosives, sailed straight into an enemy ship, and then ignited. It was equally dangerous for the men who sailed her and set her afire.

On April 27, 1669, the 13 pirate ships—anchored just out of range of the Spanish—sailed. They had waited until the wind and tide were favorable to make a run to freedom. Espinosa was prepared. With the water in the channel so shallow, he let the pirates come to him. He ordered his men to stand ready to cut the anchor cable and furl all sails if the battle turned against them.

Morgan's Ruse

Morgan's banner flew high on the main mast of the Cuban flagship. Its deck was crowded with men. Two small frigates flanked the flagship. The fire-ship sloop was not seen. When within range, the two frigates, with all guns firing, broke ranks and sailed to either side of the *Magdalena*. Morgan's flagship continued firing and steered straight for her center. As they crashed, pirates grappled onto the Spanish flagship, then jumped overboard to a waiting canoe. Within seconds Morgan's flagship exploded, then erupted in flame. The winds fanned the fire and enveloped the *Magdalena*. Within minutes she was destroyed. As his men jumped into the water, Espinosa stayed aboard his burning vessel. He flung loose planks overboard to try and save his seamen who would otherwise have drowned. In the last seconds, he leapt over the side and was picked up by his longboat.

Espinosa's Plan Unravels

Unable to help save the flagship, the captain of the *San Luis* cut anchor and sailed toward the safety of the fort. He ran her aground on a sandbar. Quickly grabbing as much ammunition and provisions as possible, his men abandoned ship and found

Ships under pirate attack.

safety in the fort. Before joining his men, the captain torched the *San Luis.* The captain would not allow it to become a prize.

The captain of the *Soledad* was not as fortunate. Attempting to keep his ship out of harm's way, he ordered the cable cut and sails set. One of the sail-lines jammed in its pulley. Unable to maneuver the vessel, it drifted out of the protective range of the fort's cannon. Eight ships and dozens of canoes filled with buccaneers hotly pursued. Unwilling to risk capture, most of the *Soledad*'s crew jumped overboard. She ran aground in the swamp. Her captain barely escaped. He then watched in horror as the buccaneers boarded their prize.

Don't Mess with a Master Tactician

Morgan's ruse worked. His Cuban flagship was the fire-ship. He was certain there were spies ashore as they prepared for battle. The buccaneers made sure specific misinformation got back to the Spanish. Morgan knew they would expect him to outfit a flagship with more guns. So his carpenters cut fake gunports along her hull. The extra guns they had aboard were merely logs painted black. His men hollowed out the wood and jammed them with explosives and short fuses. Every part of the ship was then treated with a combustible mixture of tar, pitch, and brimstone. Barrels of gunpowder and anything else they found in the town that would burn was packed aboard.

Only 12 men sailed her and grappled onto the *Magdalena.* The additional "seen" crewmen were upright logs tied to the railing dressed as sailors with painted faces.

Repelling the Pirate Invaders

The buccaneers now stormed the fort. It proved far more difficult than anticipated. The fort commander was experienced and competent. Now manned by a full complement of enraged soldiers, militiamen from the hills, and the surviving seamen, they managed to repel the pirates' every assault.

As leader, Morgan had to come up with a solution. The entire buccaneer fleet with all their accumulated treasure would be an easy target if they attempted to flee. Doubtful the offer would be accepted, he attempted to negotiate a truce. By this time, Espinosa had arrived at the fort, and—as ranking officer—assumed command. Espinosa, of course, rejected Morgan's peace overtures. With the pride of the Spanish fleet now destroyed, he knew that once back in Spain he was a dead man. Therefore he had no intention of letting the pirates escape. To save himself and his career, he was determined to bring Morgan and his brigands triumphantly back to Spain, dead or alive.

His peace terms rejected, Morgan kept his mates occupied by salvaging the *Magdalena* for any sunken treasure. It proved a successful endeavor that also afforded him more time to think. While his men were restocking their ships with provisions, Morgan came up with a plan.

Now You See Them, Now You Don't

From his Spanish prisoners, Morgan learned that only six cannon in the fort were operational. He surmised that with so large a fleet, six cannon couldn't possibly sink them all. If they fled under cover of darkness at high tide, there would be an even better chance. Morgan took their entire treasure and shared it outright then and there among the men. Better to lose a small amount if a ship went down then the entire haul. Then he surprised his mates by loudly ordering them all to their ships.

Later that day, Spanish sentries observed canoes of armed buccaneers being rowed to the swamps just out of sight of the fort. The canoes returned to the fleet empty with only the paddlers. They would emerge again ferrying more men ashore.

Espinosa surmised the pirates were going to attempt a land assault on the fort. He felt they'd likely attack at night. Preparing to foil their plans, he ordered most of the cannons repositioned to cover all possible alternative routes. Guards watched from every angle of the fort waiting to see from which direction the pirates would break cover.

Slipping Back Out to Sea

When darkness fell, the entire buccaneer fleet cut their anchors. With sails furled, the ships drifted with the tide across the channel. They were spotted immediately and the fort fired the cannon pointed toward the sea. By the time Espinosa's men repositioned the other cannon, the fleet had drifted past their firing range with only minimal damage to the ships.

Morgan had played an old buccaneer trick. Each time the canoes emerged from the swamp the boats were still full. All the men, with the exception of the paddlers, were lying flat under the canoe thwarts, the paddlers' wooden plank seats, giving the appearance of an empty canoe.

Freeing their prisoners the following morning, Morgan's men sailed back to Jamaica on his new flagship, the *Soledad*. One more remarkable expedition was added to his reputation.

Modyford Puts the Brakes on Morgan's Raiders

Reporting to Governor Modyford, Morgan received the official order: with the peace so strained between England and Spain, all buccaneer raids against any Spanish ship or settlement must cease. Ironically, as Morgan was ordered to cease attacks, the queen of Spain was doing just the opposite. For years the English government had evasively refused Spain's constant demands to curtail the English buccaneer raids in the West Indies. In April 1669, an edict went out to all of Spain's colonial officials declaring all-out war with the English in the Indies.

Governor Don Juan Perez de Guzman was thrilled with the edict. He expected Spanish privateers to rally. No one answered. Spanish raiders knew firsthand the ferocity of the English. They had no intentions of attacking them outright.

Captain Manuel Pardal Rivero was a Portuguese corsair seeking a reputation as well as wealth. In 1670, he began by attacking English ships. Guzman rewarded his successes, which convinced Spanish privateers to do the same. Thrilled by the governor's attentions, Rivero had the audacity to set his sights on Jamaica. He raided a number of settlements on the northern and southern shores. In his insolence, he left a bold challenge for Morgan while admitting he was the single perpetrator of the raids.

The insult was too great for the entire population of Jamaica. The council of Jamaica met to discuss how to handle this backhanded challenge to the entire island. Not yet hearing the news concerning the Spanish edict, the population of Jamaica was stunned by the recent attacks on their commerce and island. They had just openly declared peace in the Indies. They considered this the Spanish answer to their olive branch. The council began to pressure Modyford to let the buccaneers sail against direct orders from England. They reminded Modyford that the king had given him permission to deal with extraordinary situations with whatever extraordinary means he deemed necessary.

Dead Men's Tales _____

I, Captain Manoel Rivera Pardal, to ye chiefe of ye squadron of privateers in Jamaica … I come to seeke Generall Morgan … I crave hee would come out upon ye coast to seeke mee, that hee might see ye valour of ye Spaniards … And because I had noe time I did not come to ye mouth of Port Royall to speake by word of mouth.

—Captain Manuel Pardal Rivero, in a note delivered to Morgan, July 5, 1670

An Open-Ended Commission to Attack Spanish Shipping

Modyford bent to the council's will and issued a letter of marque to Morgan and a buccaneer fleet. Carefully worded, the letter basically gave Morgan and his men permission to sail anywhere and do anything against the Spanish as long as Morgan had the slightest hint the Spanish he attacked might own weapons or ships that could even be considered capable of invading Jamaica. The governor of Curaçao provided justification for Modyford. He sent him a copy of the queen's declaration of war in the Indies.

The Largest-Ever Buccaneer Fleet

Henry Morgan put out the word. He had a legal commission for any pirate interested in going on the account with his fleet. The location of the rendezvous would be Isla Vaca. French corsairs along with English buccaneers flocked to the site. Buccaneers earlier forced to retire were able to acquire credit from eager merchants to make their ships once again seaworthy. More than 2,000 men and 36 ships arrived. To date, it was the largest buccaneer fleet to assemble. At Morgan's council of war, he left it up to his captains as to where they would attack. The resounding consensus was "Panama!"

Morgan's Dream Expedition

Morgan knew they had to act swiftly if they were to accomplish this goal. Modyford had gotten word that Spain and England were once again in peace talks. His fleet sailed first to New Providence (Nassau). Recently captured by the Spanish, the governor quickly surrendered. He asked Morgan to stage a fight so he could save face. Morgan obliged. His fleet now had a staging area closer to Panama. With a hand-picked body of 470 men, Morgan advanced to the castle at San Lorenzo, which guarded the Chagres River that led into Panama. Morgan saw at once the fort outgunned his ships. Upon landing, the men had to hack through jungle to capture the fort. When there, the soldiers put up a valiant fight. It wasn't an easy victory for Morgan. He lost more than 100 men. He left 370 men to guard the fort. He was not going to make the same mistake as he did at Maracaibo. The privateers believed the route to Panama would now be easy. They were wrong.

The Famous Trek to Panama

One thousand five hundred buccaneers with canoes, 7 shallow draft sloops, and 36 riverboats meandered up the Chagres River. The first 24 hours went as planned. Then the expedition hit its first snag. The rainy season was at an end, and the river was shallow. First Morgan had to abandon the sloops; the riverboats went next. Soon the men had to walk with only the provisions in the canoes. Five times the water table dropped, forcing the men to carry their canoes. By the fourth day, the river was nothing more than a bed of mud. The men abandoned everything except for their ammunition. Setting out on foot, they had to hack their way through dark, snake- and mosquito-infested bamboo swampland.

By the fourth day of their march, they had hoped to find food at the military post of Torna Cavallos. But the troops, knowing they were coming, had fled, tearing down their barracks and leaving nothing behind but a few empty leather bags.

The men dreamed of reaching the village of Venta de Cruces and provisions. They would be disappointed. The village turned out to be nothing more than a series of smoldering woodpiles, and it was deserted. Worse, Morgan knew that the Spanish knew he was coming. After having endured what might've been called "hell week," the men could only proceed. It took two more days before they emerged from the unforgiving jungle onto an open savanna. The advance guard reported good news. They had seen the city of Panama. Even better, they had spotted a herd of cattle. When fed and briefly rested, and with their spirits high, the men marched on.

Dead Men's Tales

Being angry at this misfortune ... (they) fell to eating the leathern bags, as being desirous to afford something ... to their stomachs ... For these first took the leather, and sliced it in pieces. Then did they beat it between two stones, and rub it, often dipping it in the water of the river to render it by these means supple and tender, Lastly they scraped off the hair, and roasted or broiled it upon the fire. And, being thus cooked, they cut it into small morsels, and eat it, helping it down with frequent gulps of water, which by good fortune they had nigh at hand.

—Alexander Exquemelin, *Bucaniers of America* (1684)

Movement to Contact

By nightfall they sighted the Spanish battle lines. Stretched out before them were 600 cavalrymen and 2,100 soldiers commanded by none other than an ailing Guzman. Both forces camped. The fate of Panama would be decided on the morning of January 28, 1671. Overnight two thirds of the Spanish force fled. Guzman had no choice but to retreat to the city and make his stand. Rallying an additional militia of 1,700 men, he positioned his troops for the coming action. Guzman placed his artillery in the center and his cavalry on the left. He believed his right flank to be secured by a steep hill.

The Hollow Sacking of Panama

Morgan instantly recognized the plan's flaw. With the sun glaring down on the Spanish, he sent men up the hill unseen. A jittery cavalry officer broke ranks and charged with his unit. The French corsairs—all crack shots—calmly picked them off. Morgan's men successfully took the hill and surprised the Spanish troops. Most of the Spanish soldiers broke ranks and fled. A desperate Guzman then stampeded a herd of wild cattle forward and through the buccaneer ranks, expecting the men to be trampled. The cattle, spooked from the gunshots, scattered in every direction. Privateers shot the ones who got in their way. Defeated, the Spanish ran. It took Morgan just two hours to capture Panama, but his triumph was short-lived.

The majority of Panama's citizens had fled days before with their valuables. Captain of artillery Don Balthasar Pau y Rocaberti had remained in the city. His orders were simple if the battle turned against them. Spike the cannon and torch the powder magazines that were scattered throughout the city. With few exceptions, Panama was a city built from wood. Rocaberti carried out his orders. The wind did the rest. In mere minutes, Panama was engulfed in flame. Buccaneers found themselves busy putting out fires, not plundering as they would have preferred.

For the next 20 days, the buccaneers picked through rubble and sought captives for their valuables. The treasure heap looked impressive. Again Morgan chose to share out then and there. But discontent within the ranks quickly rose.

Grumbling Within the Ranks Forces Morgan's Hand

Depending on the source for all the hardship they endured to capture Panama, the common share was stated to have ranged somewhere between a paltry 15 to 100 pounds sterling. The men cried foul and accused Morgan of holding back treasure.

Morgan made a big show of displaying all he had on his person and forced the French corsairs searched, too. Though no additional booty was found, the buccaneer captain lost the trust of the brethren—and he never regained it.

Not comfortable with the dangerous mood of his men, Morgan departed immediately for Jamaica without signaling the rest of his fleet to follow. Historians speculate that he wished to arrive home first with his version of the expedition to be believed before others returned with their versions. However, most of the men who sacked Panama with Morgan did not sail back to Jamaica, but sailed for more plunder throughout the region. Those who later returned to Jamaica continued to grumble over their paltry share and Morgan's duplicity.

> **Treasure Chest**
>
> Exquemelin sailed with Morgan and portrayed him in print as a cheat and villain. As a devout Catholic, would he have been horrified over Morgan's decision to use clergymen as human shields in addition to feeling cheated of his proper share from Panama?

A Less-Than-Triumphant Return

The Treaty of Madrid was signed on July 18, 1670. Spain now officially recognized England's holdings in the Caribbean. The news did not reach the West Indies until May 1671, and the buccaneer fleet had already sailed. Mail and official government caches were distributed to the West Indies by the only transportation available: ships. Therefore governmental documents took months or even years to reach their destination. To keep the peace, Charles II was forced to arrest Modyford, who spent two years in the Tower of London. With the duke of Albemarle's death it appeared Modyford and Morgan had no ally in the government. The new governor of Port Royal, Sir Thomas Lynch, arrested Morgan on April 4, 1672. Sent back to England, the government treated him like a celebrity rather than a prisoner.

Charm and Daring Wins Every Time

Morgan would remain in England for two years but was never imprisoned. A hero to the English population, he made good use of his time by charming the English court. His intelligence, charisma, and boldness won him friends in high places. Secretary of state Lord Arlington urged Morgan to prepare a memorandum for King Charles on Jamaica's defenses and his suggestions for improvement. With time and continuing peace between Spain and England, Morgan became less of a political embarrassment. When the new governor of Jamaica was appointed, Morgan was awarded the post of lieutenant governor. Charles II knighted him on January 23, 1674, before he departed for Port Royal.

To Catch a Thief

Morgan's freedom and laurels did not come without a price. King Charles issued specific orders: privateering and pirating must stop throughout the West Indies. With this royal command, Morgan ceased issuing letters of marque and withdrew the commissions already granted. He considered himself a buccaneer and a privateer, not a pirate. He never sailed without a commission, and he attacked only those considered an enemy of England. If he had to capture and hang an old mate who refused to obey the law, he did so with a heavy heart. Many called Morgan a turncoat, whereas others shared his philosophy and retired from the sweet trade.

Living Well Is the Best Revenge

Now stifled by inactivity, Morgan spent his remaining days in assembly council meetings or drinking with his mates and reliving past adventures. Becoming acting governor for a short time, Morgan used the opportunities afforded by the post wisely. With a threat of possible French attack, Morgan mobilized a militia and built two forts to protect Port Royal. On August 25, 1688, at the age of 53, his extravagant lifestyle of drunkenness and carousing caught up with him. Sir Henry Morgan was given a state funeral accompanied by a series of 21-gun salutes.

The Least You Need to Know

- François L'Ollonais, indentured to cruel masters, turned psychopath. He was feared by the native Indians as well as the Spanish.

- So unpredictable when drunk, Rock Brasilliano frightened everyone, friend and foe. The governor of Jamaica moved his residence to live as far away from him as possible.

- Bartholomew the Portuguese, though unlucky in acquiring treasure, was clever enough to extricate himself from prison using empty jars as flotation devices.

- Though growing up a slave, once turned to piracy Red Legs Greaves was known for his humane treatment of prisoners.

- Henry Morgan was a brilliant military leader who successfully executed a raid on Panama. Turning from buccaneer to enforcer, he not only halted pirate raids in the Caribbean, but convinced King Charles II that Jamaica was strategically important.

Weighing Anchor: Why Go to Sea?

In This Chapter

♦ Job openings available at sea

♦ A boy's journey into manhood

♦ Legalized kidnapping

♦ Independence for females in breeches

♦ Hellish conditions aboard ship

♦ A disgruntled seaman's only recourse: desertion or mutiny

Why would anyone willingly risk life or limb by going to sea, particularly during an era when naval wars and pirate attacks were the normal state of affairs? But many did so, and for a variety of reasons.

Of those reasons, nearly every member of a ship's crew—during the period from the fifteenth through the eighteenth centuries—fell into one of four categories: the call of adventure was too strong to ignore; they were running from the law, or they felt there was no other economic option open to them; they were forced into service and had no say in the matter; or sea service was a family tradition.

Seeking a Better Life

During the golden age of piracy (1692–1725), men had a few more options open to them than either women or children. Typically, a man remained within the social stratum to which he had been born. Illiteracy was the norm. Breaking the social class structure was difficult. A man of intelligence and fortitude, however, did have a chance to improve his life.

Economic conditions were a major contributing factor in one's decision to seek a better life. Three quarters of the people in England lived in rural communities. The majority came from the lower class and extreme poverty. If a man lived on a noble's estate as a tenant farmer, he did backbreaking fieldwork for food and little money. His livelihood and very existence hinged on how well his landlord managed the overall estate. *Serfdom* began to disappear in the fifteenth century. Freedom of career choice and decent living wages as a viable concept, however, were slow to catch on.

Knowing the Ropes

Serfdom was the hereditary attachment of peasants who labored on an allotted area of land belonging to an estate of an aristocratic lord. Serfdom differed from slavery in that serfs could not be sold to a new master. However, a serf's loyalty and obligation would be transferred if the property was inherited through death or purchased by another lord. Serfs generally never left the land on which they had been born.

Mother Nature didn't help matters either: drastic weather changes and severe storms caused widespread loss of livestock and ruination of crops. Starvation was rampant. Once-honest people were forced into thievery to survive.

Still, many men left the countryside to first try their luck in the towns and cities before their thoughts turned to the sea.

Moving to a city without references and finding a job was tricky. With luck one might apprentice to a skilled craftsman. Other possibilities for employment might be found in a shop, a tavern, or as a member of a household staff. Sporadic paying work could tide a man over for a few days. His workday would be long and hard, and his wages low. Worse, a country lad had to compete with the men and boys already in the city. When hunger became overwhelming, his choices were to slip into the underground criminal life to survive or go down to the docks for work.

Competition for Jobs: Sign On and Learn a Trade

Throughout much of Western Europe, Spain's constant wars for territory and Catholic dominance drove people from their homes. England became the only safe haven. Refugees flooded in from every country and ethnic background. By the 1560s, England supported a huge influx of Dutch, French Huguenots (Protestants), Flemish and Walloons (Belgians), Irish, and even Spanish immigrants. Englishmen faced a sudden lack of available jobs as these foreigners snapped up all of the good employment opportunities.

One bright spot, however, was the legitimate merchant shipping business, which expanded with so many people entering the country. This created a need for sailors. One of the alluring factors of signing on to a merchant or naval ship was acquiring a viable trade. On a naval vessel one would learn to become a seaman, a crewmember (not a commissioned officer) who knew the workings of a ship (handling line, sails, etc.).

On a merchant ship, a man learned the tasks needed to sail. When a man became an experienced seaman on a merchant ship, he could hire on to another vessel and receive higher wages. If skilled, he could learn the cooper's or carpenter's trade. This afforded him a greater chance of employment on land. An ambitious seaman might find someone aboard who could teach him to read and write. If fortunate, he might convince the navigator to instruct him in the art of reading sea charts and navigational instruments.

A Perilous Life Under Sail

The average life expectancy of a sailor was not long: 30 to 35 years of age at best. (Depending on the individual and their circumstances, the average life expectancy of a nonsailor was the late 50s.) It was a harsh reality based on dangers associated with sailing, combat, and disease. Daily life aboard a ship was hazardous to say the least. Falling from a great height was all too common. The daily chore of clambering up ratlines (small rope rungs of the rope ladders that led up the mast and rigging) was potentially life threatening. While climbing some 50 to 150 feet (depending on the ship's design), a man could lose his footing. It was not uncommon for an inexperienced seaman to fall onto the deck, breaking his back,

Pirate Yarns

The classic movie scene in which the pirate is seen swimming toward an enemy ship with a dagger clenched between his teeth is misleading. The vast majority of sailors and pirates could not swim. When a man hit the water (from any height), he usually drowned.

or land in the water and drown. During a storm or battle, even an experienced sailor could lose his balance and fall to his death.

Despite the risks, the lure of the sea for many had a special, almost-hypnotic appeal. The mysteries that lay on the other side of the horizon called out to many men from all social classes. Without realizing the harshness of life aboard a merchant or naval ship might be far worse than on land, these would-be adventurers willingly signed aboard to make their fortunes and see the world. When the lack of fortune and daily life became a reality, many sailors turned to piracy.

From Boy to Man

Cities were dangerous places for the hundreds of unwanted or orphaned boys. It was common practice for orphanages or parents to sell a child to anyone who offered the highest price. The jobs they worked were hard, dangerous, and varied.

As a chimney sweep, for example, a boy would spend his days climbing into soot-filled claustrophobic fireplace flues. If agile, he might avoid being stuck inside for hours. Often the coal embers still glowed hot and he got burnt. Many died from burns or lung disease at a very early age.

Considered to be a social "step up," being sold into apprenticeship—to a shop or tradesman—a boy was virtually owned until adulthood (his twenty-first birthday). The only provision the law required was that he be fed (usually table scraps) and be given a roof over his head. Depending on the master, a boy could be treated worse than a slave.

For many boys, life on the street was all they knew. This consisted of begging, stealing, or simply starving to death. If caught committing a crime, the law did not consider a boy's age or the circumstances surrounding the crime. Depending on the severity of the offense, a boy could be thrown in jail for life or hanged. The lure of adventure, seeing new places, fresh air, guaranteed meals, a place to sleep, and wages drew these street boys to ships.

Cabin Boys

Eight years is the earliest age recorded for a naval cabin boy. By that time, a lad understood rules and regulations and could react promptly to the urgency of commands. Many a lad wasn't yet tall enough to hop into his hanging sleeping hammock. He'd need a step or a helpful push from a fellow shipmate.

A boy's duties were varied. He would assist with the domestic chores, sweep and wash the deck, polish the brass, and help wherever else he was needed. He might be assigned to the captain or another officer as assistant steward.

Boys between the ages of 10 and 12 were completely integrated into all aspects of shipboard life. Age was not a consideration. A cabin boy was the lowest seafarer in the chain of command and, by the early-seventeenth century, his wages (6 shillings) reflected such. To deter desertion the navy paid their crews six months in arrears. A ship the size of a *man-of-war* might billet (bunk) up to 12 boys, all of whom would receive instruction from the ship's schoolmaster (who also taught the midshipmen).

Knowing the Ropes

The **man-o-war** evolved from the galleon. The Dutch and English were the most aggressive designers and developers of these vessels. Removing the fore and aft castles, a covered gundeck was added. A heavier keel assured the vessel could support the extra gun weight. The deeper draft kept the ship steady when the guns recoiled after firing. The maximum breadth of the hull was forward of the midship in a "cod fish head shape" tapering to the aft like the "tail of a mackerel" for stability. The length of the keel evolved through the years. From 110 feet in a 1588 Armada ship to the 150-foot keel of the HMS *Victory* (1765). Depending on the ship, they carried upward of 120 guns of varying poundage.

Careers for Nobility's Second Sons

Not every lad who had a sailing career was orphaned or poverty-stricken. In most Western European countries, the second son of titled nobility already with a family naval tradition joined the service. Depending on his father's whim, a boy as young as 10 might have a *purchased* commission, enabling him to serve aboard ship as a midshipman (cadet) and work his way up to commissioned officer. If his parent paid the admiralty enough money, a teenage boy might be commissioned into naval service at the rank of lieutenant. These bought commissions often took place whether the boy was intelligent, competent, or not. Noblemen who ran the naval departments of most countries believed that only titled, property-owning men (gentlemen) or the sons of gentlemen were suitable to lead others.

Powder Monkeys

The speed, coordination, and dexterity of boys were assets at sea, especially during times of combat action when they served as gunpowder-bearing "powder monkeys."

Highly volatile gunpowder was stored loose in barrels on the lowest deck (called the *orlop*). This dry room, known as the *powder room, powder magazine,* or *magazine,* was approached with extreme care. Gunpowder was so dangerous that large quantities of ammunition were prepared only when needed and only by an experienced gunner.

The calculated amounts of gunpowder differed for cannons, pistols, and muskets. Measured powder was carefully poured onto paper and rolled into a cartridge. Placed carefully in canisters made of leather or canvas, it would be carried up to the guns. The gunner shouted which weapon or ship deck it was intended for when he had a full canister ready. A boy grabbed the full canister by its handle and rushed up the companionways (stairs) as fast as he could. He needed to be quick for lives depended on that ammunition. Care also had to be taken not to spill, dampen, or get the powder too close to flame. The agility of the lads earned them the nickname "powder monkeys." Later the name applied to anyone running canisters up from the powder magazine. When a boy wished to join a pirate crew, this experience could instantly elevate him—from that of a mere cabin boy or servant on the ship—to crew and thus allow him a share of any seized treasure.

Joining the Navy

The Royal (British) Navy offered two incentives to lure a man into service. First, the navy offered two months' advance wages as a loan prior to sailing. Second, it guaranteed to keep a man out of debtors' prison if he owed his creditors less than 20 pounds sterling. However, men living in port cities knew of the brutal conditions of navy life, so few men jumped at the incentives. The navy had to come up with a solution and quickly.

"Pressed" into Service

The admiralty established the "Impress Service." It was an organization set up at every English port. According to stated regulations, the Impress Service could lawfully seize men between the ages of 18 and 55 for naval service. The regulating officer of each Impress Service office hired local men in each port. These wharf laborers—often the toughest of the tough—were paid to roam the city in search of suitable victims. Many dockworkers joined the Impress Service so they themselves would not be forced against their will to join the navy and go to sea. Thus the dreaded *press gangs* came into being.

Knowing the Ropes

Press gangs were groups of men who were legally authorized by their government to forcibly use whatever means at their disposal to recruit able-bodied men for service in the navy. It was common for them to beat, shackle, and drag men from streets, taverns, and even their homes onto naval ships. "Press" is a corruption of the French word *imprest* or *prest*, meaning "loan" or "advance." Press came to mean "forced." Gang was shortened from the term *ganger* or the "foreman" of "wharf laborers."

The admiralty paid the service whenever a man was delivered to a ship. The Impress Service was instructed to immediately pay each man they acquired his first month's naval wages as soon as he "volunteered." Needless to say, the organization rarely adhered to admiralty regulations of paying the monthly wage. No captain needing a full crew questioned whether his enlistee received his wages when forcibly brought to the ship.

A man-of-war could be seen from shore hours before it docked, allowing enough time for men and boys living in dock towns to go into hiding. This required the press gangs to travel farther inland for recruits. The Impress Service paid for travel and lodging. Wharf laborers were a rare sight in farming areas. This gave the gangs the advantage of surprise. Naval muster and pirate trial records indicate the largest percentage of Englishmen on the high seas came from Wales and farming communities. Though press gangs were feared, some towns and villages actually fought them as they dragged their men away. If wealthy enough to bribe a gang, a man had a good chance of escaping service.

By the late eighteenth century, Royal Navy warships began to assign 8 to 12 of their strongest seamen, with the quartermaster to supervise, as a press gang crew. This cut down on the expenses incurred by the naval department. Ironically, this also allowed them the option of grabbing the very wharf laborers who previously worked for the Impress Service. These tactics prompted many a conscripted sailor to piracy when the opportunity presented itself, as you'll learn in the next chapter.

Merchant Service or Privateering Won't Save You

Sailors on merchant ships or privateers weren't immune to kidnapping. Press gangs and naval captains were free to board commercial ships to conscript as many men as needed.

Technically they had to leave enough men aboard to allow the ship to sail. By law, they were not to take officers or apprentices. In many ports, the rule was given very broad interpretation. And because it was fairly easy to spot a gang of tough-looking men, it became increasingly difficult for press gangs to board and find suitable sailors.

Captain William Kidd had to contend with this naval law when he departed on his disastrous trip (see Chapter 14).

Have Another Drink

Taverns and alehouses were prime press gang traps, and their patrons were prime targets. One method was offering money to unsavory barkeeps and serving wenches who pointed out suitable victims. There was either the typical tavern brawl if one tried to resist or a more subtle attack. When the unawares victim had the tankard raised high and couldn't see anyone coming, he would be knocked unconscious from behind. When he regained consciousness, he would find himself on a navy ship, miles out to sea.

Look Before Turning Up the Tankard

The tankard shilling entrapment proved to be very effective. According to English law, if a man accepted, albeit unknowingly, the king's (or queen's) shilling (the equivalent of 12 pennies, which was a large sum of money in those days) from a naval representative, he was instantly enlisted. Many an unsuspecting chap fell for this ruse. He would be served a tankard by a barkeep and sit enjoying his ale. Soon he would notice or taste something in his drink. Upon closer investigation, the man would find and pull a shilling out of the bottom of his tankard. The press gang officer would then inform him he'd just volunteered to join the navy by accepting the crown's pay advance.

This ploy worked flawlessly, but all too frequently. Alehouse regulars became wary of every drink ordered. Soon, men were stirring drinks with anything—fingers, spoons, daggers, and sticks—to make sure no coin was there.

Honest alehouse landlords soon began to lose a great deal of business. What man wanted to drink in such a cautious, stressful environment? As a consequence, honest owners introduced the glass-bottom pewter tankard in the mid 1700s. Upon receiving his drink, a man could immediately check the bottom of the tankard to confirm no coin lurked within. A second advantage of the glass bottom was self-defense. This tankard provided an unobstructed view of someone coming toward you. Of course, if the bloke was drunk, the glass bottom most likely didn't help.

Treasure Chest

Avoiding conscription was a serious consideration for most men. Once aboard, they were technically required to serve in the Royal Navy a minimum of 18 months. In reality, that hitch stretched into years. Usually when a sailor's hitch was up, he would be aboard ship in the middle of the ocean. If a sailor managed to jump ship, he was a deserter. He'd be hunted down as a criminal. If caught, the severity of his punishment by flogging was at the captain's discretion. Punishment would always be carried out in front of the entire crew—and to serve as a lesson, was brutal and often fatal.

If He Can Sail, So Can She

If men and boys had few options open to them on land, women and young girls had even fewer. There were only a couple of morally acceptable occupations a female could obtain. Whatever her job, she was constantly in danger of having her virtue tested.

If lucky enough to have a work recommendation, there was the exhausting position of domestic servant. The hours were long, the treatment demoralizing. Considered fair game, it was not uncommon for the men of the house to press their sexual and social advantage.

The possibility of marriage for respectability and security was a gamble. A woman might find herself back on the job market having to support a husband and child as well as herself. This was also a reality if her husband was "pressed" into service or willingly joined the service. If a woman lived with her parents or a male relative, the laws of the day gave them complete control over her life.

Few Options on the Street

If a girl or woman lived on the street, there were only three survival options: beggar, thief, or prostitute. The same lure of adventure, fresh air, three meals a day, learning a trade, a guaranteed place to sleep, control of her own wages, and a sense of independence spawned a somewhat rare phenomenon: the odd teenage girl or woman who went to sea. To them the harshness of naval discipline was actually less restricting than options on land.

Haircuts and Bound Breasts

It wasn't difficult for a teenage girl or a woman to change her name and disguise herself as a boy. The disguise was easy enough to accomplish. Her first step would be simply to change her name. Tightly binding her breasts with strips of cloth and the loose-fitting clothes of the day solved the problem of correct body type. The popular hairstyle for men was shoulder-length or longer. A woman simply cut her hair shorter. (Custom dictated women never cut their hair.) She then had the option of wearing it either loose or tied back in the popular queue (ponytail). Grace O'Malley (see Chapter 5) was nicknamed by her family Grainne Mhaol (Grace of the Cropped Hair) for cutting her hair short like a boy.

At varying ages, a boy's voice changed along with the degree of facial-hair growth. All that needed to be done to solve those problems was survive the rounds of good-natured ribbing by shipmates. Seamen rarely bathed (bathing in those days was deemed un-healthy), and they slept in their clothes.

Tough daily chores kept a woman lean and muscular. She'd be quite able to pull a sail line or stand on footropes and furl sails (as they do today), keeping pace with the men. Acting and dressing the part of a young sailor convincingly would rarely cause a fellow mate reason to scrutinize her looks. However, she would have to be extremely brave and tough enough to live and survive in that harsh environment—much like pirate Mary Read, whom you'll meet in Chapter 16.

Little Respect for Sailors

Sailors had a thankless job. They risked their lives during sea battles for their country's survival—or rise to supremacy—only to be regarded as "scum," "lowlifes," dangerous, and to be avoided at all costs by the general populace upon their return.

It wasn't just the dangers associated with battle that sailors had to contend with. Besides being pressed into service, some endured maniacal captains and officers, keel-hauling, and other brutal punishments, storms, and disease. Top that off with being rejected by society, denied their back pay, and lack of opportunities for a decent job on land or advancement at sea, and many honest men were pushed over the edge. It's no wonder many turned to piracy.

To fully understand such seemingly radical decisions made by men (and women), one must first consider what daily life was like on naval and merchant ships and the total lack of basic human rights once aboard.

For a common seaman in the navy, it often didn't matter what country's flag was flying above his head. Whether he truly volunteered for the position or was press-ganged, he was owned, body and soul, by the captain of his ship until "told" his time was up.

In addition to naval regulations, captains added their own rules regarding the running of their ships. Even if the captain was a fair-minded man, life onboard was just plain intolerable. Physical work was demanding, the sleep sporadic, filth and tight living quarters the norm. Disease was rampant. Until it was discovered that vitamin C helped prevent scurvy, it was a common and devastating disease aboard ships. Seasickness affected many. Ship rules and infractions would be reasonable, yet punishment carried out immediately. This kept the officers in control.

Captains of merchantmen were also under the naval laws of the office of the admiralty, yet like their naval counterparts, when past the shoreline they had total authority over the lives of his crew.

If the Work Doesn't Kill You, the Captain Might

For seamen serving under psychopathic or sadistic captains, life wasn't just grim, it was often deadly. History is rife with accounts of captains having it in for a crewman and subsequently working him or beating him to death. There were many ways this could be accomplished aboard a ship. The captain could have the man continuously running up and down the ratlines until, exhausted, he would literally lose his footing and fall to his death. Another command could have him running around the entire length of the ship's deck for hours until he dropped dead of exhaustion.

This particular punishment was adopted and refined by the pirate Francis Farrington Spriggs (see Chapter 19). Upon capturing a Portuguese ship and taking its cargo, the pirates amused themselves with "sweating" their captives before setting them free. Lighting candles along the decks and mizzenmast, each victim was forced to run a gauntlet around the decks while pirates pricked him with sharp objects, enough to draw blood until the man fell exhausted.

Shackled and Starved

There was always the old standby of throwing the seaman below deck in shackles and chains without food and water. Captains could order a seaman tied to a dangling rope secured to a mast. Death was caused by internal injuries from slamming against the mast, sun exposure, or starvation (as recorded in admiralty records). Pirates adopted many of these tortures as their own, especially against captured naval officers.

Because captains had complete charge aboard ship, no one had the authority to stop them from abusing and even killing members of the crew. If a compassionate officer attempted to intervene, the officer would be putting himself in physical danger. This was not exclusive to state navies. Merchant fleets followed the same harsh rules.

Dead Men's Tales

The system placed violence and discipline at the heart of the social relations of work and reproduced that violence by creating a powerful dynamic of aggression and counter-aggression, a strong tendency toward personal vengeance … many captains believed with Nathan Uring, that seamen were "unthinking, ungovernable Monsters … wretched ungovernable Creatures … when there is no power nor Laws to restrain them."

—Marcus Rediker, *Between the Devil and the Deep Blue Sea* (1987)

If a sailor survived a brutal beating or wished to report a wrongful murder against a captain, be he navy or merchantman, to the high court of the admiralty, the sailor had to be willing to part with a large sum of his wages for the case to be legally presented. Even with that deterrent, cases of alleged excessive violence and deliberate murder presented in the high court of the admiralty between 1700 and 1737 were numerous.

Flogging

The most common punishment onboard ship was flogging (whipping). A man might be flogged for the slightest infraction of a ship's rules, such as an incorrect salute to a superior officer.

The number of strokes meted out was at the captain's discretion (although a formal schedule of regulated lashes meted out per infraction was established in 1755). Generally, the minimum was 10 lashes—12 if caught drunk on duty. Fifty lashes might cripple a man for life. One hundred after being accused by a formal court-martial could kill him. A man's flesh could be opened to the bone depending on the strength and force behind each lash. Saltwater was then poured over the exposed flesh. It not only prevented infection, but also became an additional excruciating reminder of his infraction. Not surprisingly, under these circumstances many men jumped ship for the chance to become pirates.

The cat (cat-of-nine-tails or cat-o'-nine tails) was the name used to describe the whip. It was made from hemp rope, sisal rope, or leather strips with nine separate lashes extending from the handle. Each whip was handmade and the lash strips ranged from 12 to 24 inches long. A minimum of three knots, called blood knots (because they drew extra blood from their victim), were tied to the end of each lash, spaced ½ to 2 inches apart. For additional severity, jagged strips of metal were sometimes tied into the knots.

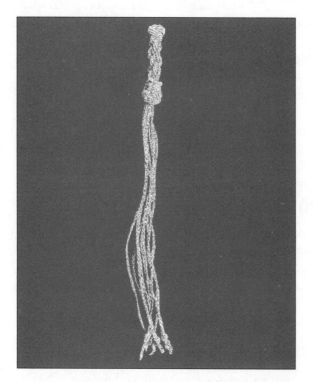

Cat-o'-nine tails.

(Photo: William Perlis)

The dreaded cat-o'-nine tails in the Royal Navy was kept for all to see in a blood-red bag attached to the main mast. (Ships in the American Navy kept theirs in a green bag.)

Interestingly, the slang expressions used by seamen and sailors connected to flogging have filtered down into our daily vocabulary with their original meanings evolving over time. For instance, no crewman wished the captain to give the order to "let the cat out of the bag." When the offender was stripped to his waist and tied to either a hatch grating or mast, a silence normally enveloped the ship. Officers often chided the men, saying, "cat got your tongue," because as a group they were afraid to speak. If a ship's deck was not wide enough for a strong man to give a proper arch to the whip, it was said that the ship had "no room to swing a cat."

Because each flick of the lash delivered nine strokes to a man's back, a punishment as light as 10 lashes was in reality 90 lashes against exposed flesh. As friendships formed among crewmen, it was not unusual for seamen to make private agreements. If they were to swing the cat, they would make it appear to have great force behind the swing. In reality, a light blow would be delivered that scratched the first layer of skin to make it bleed. Friends agreed with each other, "If you scratch my back, I'll scratch yours," and you'll get away, "no worse for the wear."

> **Pirate Yarns**
>
> Seamen and sailors were a superstitious lot, and believed a flogger would not want to cut the cross of Jesus. Hoping the lash strikes would be lighter, many had a large black cross tattooed onto their backs.

Flogging was practically a daily occurrence on some naval ships. But when a man signed onto a pirate ship, he knew that only a severe infraction to their articles of rules brought out the cat, and that the entire pirate crew had to vote and agree on that punishment (see Chapter 10).

Shipboard Defense

The threat of a mutiny meant that seamen and sailors were never issued weapons for personal use. They were taught to shoot or wield swords (at the discretion of their captain) for the sole purpose of defending their ship during battle. All weapons were locked below deck. Only certain officers had the keys to the weapons locker and powder magazine.

"A Few Good Men"

Marines were assigned to the men-o-war for shipboard defense. They were professional soldiers who were also familiar with the duties of ordinary seamen. (Royal Marines were officially under the British army until 1755. American Marines, which were founded in 1775, were officially under the Continental Navy.) Throughout the age of sail, marines were usually considered more loyal and thus more dependable than the sailors themselves. Consequently, one of their primary missions was to act as shipboard policemen and bodyguards for the ship's officers. Sailors rarely attempted a mutiny if marines were aboard. Marines had a number of other functions aboard ship. They served as sharpshooters, who provided small-arms fire (musket and pistol) to defend the ship against hostile boarders. They also manned one or more of the big guns if needed. They led shore parties, whether raiding or foraging for food. Depending on the mission, they could be assigned to other naval vessels.

If ever allowed off the ship, a seaman's only weapon was his fists or a spare belaying pin (the pin that secured sail lines; pictured in Chapter 12) that he managed to smuggle off the ship.

The Sailor's Knife

Seamen and sailors owned a special knife for necessary shipboard chores. An ordinary knife could not stand up to the required ship demands. The bottom edge of the knife blade was razor sharp. The top of the blade was flat, thick, broad-backed and blunt to withstand heavy usage. This made the knife an all-purpose tool (which is still in use today). The quickest and cleanest way to cut rope aboard ship was to use a mallet to pound this knife through the rope. The point of the knife was dull. The knife was designed this way to protect a man from accidentally injuring himself with a sharp point. Consequently, the knife could not be used as a stabbing weapon. If a man was caught with a sharp pointed knife, an officer would immediately cut the tip off and the man would be punished. The knife handle had a lanyard hole attached with a very long lanyard, made of either cord or leather, secured to the seamen's belt at all times. In case a man was topside and needed to use the knife one-handed, he did not have to fear the knife slipping from his hand, hurtling to the deck, and accidentally killing someone.

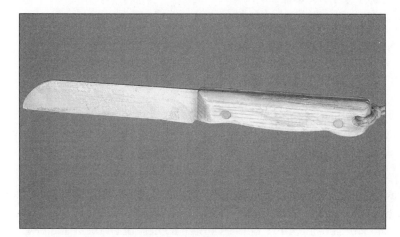

Sailor's knife.

(Photo: William Perlis)

Sustenance Aboard Ship

In terms of quantity, naval rations for the average seaman were surprisingly generous. The quality, however, was dismal. Breakfast was gruel, watered-down oatmeal the crew referred to as "burgoo." The main meal at noon was salt pork or beef, hard cheese, beer, and biscuits. When the salted meats ran out, the seamen ate the ship's rats. The lack of fresh fruits and vegetables proved to be a problem on long voyages, resulting in frequent cases of scurvy. And the drinking water was almost always brackish. Sickness and disease from poor nutrition plagued the men. What the men did look forward to was their daily grog ration (rum and water) doled out to each man after dinner (the noon meal) and supper (the evening meal).

The officers' fare was often far better than what the crew had. Officers purchased and brought aboard their personal food stocks. Thus, they were served generous portions of quality meats freshly butchered, and fine wine when available. They would share in the crew's menu only when all other stores ran out.

On a merchantman (a commercial ship of varying size that carried cargo for profit), a captain had complete control over the food. He could order the crew served meager and barely edible food portions as a means of discipline or to save money for the ship's owners and therefore receive a bonus at the end of the voyage. The daily alcohol ration was small and regulated.

Only the Clothes on Your Back

The clothes on one's back when boarding were worn until they were in tatters. If the clothes got damp or soaked from rain or ocean spray, so be it. The clothes a man owned, he worked in and slept in. There were no luxuries such as nightshirts. A night-shirt would be impractical to wear onboard even if a man could afford to own one. Because seamen were expected to rouse at a moment's notice to handle the sudden needs of the ship, sleeping in one's clothes and "all-standing" was the norm. Washing garments (with the captain's permission) was done in seawater (freshwater was far too precious to waste) and only when the weather became warm enough to allow the clothes to dry quickly.

The ability to purchase new clothes aboard ship didn't come about until 1632, at least for the English. (With the exception of officers and marines, there were no official uniforms issued until the late 1800s.) Ships' pursers stored a chest of clothes called the *slop* chest. Within the chests were shirts, breeches, coats, and stockings. But this wardrobe came at a heavy cost. The purser deducted two months' wages for an entire wardrobe. So expensive were these garments to the average seaman, they were worn until they also turned to rags.

Knowing the Ropes

Slop or **slops** is the name for ready-made clothes. The word comes from the Old English sloppe or breeches and were pant coveralls.

Officers, because they were of the noble class, boarded ships with their own chest of uniforms. Officers' clothes were individually tailor-made and paid out of pocket. The contrast of seamen's filthy ripped raiment and the nearly spotless attire of the officers who could afford their uniforms added yet another grievance to the already disgruntled crews.

Mutiny or Desertion?

Life for many seamen was appalling. And most men desiring an "out" saw only two courses of action available. The easiest was desertion. If a man saw an opportunity when his ship was in port, he hoped to be able to slip away unnoticed. However, most captains were aware of this fact and were more than prepared to retain their crews when anchoring in a harbor for much-needed supplies.

It was not uncommon for captains to lock the entire crew in the hold until his trusted officers had restocked their supplies. Only then, while his officers (or marines if he had them) guarded the crew with loaded weapons, would he release his men. The wiser captain, while still refusing to let his men disembark, had prostitutes and barrels of alcohol brought aboard while the ship was restocked.

Mutiny was the other alternative. This required a great deal of trust, secretive meetings, and strategies among seamen on how to disarm the officers and marines and arm themselves. The man who instigated a mutiny had to believe he had the power and charisma to sway enough of the crew, and the ability to scare men into not revealing the dastardly plans.

There are many accounts of successful mutinies where the men sailed off making a name for themselves as pirates. Conversely, there are just as many accounts of the captain and his officers fighting off the rabid crews and gaining the upper hand. Those disastrous attacks ended with hangings to dissuade others from trying such tactics again.

Though still quite dangerous, it was far easier for seamen on merchant ships to mutiny. The conditions aboard a merchantman were almost identical to that of a ship of the line (a navy ship). The differences were a marginal security force (no marines served aboard merchantmen) and the fact that the ships varied in size. Smaller vessels were more conducive to the success of a mutiny.

When a sailor successfully mutinied or deserted, he was by law a criminal and hunted man. He had only a few choices open to him. Turning pirate and heading for a pirate-friendly harbor was the easiest option.

The Least You Need to Know

◆ For the majority of men, the only jobs available were at sea.

◆ Boys escaped wretched conditions by running away to sea.

◆ The naval equivalent of the draft was legal kidnapping.

◆ Seeking a better life and independence, a few brave women and girls posed as boys to get onboard ships.

◆ Conditions on a navy or merchant ship were brutal. Many seamen felt the odds of survival were better as a pirate than serving in the navy.

◆ Dissatisfied sailors faced two choices: mutiny or desertion.

Joining a Pirate Crew

In This Chapter

- ◆ Joining the pirate ranks
- ◆ Men eagerly sign on for adventure and riches
- ◆ Not everyone willing to join
- ◆ Roles on a pirate ship

Choosing to live or die beneath the infamous "black flag" was not for everyone. Only the most adventurous, courageous, often the most aimless, and perhaps the hardest-of-hearts need apply. Those who signed on for pirating were motivated by riches—often beyond their wildest dreams. Others hoped to see the world, prove their manhood, escape criminal prosecution, or, in some cases, exact revenge upon personal enemies.

The risk was high, as was the shipboard mortality rate. Thus it was not unusual for a pirate vessel as small as a hundred-footer to bunk 200 men or more at the beginning of a voyage. And all men were trained to fill the gaps of others who might be lost to storm, disease, or combat action. Green kids learned from seasoned shipmates how to haul line, scrub decks, brave heights in the rigging, fire weapons, and wield swords.

There were other crucial positions and important duties (we will get to those in a moment) that needed to be assigned before a ship set sail. But if billets were not filled at the beginning of a voyage, pirates had their own unique way of remedying that situation.

The Pirate Ranks

Pirates came from all nationalities, circumstances, and backgrounds. From trial records and ships' logs, it is interesting to note that the majority of pirates during the golden age of piracy were Welsh. After the Welsh—in descending order—were the Irish, the English, and the Scots. The breakdown continues to be a social testament of the troubles and dissatisfactions of nations.

French and Spanish pirates counted an almost equal number. A smattering of German, Italian, Greek, and Dutch pirates also sailed. Rare, but not unheard of, were a few South Seas natives and North American Indians.

African Slaves Turned Pirates

"Cimarron," the name given to all runaway black slaves owned by the Spanish, swelled the cutthroat ranks. They accounted for approximately 25 to 30 percent of the estimated 5,000 pirates known to be sailing in the years between 1715 and 1726. Pirates considered runaways as equals within their community. Nevertheless, if pirates captured a slave ship, they would think nothing of selling its human cargo.

Cimarrons could be counted upon during battle to fight with great ferocity in order to keep their precious freedom. There are a number of famous black pirates who plagued the Caribbean. Diego Grillo, a Spanish-African slave, escaped Havana in 1668. Nicknamed "Lucifer," he and his crews attacked the Spanish. Lauren de Graff sailed between 1680 and 1690. His raid on Vera Cruz in 1683 was more destructive than Henry Morgan's attack. Edward "Blackbeard" Teach (see Chapter 17) at the height of his piratical career had more than 60 black men under his command.

The Spanish did not consider blacks to be human beings, rather beasts of burden. Thus, if recaptured, the punishment meted out was usually aimed at setting an example to other slaves. In most cases, the recaptured black runaway faced castration or the torture of being roasted alive.

Men Signing On in the Frozen North

During the spring and summer months, pirate ships and fleets plundered the eastern coast of North America, ending their voyages in Newfoundland, Canada. The fishery owners, merchants, and townsmen were naturally unnerved whenever a pirate ship was sighted. The people never knew whether an anchoring pirate ship was going to plunder or trade.

Poor men from the west of England contracted to work as "slitters" in the fisheries looked forward to the pirates coming as a way out. The slitters' wages were low. Room and board was not included, nor was the fare home. Usually by the end of the season they had no money to pay for anything, much less their return fare. Thus they contracted to work the winter fish runs, and the cycle for them continued. The work of catching, splitting, and drying fish all day was exhausting. For hundreds of men, watching these men depart their ships with money to spend and fancy clothes, piracy seemed a far better life than what they'd previously contracted and a chance to eventually return home. Thus pirate crews swelled in number when their ships, well-stocked with provisions and water, pulled up anchor and left Newfoundland.

Pirate attacks against ships and settlements on Newfoundland persisted well into 1724. After Captain John Phillips's crew (see Chapter 7) mutinied and threw him overboard, they continued to plunder Newfoundland and eventually sailed into Boston. The crew was apprehended and tried for piracy by a special admiralty court on May 12, 1724.

> **Treasure Chest**
>
> In 1612, Captain Peter Easton (Peter Eaton) arrived in Grace Harbor, Newfoundland, with a fleet of five pirate ships. He plundered settlements along America's eastern seaboard, adding five more ships to his fleet, provisions, weapons, ammunition, and valuables. He kidnapped or persuaded at least 100 fishermen to join his crews.

"It's Not Just a Job; It's an Adventure!"

In the late twentieth century, a U.S. Navy advertising campaign targeted young Americans by promoting sea service as "not just a job," but "an adventure." It was not the first time sea captains had appealed to a potential recruit's sense of adventure as a means of swelling the ranks of ships' companies.

Pirate Recruiting

During the golden age of piracy, whenever a buccaneer captain decided to mount a treasure-hunting excursion, he put the word out that his ship was "going on the account." Throughout the harbors and coastal towns frequented by pirates and other seafaring hopefuls, news of where the ship intended to sail, its purpose, and how long she'd be out became the major topic of conversation in taverns, brothels, and alleyways. Those interested in the expedition eagerly signed on. If the captain had been successful on previous journeys, former shipmates would be first in line.

The buccaneer captain's reputation also enticed others to join. His personal sailing and combat experience—as well as reputed courage and physical prowess—were of utmost importance.

The captain signed as many competent men as were willing (and some who were not). While the ship was being outfitted with supplies for the journey, those men "lucky" enough to be chosen prepared what they needed to bring. This was similar to preparations for a privateering venture—the fundamental difference being pirates attacked ships of all nations.

Weapon-Worthy

In most cases, the minimum requirement for each man consisted of a pistol, a measure of *blackpowder* and *shot*, and a sword. Those men fortunate enough to possess additional weapons were considered more valuable to the captain, and were consequently moved to the front of the selection process.

Knowing the Ropes

Blackpowder was a sulphur- and charcoal-based gunpowder (later replaced by the faster-burning smokeless powder) stored in a portable protective case that came in many designs and sizes. A pirate owning a pistol needed to bring enough blackpowder to fire at least one **shot**, which was the lead ball (predecessor of the conical bullet) fired from the pistol. Powder and shot were expensive. Any pirate-hopeful in possession of these items and willing to bring them along was deemed a man committed to the forthcoming journey.

Crews could be at sea for months. Consequently, all worldly possessions had to be packed for the journey. Whatever a man owned in terms of extra clothes (if any), small personal weapons, and booty from previous treasure hunts he hadn't sold or given away were stuffed into a "ditty bag." Because pirates squandered as much as they acquired, possessions were few. Large weapons used during battle, such as muskets and axes, would be hand-carried aboard, then stowed along with those of his shipmates.

A pirate carried a vast array of weapons (as you'll see in Chapter 12) upon his person. Besides their obvious use, a pirate's weaponry served to intimidate both his potential enemies and his victims.

Pressed into Piracy?

For lengthy, dangerous voyages, shipmates with special professional skills, such as surgeons or carpenters, were needed to round out an efficient crew. However, few professional men would agree to join a pirate expedition. Pirate captains solved this problem by simply following the example of the Royal Navy: they seized them. But unlike the navy, which pulled most of its unwilling crewmembers from harbor towns, pirates seized men on the high seas.

First, the Officers and Crew

Whenever a ship was taken, the officers and crew were initially lined up on deck separate from the passengers. The pirates then asked all crewmembers if any were wanting or willing to "go a pirating." Considering the common sailor a kindred spirit, pirates generally made a point of not forcing a simple seaman into the trade. The exception was a man who was musically inclined (which we'll talk about later in this chapter).

Conditions aboard naval and merchant ships were harsh. So it isn't surprising that many men jumped at the chance to become pirates. That said, because detailed log records were kept, sailors eager to join would attempt to make their decision as inconspicuous as possible. This was done as a safeguard. If arrested, the sailor-turned-pirate wanted the ship's log to reflect that he had been taken by force and would therefore be innocent of any charges brought against him.

Then, the Passengers

Pirates then turned their attention to the passengers. As mentioned, pirate captains needed men with specific occupational skills. A high percentage of those men were kidnapped. If the professional men needed by the pirate captain did not immediately step forward and volunteer their services, the pirate crew would mercilessly interrogate the captured officers and passengers until someone disclosed who the sought-after professionals were. The interrogations included whippings and other tortures, executions by hanging, and throwing victims overboard.

Appalling accounts of torture by former captives began circulating in publications. Such accounts both horrified and fascinated the public to such an extent that many ships sighting a pirate flag would surrender without a fight. To prevent harsh treatment of those aboard, professionals often acquiesced with little resistance.

A Pact with the Devil

Once pressed into piracy, captives were required to sign "shipboard articles of conduct." Though the captives had no say in the original formulation of the articles, they nevertheless were bound by them.

By law, if seized and sent to trial, every man had the opportunity to defend himself before judge and jury. As such, the signed articles often were produced as a means of defense for the common pirate, and judges usually permitted the documents to be entered as evidence. The articles offered proof that such men—even if forced into piracy—were compelled to follow orders.

Soft-Hearted Pirates?

Somewhat ironically, pirates had such a strong sense of democracy and fair play that they were known to acknowledge that some of their brethren had been forced aboard even if they themselves had not. In fact, the published proceedings of a number of historic trials reveal that pirates were so bound by this code of honor that they often stood as witnesses on behalf of those who had been forced against their will into the trade. And because such a vast number of men were truly kidnapped, the combination of pirate witnesses and inscribed articles more often than not saved impressed pirates from the hangman's noose.

> **Pirate Yarns**
>
> Despite the tales, there is no documented evidence that any pirate ever forced a prisoner to walk the plank (the plank being the ship's gangplank). Major Stede Bonnet, a successful plantation owner who turned to piracy, was rumored to have invented this torturous death. However, this method of execution was never substantiated.

Unlike naval vessels, at the close of a pirate expedition (whether treasure had been secured or not), every crew member of a pirate ship was free to leave the ship's company. Interestingly, quite a few of the skilled men who had been kidnapped and pressed into service chose to remain in the profession of piracy.

Who's Who on a Pirate Ship

It took many experienced men to keep a ship afloat, on course, and ready for action at all times. Aside from the ordinary sailing men, these included the captain, the surgeon, the navigator, the quartermaster, the boatswain, the master gunner, the cook, the carpenter, the cooper, and even the musicians (important for the morale of the crew). Let's take a look at some of the more important positions and the individual crew members' responsibilities.

The Captain

Of the thousands of pirate captains who sailed, only a handful resembled the iron-fisted and colorful pirate captains we've all seen on the silver screen. Granted, these few captains certainly possessed the charismatic personalities needed to lead a full complement of brutally violent men. However, the only real reason most pirate captains were able to maintain their positions was because they had a reputation for delivering incredible wealth.

An Elected Officer

For the majority of pirate skippers, the supreme post of "captain" was bestowed by a pirate crew's majority vote. All had an equal say in the process, including the youngest boys. This democratic insistence stemmed from the pirate crew's aversion to strict naval protocol where naval captains—regardless of competency or lack thereof—were deemed lord and master.

> **Dead Men's Tales**
>
> They [the crew] only permit him to be captain on condition that they may be captain over him.
>
> —Captain Charles Johnson, 1724

Once elected, most captains were essentially "first among equals." They had proven themselves under fire and sail. They knew where to go, how to fight, and the ultimate objective of the journey. But—unless they were the domineering personalities who few risked challenging—they could be ousted from power as quickly as they had been placed.

What Pirates Demanded of Their Captains

The pirates' criteria for a good captain were simple. They wanted a man shrewd enough to find treasure and keep them all alive. This meant the candidate had to be first and foremost an excellent battle tactician. Boldness and daring were other traits that endeared the elected captain to a ship of cutthroats. Contrary to novels written during the golden age of piracy up through today's popular fiction and movies, it was a rare additional talent if the captain was also a good navigator.

Unlike the authoritarian rule naval captains had over their crews, the average pirate captain actually had little privilege and no real power over his men's actions. Of course, the pirate captain bunked in the large captain's quarters. Yet any man aboard ship could enter at will, eat off his plate, drink from his goblets, or even sleep in his bed. The greatest compensation a captain received was one of the highest shares of booty. This was his reward for finding and successfully acquiring the prize.

> **Dead Men's Tales**
>
> The captain had absolute power in battle and when fighting, chasing, or being chased, but in all other matters he was governed by the majority wishes of the crew.
>
> —David Cordingly, *Under the Black Flag* (1995)

Pirates wanted quick results or the possibility of wealth great enough to compensate for the harsh conditions at sea. When the success of locating and acquiring treasure dropped to an unacceptable level, the responsibility for the calamity fell directly onto the captain's shoulders.

Voting the Boss Out of Office

Pirates didn't take kindly to losing treasure or getting into close, bloody scrapes with enemy ships. Woe to the captain who after a battle didn't deliver the goods as expected. If the majority became unhappy, the captain could easily be voted out of office. Another shipmate, displaying the pirate-admired leadership traits, would quickly take his place.

If sensible enough to step down graciously from the captaincy, the pirate leader's status would simply become that of an ordinary crew member. If he became argumentative and refused to relinquish control, he could be executed. If a captain was savvy enough to survive numerous actions and sail back with satisfied crews, he was considered "pistol proof."

Interestingly, the only time a vote for a new captain was prohibited was 10 minutes before battle. It would have been too disruptive when all the crew was preparing to fight.

Infamous captains, such as Blackbeard, were so confident that they could bully or kill anyone who dared argue with or attempted to usurp their power that they thought nothing of having to confront disgruntled crewmen. This was not the norm. But if a pirate crew member under the command of such a captain became unhappy with the captain's command—and if that crew member valued his life more than the risk of attempting to elect another man to the office of captain—the pirate simply disembarked at the nearest port and signed "on the account" with another pirate ship.

The Navigator

The navigator, sailing master, pilot, or sea artist—whatever the crew chose to call him—knew the science of the stars and waterways. Mathematics, literacy, and a crude ability to draw were essential to the job. He had to plot a course through the many reefs, sandbars, and shoals that could sink a vessel. A navigator was so vitally important, he became the first person kidnapped when a ship lost its own navigator in battle or through disease.

Tools for Plotting the Ship's Position and Course

Though techniques were primitive, the navigator had a number of instruments at his disposal to calculate and chart a ship's position and course. One of the oldest and most important tools was the compass.

Other items used to steer the ship were the ring sundial, the wind vane, and the telescope. The telescope was nicknamed the "bring 'em near" for obvious reasons. The astrolabe, the precursor to the sextant, calculated the altitude of the sun and stars. Log lines estimated how fast in nautical miles, or knots, the ship traveled. Sounding leads not only measured the depth of the water but also the consistency of the ocean floor.

The backstaff, one of the great advances in navigation, was invented in 1595 by John Davis. Previously men had to stare into the glaring sun to calculate latitude. Now with his back to the sun, the navigator marked the angle of the sun above the horizon line by measuring its shadow.

> **Treasure Chest**
>
> Though placing great value on the compass, sailors, who tended to be superstitious, were somewhat afraid of it. Because the lodestone was magnetized to the north, they felt the instrument held magical properties. To allay their fears, the compass was housed in a small wooden box known as a *binnacle*, from the Latin *habitaculum* for "little house." The term is still used today.

The Most Critical Navigational Aids

A navigator's most coveted and guarded possessions, especially during times of war, were his sea charts. If unfortunate enough not to own one that mapped the area he was sailing at the time, the navigator drew his own charts for future voyages.

Backstaff.

(Photo: William Perlis)

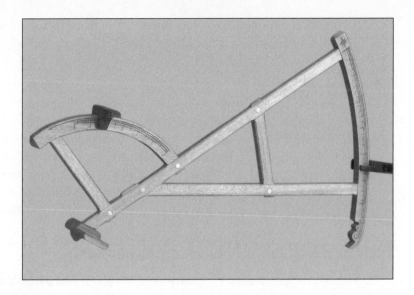

The Ship's Surgeon

Surgeons (also called barber-surgeons because they were combined into the same guild) were scarce and consequently considered to be quite the catch, whether they signed on voluntarily, as did Alexander Exquemelin, or were forced aboard, as most were.

The surgeon constantly treated the men with mercurial compounds for venereal diseases. Brought back after the second voyage of Columbus, they were given various names, such as the French pox and Spanish disease. Unfortunately, with the limited medical knowledge of the time, he could do only so much to help those with major illnesses such as malaria, yellow fever, typhus, and dysentery.

Whenever they ventured ashore, surgeons studied cures used by native inhabitants. Many of the natural herbs and flowers used in medicinal teas, salves, and ointments were as poisonous as they were helpful. The correct ratios became known through dangerous and often disastrous trial-and-error experiments. Successful measurements were always noted in a medical journal for future use.

The Surgeon's Medical Chest

The surgeon's medical chest consisted of vials of tinctures (a medicine mixed with alcohol) and ointments labeled in Latin. If pirates stole a medical chest and had no surgeon to translate, using what medicines they had stolen became pure guesswork. Standard items included the ever-present vanilla bean, castor oil, and glycerin for mixing a medical base.

The Instruments of His Practice

Surgical instruments were crude. The capital saw for major amputations of the leg or arm had frequent use. A competent surgeon could amputate a leg within four minutes. Various curved- and straight-razor sharp knives—in varying sizes—amputated different body parts such as fingers, toes, or hands. Scalpels would be used for flesh wounds, along with suture needles and catgut. The sharp-hooked tenaculum and retractors would separate flesh. Probes, a syphilis syringe to directly inject mercury into the penis, syringes, and tourniquets completed a kit. Even if opiates were available, surgery was done without any anesthesia for fear the patient might die of a weak heart during the operation. The patient—fully awake and in unimaginable pain—would be held down with either leather straps or by strong men. Opium or rum would be administered afterward to alleviate the pain. If no infection set in after surgery, a man had a decent chance of surviving. Hooks to replace hands and wood to replace legs were available. However, hooks were expensive, as were fitted wooden legs, and therefore rare. Men improvised as best they could.

Pirate with wooden leg.

(The Pirates' Own Book, *Charles Ellms, 1837*)

Sawbones, or Bones, was a nickname often given to surgeons because amputations became so frequent during and after a battle. The surgeon dressed wounds, did amputations, and fought against infections and the dreaded gangrene.

If a surgeon wasn't aboard and amputation was required in the hopes of saving someone's life, the ship's carpenter would be enlisted to do the job with his wood saw. Fortunately—perhaps unfortunately for the patient—the tools of both professions at that time were basically the same.

The Quartermaster

The quartermaster, who, like the captain, was elected to his position by the entire crew, held true authority aboard ship. Though technically second-in-command, his responsibilities were varied and impressive. He supervised the daily running of the ship. Even the captain needed his approval concerning certain decisions.

Trial Judge

The quartermaster was the one with the judicial power to dole out punishment for minor offenses as per the ship's articles. Offenses ranged from neglecting equipment to fighting among the men. If a serious offense was committed, the quartermaster officiated at the trial as judge with the captain and crew as jury.

Dead Men's Tales

[The quartermaster] is the trustee for the whole ship's company ... for the captain can do nothing which the quartermaster does not approve of ... for he speaks for and looks after the interest of the company.

—Captain Charles Johnson, 1724

A Leader in Action

In the heat of battle, the quartermaster often was among the advance elements boarding a prize. (The captain usually *led* the advance elements.) When necessary, the quartermaster manned the helm. His duties included accumulating all the plunder and laying it out on the deck. First he would separate whatever goods he felt could bring the best prices when they sailed into a friendly port. Then he kept a watchful eye while the crew members chose from what remained, making sure each man took only his fair portion.

Other Crew Members

The two primary functions of a pirate ship were to sail from point A to point B, and to fight and survive in actions against prizes. The boatswain made sure the ship could sail. The master gunner ensured the ship could fight.

But no pirate could sail on an empty stomach: his food needed to be properly prepared and safely stored. Preparation and storage were the responsibilities of both the cook and the cooper.

A pirate ship had to constantly be repaired and portions of the vessel were often being reconstructed, particularly after a long voyage in poor weather or combat action. This was the responsibility of the carpenter.

Shipboard entertainment was vital to crew morale. This was ensured with the help of musicians.

The Boatswain

The boatswain (pronounced bosun or bos'n) handled the overall daily maintenance and inventory. These items in the ship's stores consisted of cordage, tar, pitch, tallow, extra sails, oil, brimstone, tackle, and sail needles. He made certain that sails were repaired, and rigging tarred properly to protect against dampness.

The Master Gunner

The master gunner made certain all the ship's cannons and personal weapons were clean and in good working order. He stored all the explosive gunpowder below deck, and constantly checked to ensure that it remained dry and that the supply never ran too low. He trained the gun crews to become cohesive teams, working seamlessly together and always ready for action.

The Cook

The cook was often known as "Slouchy," as he was usually a pirate maimed during battle and so named for his general disfigurement. This is the pirate's variation of the nickname cooks were given in the British navy. They were given the nickname "Slushy" after the greasy liquid accumulating on the top of cooked salted meats. After recovering from his wounds, if no designated cook already claimed the position, he'd be given the job. This enabled the man to continue sailing and still receive a portion of any future prizes. Quite a few pirates who lost an eye, leg, or arm regularly signed on the account knowing they'd get a fair share as long as they could do their work.

The cook had the task of both preparing palatable meals and ensuring the stores of food aboard ship were fit for consumption. Because voyages were long, this was often difficult. Underway, in rough weather, cold meals were the norm. Storage also was a problem. Despite the best efforts of the barrel maker, food items quickly deteriorated and rotted within the first few weeks. This required the cook to become quite inventive with vittles.

The Carpenter

From an early age, boys began apprenticing in shipyards. Many became qualified shipwrights, and their knowledge of detailed shipbuilding was quite impressive. Because ships were wooden, and wear and tear from hard use and weather took a constant toll on the vessel, the ship's carpenter was always working. He needed to maintain the entire ship, from the hull to mast-top and everything in between.

In battle, the job of the ship's carpenter was vital to the survival of the ship. He, and others he had trained, quickly patched holes so the ship wouldn't sink, and replaced any broken gear so the ship could continue to maneuver quickly.

Knowing the Ropes

To **careen** the ship meant laying the entire ship on its side for repairs. After finding a secluded inlet or harbor the ship would be grounded. With rope, block and tackle, and sheer muscle, the en-tire crew would literally pull the ship over until it was laying on its side. After repairs on one side were completed, the crew would completely flip the vessel over on its other side and begin the repair process again.

When the ship was severely damaged—whether by high seas, rocks, extreme weather, teredo worms, or combat action—the carpenter had the crew *careen* the ship. He supervised the repairs so they were done properly and promptly. Conducting major repairs at sea or on land was dangerous work, as the ship was vulnerable to attack and would have little chance of escaping a swift-moving opponent.

The Cooper

Though not considered a position of life-or-death importance, the job of barrel maker, or cooper, was indeed vital to the well-being of the crew. Barrels were the standard storage unit on a ship. Everything from lamp oil to extra sails to gunpowder was stored within a barrel or cask. The cooper attempted to keep all food provisions stored safely. Virtually all food and drink, beef, hard-tack biscuits, water, beer, wine, and liquor were stored in wooden barrels. The food barrels—stored in the darkest, lowest, dampest portion of the ship's hull—had to be monitored daily. The erratic weather changes caused the barrels to expand and contract. The cooper constantly battled to keep the barrels as airtight as possible and to protect them from rats and moisture. Depending on what other barrels contained, they were checked at regular intervals. He often built new ones aboard ship.

The Musicians

The most popular sailors aboard ship were the musicians. Sometimes they were pirates with musical talent. Many navies maintained drum-and-pipe corps aboard ship. These band units became prime targets of pirates. The lives of sailors on newly seized vessels who could play even the simplest penny whistle were usually spared if they agreed to jump ship. Naturally, most agreed.

Pirates forced the musicians to play during communal meals and impromptu ship dances. Jigs and nautical shanties were common favorites. During battle, bands were ordered to play loud martial music while the pirates yelled, sang, and yodeled in hopes of frightening the enemy and boosting the spirits of their own crewmen. The most sought-after musicians owned concertinas, lyres, and bagpipes.

The Least You Need to Know

- ♦ Many men eagerly joined the pirates for wealth, adventure, and to escape the brutal life aboard naval vessels.

- ♦ Pirates often kidnapped surgeons, carpenters, navigators, and musicians to fill those positions aboard ship.

- ♦ To join a pirate crew one had to provide the minimum armament of pistol, ammunition, and sword. A man's pistol was his most prized possession.

- ♦ Pirate captains were elected, and the majority of them did not have absolute control over the ship and its democratic crew.

- ♦ The job of navigator was considered the most important post aboard ship.

- ♦ From cook to cooper, everyone onboard a pirate ship had an important job to do.

Chapter 11

Life Aboard a Pirate Ship

In This Chapter

- ◆ Dismal living conditions above and below deck
- ◆ Battling the weather and the doldrums
- ◆ Eat, drink … and drink some more
- ◆ Boredom between prizes
- ◆ Common pirate attire

There were as many reasons to willingly join a pirate crew as there were reasons not to. There was the lure of a life of freedom on the open sea, the chance to breathe clean air (although only on the main deck), to enjoy previously dreamt-of vistas stretching from one horizon to the next, and to perhaps see new lands—new worlds. There was also the camaraderie of sailing with likeminded mates from one adventure to another. A chance to prove one's self as a man. And an opportunity to find wealth and treasure enough for three lifetimes, if one could survive long enough to spend it. But when most of us consider the adventurous life of pirates, we often fail to fully understand the downside of their existences. Fact is, aboard ship, pirates lived in extremely cramped quarters. Adding Mother Nature—and the fact that pirates were global outlaws—to the mix, piracy was one of the world's most dangerous professions.

Weeks or months might pass by where no prizes were sighted. All too frequently, days passed with no wind to fill the sails. Boredom and drunkenness (while the booze lasted) was the norm.

Though the Caribbean was their primary operational territory, pirate ships could not anchor everywhere at anytime. Pirate-friendly governors and locals fluctuated as rapidly as wars and treaties did among the great nations. When food and drink began running low, a pirate captain's worse fears might come true: fighting amongst his crew or a mutiny culminating perhaps in his own death.

Conditions Aboard

The ideal number of men on a pirate ship was two to three times greater than the number of men needed to sail under normal circumstances.

Why?

Battle casualties, fever from infections, and gangrene rapidly depleted the pirate ranks on a long voyage with a lot of action. Additionally, crew numbers diminished as a result of the many diseases (brought on by the humid mosquito-ridden climate of the Caribbean) that often ran rampant among a closely quartered crew. Malaria, yellow fever, cholera, typhus, scurvy, dysentery, and typhoid fever, not to mention venereal disease, killed many a pirate. Surgeons usually spent more time and effort attending to diseases than they did battle wounds and deck (sailing) accidents.

No Wonder So Many Sickened and Died

Pirate crews were not nearly as hygiene-conscious as crews on naval or merchant ships. Decks were rarely if ever washed. If food fell to the deck, it would be picked up and eaten. Any food crumbs that dropped would only nourish and breed rats.

Men could urinate in the *head* or just over the side of the ship (as long as it wasn't to the windward side!). Taking an example from naval vessels, they also used "piss-tubs"—urine buckets situated in corridors or corners of the ship. This guaranteed a quick supply of liquid to put out any emergency fires. It also added to the distinct aroma aboard ship and increased the chance of contracting and spreading disease. If it was known that a man had syphilis he was not allowed to use the piss-tubs.

Knowing the Ropes

The **head**, or ship's toilet area, got its name because it was situated on the beakhead. The beakhead was a small platform or plank of wood with cut holes used to defecate. The beakhead was secured to the outer section of the ship near the bow (front) of the uppermost deck (the deck in front of the foremast). It was fastened to the stem (curved upright bow timber) and supported by the main knee. The knee was a right angle shaped timber used to secure parts of a ship together, especially the beam (horizontal timber).

The Tougher the Man, the Better His Sleeping Accommodations

Sleeping space was limited. Those who—by intimidation or brute force—were able to secure a sleeping hammock, had only a 14-inch width upon which to stretch. Rows of hammocks were slung below decks across the entire length of rafters mere inches apart.

With so many jammed in a tight area, tempers frequently flared. So overcrowded were the ships, many men and boys were forced to sleep up on deck wherever they could find a flat surface or space to lean against. Even in good weather, the morning air at sea was damp, which kept clothes wet. It was far better and more comfortable to try and fight for a dry hammock on the off chance you'd win at least one night of decent sleep.

Far Worse Below Decks

The foul air below stank from unwashed bodies, rotting food, urine buckets, and the putrid water in the bilge, the lowest bottom of a ship's hull. No matter how carefully the ship's wood planks were caulked, water seeped in and collected in the bilge. The putrid standing water and spilled refuse simply added to the stench.

Lower decks were constantly dark and dank. Water from rain or rough seas ran down hatchways and flooded lower decks. Once wet the lower decks remained musty along with any damaged personal items. Contingent on the geographic location and season they sailed, nothing aboard fully dried. These conditions were a terrific breeding ground for other living things: lice, cockroaches, beetles, fleas, maggots, weevils, and rats. This was especially true during the long privateering voyages of Sir Francis Drake (see Chapter 4) and Sir Henry Morgan (see Chapter 8).

One Ship to the Next

Typically, pirates performed only minimum maintenance on the ship to keep it afloat. Their ship was merely a means to an end. If a captured vessel was deemed better to fulfill their purposes, pirates simply took it over. Frequently they would strip a ship of necessary items such as tackle, sail, rigging, line, etc. for ship repairs. They also burned ships they no longer wanted or needed.

Another option frequently employed with captured vessels was that of the establishment of a pirate fleet. The pirates would promote one of their own to the captaincy of the new vessel, which would be subordinate to the primary (flag) ship. As discussed in Chapter 10, depending on the pirate crew and its mood, all captive crews would either be forced to join in piracy, killed, put ashore, or set adrift in longboats.

> **Treasure Chest**
>
> The ship's bell was struck on the half hour. The time was kept by using a half-hour sand glass. When the sand ran out of the top the bell was struck and the glass turned over to begin counting again. Eight bells signaled the end of a four-hour watch.

A Watchful Eye

Depending on the specifics within their ship's articles, if a crew chose to sail in a somewhat organized manner they would set up watch.

The watch was a set number of men on deck who actually sailed the ship and kept lookout. Crews alternated watch every four hours. Time was kept by ringing the ship's bell. If a pirate wasn't in the mood to stand watch, he felt it his right not to do so. However, ship's watches were extremely diligent when tracking prey.

Weather: A Blessing and a Curse

An experienced pirate navigator learned each season's weather patterns to determine the best time to sail, which direction, and under what conditions. If he owned sea charts to each region noting the currents and tides, he'd be as prepared as any sailing navigator.

During the fall and winter months, the Leeward Islands of the West Indies, South America, and the European sea trade routes were the prime targets. These were the seasons when fully loaded ships were departing from or arriving at the islands or the Main. Pirates had their choice of attacking ships or settlements. In the spring and summer months, they plied the Windward Islands of the West Indies, up the coast of

Florida, the Carolinas, New York, New England, all the way to Newfoundland. They either plundered cities, refitted their ships and replenished their supplies in friendly towns, or traded or sold goods they had acquired as booty.

The Horror of the Hurricane

The hurricane season ran from summer to early fall in the Caribbean. During this weather pattern, tropical storms materialized without warning. Ships tried to avoid the region or put into a safe harbor long before the storms were forecast to begin. But no one was able to predict exactly when a wind would whip up. These deadly acts of nature caught many ships unawares. In such circumstances, the only hope was that the masts would not split and crash onto the deck, or that the seas would not capsize the ship. Another horror facing a crew was the distinct possibility that the mighty force of pounding waves and winds might literally snap the vessel in half, killing everyone. Lucky was any crew that successfully outran a hurricane.

Knowing the weather patterns did not always ensure a ship's safety. Gale-force winds could suddenly gust from nowhere, blowing a ship off course. It could take days before the navigator was able to recalculate the ship's current position with no reference points for aid. If experienced and skilled in his art—and with the possession of a little common sense—the navigator might be able to avoid hidden sandbars, sharp reefs, rock outcroppings, and other subsurface and surface dangers. But he could not predict the wind and weather.

Changeable Winds

A favorable wind was a blessing for a pirate ship. It filled her sails, enabling her to travel from point to point. It gave her the ability to maneuver quickly in battle. It powered her during an escape from a naval vessel with greater firepower. And it increased her speed as she bore down on a prize.

Then there was the mind-numbing period of calm without even so much as a slight breeze. There was no particular season when the wind simply refused to blow. It could happen in the warmer climates with the hot sun beating down onto the men or in the colder regions near Newfoundland. Days and even weeks could pass before the winds returned.

One minute the wind billows through the sails, the next moment all is becalmed. The canvas sails instantly collapse and flop against the wooden masts. The ship wallows, rolling heavily in the water without getting anywhere. Not a ripple of a wave, just a sickening swell. And there was nothing any man onboard could do but curse and wait for a breeze, any breeze. The crew needed the ship to move before their fresh water and food stores ran out and they died an agonizing death of thirst or starvation.

Feast or Famine

Food and drink was literally a matter of feast or famine and an inventive affair for the cook aboard. Supplies were plentiful when a ship set sail. Live hens would be kept on deck for eggs and meat. Barrels of salted fish, meat, pork, dried potatoes, rounds of cheese, *hard tack*, fresh water (pirates drank water only as a last resort), cabbage marinated in vinegar or salt water, and beer would be stored below. In the humid environment below deck, much of the food quickly rotted and bred numerous varieties of insects. The cheese got so hard and inedible that the men carved their portions into buttons and other items. Any captured ships were immediately relieved of their entire food supply, including salt, pepper, and other spices. For that reason alone, a merchant ship's cargo was as prime a target as a galleon's gold treasure.

> ### Knowing the Ropes
>
> Aptly named, **hard tack** was a large round biscuit made with flour, water, and salt. The simple ingredients were mixed, then baked until rock hard. In fact, it was so hard and dry that it could—and often did—break teeth if not first soaked in some liquid.

Black-headed maggots and weevils also fed on hard tack and other perishable food items. It was easy to determine if maggots had gotten into the hard tack barrel. The bugs perforated the biscuits with holes as they fed. The crew first tapped the hard tack on the table, then waited for the tiny, uninvited guests to crawl out before they ate the biscuit. Sometimes the men sat in the dark so they couldn't see what they were eating. It was believed that if maggots were gray and thick when they crawled out, the food still had some taste and nutritional value. If the maggot was white and thin, the flavor and nourishment was gone.

The men knew well when weevils got to the hard tack instead of maggots. If not removed early in their infestation, weevils ate more of the biscuit than maggots, which caused the hard tack to completely crumble when tapped on the table.

Provisioning Was Easier Said Than Done

Being "wanted men," pirates were unable to sail into just any port when their supplies ran low. In the Caribbean, for instance, pirates deliberately avoided the large landfalls and anchored off the smaller islands in their quest for additional provisions. At the beginning of Spain's conquest, many islands were colonized and then quickly abandoned. On these islands, as fate would have it, they found an abundance of wild goat and boar. Horses and dogs ran wild in some locations. Also plentiful in the area were pheasants, parrots, monkeys, and doves.

A variety of fruits and vegetables grew in abundance along the Spanish Main. Figs, limes, dates, white cabbages, papaya, grapes, garlic, onions, and plantains (a type of banana) were common. Being unfamiliar fare, most of the men were initially suspicious of these foods.

Turtles to Rats

As food supplies dwindled at sea, the men fished or hunted for sea turtles and their eggs. The green sea turtles were plentiful and extremely slow after they crawled onto land. Pirates easily rounded them up in large numbers. Cooks kept the turtles alive for weeks by flipping them over onto their backs (turtles can't right themselves) and storing them in the ship's hold. This assured the crew of flavorful fresh meat.

Pirates did not have the option of fishing off the side of the ship. Small fish tended to avoid large moving masses like ships. When starvation hit, desperate pirates ate the ship's rats and bugs. The irregular unbalanced diet resulted in a pirate's spending a lot of time on the head, as he would either be suffering from constipation or diarrhea.

Salmagundi and Lobscouse—the Everything Meals

Salmagundi was a form of cold salad that could also be served hot. The name is a bastardization of the medieval French *salemine*, meaning "highly spiced" or "highly salted." Anything and everything edible was chopped up, thrown into a large pot, and served. Its primary ingredient was salt. The dish contained spices gathered from merchant journeys from around the world. It was not unusual for salmagundi to consist of eggs, meats, cabbage, wine, olive oil, garlic, onions, salt, peppers, mustard seed, and any other edible items on hand.

Another traditional mariner's meal was lobscouse. Some say it dates back to the Viking pirates. Made from spiced salted meats, vegetables, and biscuits, its modern variation might be considered a version of corned beef hash.

Yo-Ho-Ho and a Bottle of Rum ... or Wine

Alcoholism was rampant and excessive in the pirate community. The liberty to drink large quantities of alcohol whenever and wherever he chose—especially aboard his ship—was proof a pirate was his own free man. Being in a continuous drunken stupor became his God-given right.

Treasure Chest

There are no records of the number of pirates who died of alcoholism. Drunkenness also resulted in numerous pirate deaths during surprise attacks. Captain Edward "Blackbeard" Teach, Captain John "Calico Jack" Rackham, Mary Read, Anne Bonny, and Captain Bartholomew Roberts—once infamous, now famous—were just a few of the pirates who, when cornered by the authorities, they or their crews were simply too drunk or hung-over to put up a good fight.

Wines, brandy, sherry, beer, and Madeira from Europe and Africa were naturally popular. When barrels were taken as part of a prize, they often were consumed by the pirates—quickly and in celebration—before the alcohol could be transferred to their own vessel. Such is the 1719 account given by Captain William Snelgrave in his book *A New Account of Some Parts of Guinea and the Slave Trade* (1934): "They hoisted upon deck a great many half hogsheads (cask or barrels containing 140 gallons) of claret and French brandy, knocked their heads out, and dipped cans and bowls into them to drink out of. And in their wantonness threw full buckets of each sort upon one another. As soon as they had emptied what was on the deck, they hoisted up more. And in the evening washed the decks with what remained in the casks."

Pirate Yarns

Rumfustian, another popular drink of the time, earned its name cryptically, for the fact that rum was not an ingredient. It was made from raw mixed eggs, beer, gin, sherry, cinnamon, nutmeg, and sugar, and served hot.

Natives taught pirates to brew local wines. On the high rocky mountains of Hispaniola grew a palm tree the pirates dubbed the "wine palm." Collecting the sap from the trunk and fermenting the liquid quickly produced a very highly flavored and extremely alcoholic inexpensive wine.

Rum was the most popular alcoholic beverage. Made from molasses, it is first mentioned (circa 1650s) in Spanish records from Barbados. Rum didn't sour like beer or wine, and its potency remained constant. It was served hot or cold. Many concoctions were mixed using rum, spices, and other flavorings. The popular drink, bumboo, is believed to have been imported by African slavers to the West Indies. It consisted of a mixture of rum, water, sugar, and nutmeg.

Battling Boredom

Pirates were constantly searching for prey. Being on a ship for months at a time with little or no success led to extreme boredom and frayed nerves. To avoid going stir-crazy in such confined spaces, the men devised a variety of distractions.

Pirates Dancing a Jig

If a ship was lucky enough to have musicians aboard, there would be music. Musicians were constantly directed to play jigs. The jig was a lively country dance known to the lower classes—with slight step variations—in all European countries. If a man didn't know the dance steps, he simply made them up.

To fight boredom or when extremely drunk, any one pirate could command one or all the musicians to play at any given moment, even waking them up at night to strike up a tune.

Games of Chance

Games of cards, or dice—or a combination of the two—were extremely popular. Dice were carved from wood, hardened cheese, or pounded .60 caliber musket-shot with punched dimples for the numbers. Boards were made from pieces of discarded canvas or bandanas. This made them easier to store and transport. Names such as Hazard, Sweat Cloth, Le Bete (The Beast), and One-and-Thirty livened up the play. Depending on how drunk he was at the time, a pirate could bet everything he owned from coins to clothes to weapons. The games ranged from the simplest put your bet down on a number from one to six and roll three dice like Sweat Cloth, to the more complicated One-and-Thirty, which was similar to Blackjack with a 52-card deck.

Additional Pastimes

Pirates whittled wood, bone, and hard cheese to help pass the days. They often used their knowledge of rope tying to make fancy knot-work decorations around personal items or as jewelry. Many pirates had their shipmates assist in tattooing their bodies. Seamen first saw tattoos on the natives of the Pacific Islands in the 1600s and immediately took up the practice and art. Pirates also participated in knife-throwing contests and storytelling.

A favorite pirate pastime was the mock trial. Capture and death was a daily threat hanging over these men's heads. To lighten the possible eventuality of this scenario, they reenacted a governmental court trial. Mates would be chosen to play the roles of judge, lawyer, jury, jailer, and hangman. It was a realistic exercise performed so well one might think they were actually being tried for piracy.

Treasure Chest

Charles Johnson wrote of a mock trial performed by Captain Thomas Anstis's fleet for their own amusement in 1722. (They were actually awaiting word whether their request for a king's pardon would be accepted. Unfortunately, it wasn't.) Going pirating again and cornered by the man-o-war *Winchelsea* while careening a ship on Tobago in 1723, Anstis fled in his ship and abandoned the pirates on the island to fend for themselves. Enraged by his betrayal, some of his crew mutinied (killing Anstis for cowardice), and then sailed to Curaçoa, where, paradoxically, the men who had performed a mock trial were themselves tried for piracy and hanged. Those who brought in the fleet were pardoned of their previous crimes.

Tobacco became a popular habit when first brought back to Europe from the Spanish Main. Pirates simply chewed crushed tobacco leaf and spat out the wad. If he owned a pipe with a covered lid, he would smoke on calm days. The pipe was an expensive item and treasured if chosen as a share of his swag or purchased.

Because of constant dampness in the air, keeping their weapons rust-free and ready for battle was a continual chore.

That Swashbuckling Pirate Look

The clothes on their backs were often the only items pirates ever owned. Picking garments as their share of loot, taking them off the dead, or purchasing items in harbor towns added to a man's wardrobe.

The basics were typical of those worn by common folk, and included a loose fitting long shirt, its sleeve seams low off the shoulder; and breeches either calf- or knee-length in cotton or discarded sailcloth dyed in solid colors or striped. Calico was a popular pattern. If he had been in the navy, chances are the pirate would wear a scarf around his neck as a sweat cloth.

Wearing the tricorne hats of the period while sailing was impractical. The wind easily blew the hats off. They poised a danger if a pirate had to climb the rigging. And they could be knocked off when a pirate was pulling line. While actively sailing, pirates went bareheaded or wore scarves to protect their heads from the sun. Tricornes, the Caribbean straw hat, or the wide floppy-brimmed hat might be worn as sun protection when lounging on deck.

While aboard ship many pirates wore the fine brocades, silks, and satins that they acquired, while others preferred to save the finery until they landed ashore.

> **Pirate Yarns**
>
> Besides the advantage of keeping the burning sun off their heads, pirates believed if they wore a bandana on their head or tied tightly around their forehead, it would prevent that ever-present malady—seasickness.

Paintings of pirates by famous artists such as Howard Pyle often depict pirates wearing a solid red sash or bandana. Mimicking the fashions worn by members of nobility—particularly the Spanish—pirates did wear flashy colored sashes, either under a broad leather belt or as a belt. But the sash could be of any color or patterned cloth.

Red material was extremely expensive because the red dye was so difficult to manufacture. It was made from the extract of the crushed bodies of the female cochineal bug found only on certain species of cactus growing along the Spanish Main. A large quantity of bugs was needed to produce a minuscule amount of dye. It is therefore plausible that if a pirate came upon this material, he'd flaunt his luck by wearing it upon his person.

A pirate may or may not have worn much jewelry aboard ship. That was a personal preference if he hadn't already sold it, gambled it, or given it to some prostitute. The one item a pirate definitely wore—and wore all the time, on ship and off—was an earring. He always wore at least one. Why an earring? Noblemen wore them, so a pirate did so to flaunt the fact that he—a mere commoner—could possess such an expensive item. Additionally, the earring served as a small life insurance policy. If the earring wearer was killed in action, a sailing accident, or died of disease, there would be enough value in the ring to pay for a proper burial (though most men who died at sea were buried at sea).

While sailing, a pirate went barefoot. In this way, he would have a better feel of the swaying of the ship as it cut through the water. This would enable the pirate to maintain his balance in rough or swelling seas. Going barefoot also provided him with a secure grip on the rigging or footropes. If he wore footgear, he might wear sandals made from rope. If he owned a pair of boots, the time to wear them aboard ship was when he was preparing for battle. The boot provided yet another place to store a dagger, and boots would protect his feet against battle wreckage on deck.

Typical pirate attire.

(Photo: William Perlis)

The Least You Need to Know

♦ Pirate ships were initially overmanned as a means of compensating for forecasted manpower losses stemming from battle deaths and losses to shipboard accidents and disease. Overcrowding, however, was itself dangerous as it quickly led to unsanitary living conditions and frayed nerves.

♦ Pirate crews always found themselves at the mercy of Mother Nature. Their ships might be caught in sudden storms or windless days. Consequently, weather seasons influenced sailing routes.

◆ After their initial food supply diminished, pirates had to find food from other sources. If they could not land in a friendly port or habitable island, they would be forced to seize a ship and pillage that ship's food supply, or starve.

◆ To combat boredom, pirates occupied their time aboard ship by playing games of chance, enjoying music, dancing, and participating in realistic mock trials.

◆ Pirates normally owned just the clothes on their back, a loose shirt, breeches, and rope sandals. For better balance when working on the deck, the men went barefoot.

12

Weapons to the Ready

In This Chapter

- ◆ Names of weapons change once aboard
- ◆ Cannon: the long-range weapon with the most destruction
- ◆ Flintlock pistol: making all men lethal
- ◆ Long-arms and blades
- ◆ Other close-combat weapons
- ◆ Ordinary tools become weapons of opportunity

Pirates didn't attack every ship they spotted. Vessels were first sighted hours before they were close enough to be identified. Then came the choice to either close with and attack or pass by, depending on the crew's disposition and whether the men thought they could "take the ship" successfully. When the decision was made—by a majority vote of the crew—the call for "beat to quarters" rang out. It was then that members of a pirate crew prepared themselves and their ship for battle.

Pirates had a wide variety of weapons at their disposal. There were weapons for long-range killing and weapons for close-quarters or hand-to-hand combat. Of all the attention and upkeep given to items aboard ship, nothing was deemed more important or accorded more focus than the care and cleanliness of weapons. After all, salt air and seawater were anathema to wood, metal, small working parts, and propellants such as gunpowder; and a man's survival depended to a great degree on the condition and the performance of his weapons and ammunition during combat action.

Coming to Terms

Before we look at the actual weapons aboard a pirate ship, we need to say a few words about pirate arms terminology, which can be very confusing when considering warships and weapons. Take the cannon, for instance, which we'll look at in greater detail in just a moment. Prior to the twentieth century, a shore gun—no matter the weight of the piece—was called a "cannon" and the spherical iron missile that was propelled from the cannon was simply a "cannon ball." However, when that cannon was placed on a ship, both the cannon and its ammunition changed names. Aboard ship, a cannon became a "gun" and a cannon ball became known as "shot" or a "round." Projectiles other than standard cannon balls were also referred to as "shot." On land, soldiers or marines (naval infantry) who manned and fired cannon were known as "cannoneers" or "artillerists." Aboard ship, they were known simply as "gunners." In the early 1900s, the terms began to be used interchangeably (as they are today) for guns and gunners on land and sea.

Additionally, handheld flintlock side-arms on land were often referred to as "guns," or "pistols" and—you guessed it—at sea they became "pistols." On land or sea, a musket was referred to as a "musket" or—depending upon its design—a "smoothbore musket" (or "smoothbore") or a "rifled musket" (or "rifle").

A Ship's Big Guns

The most obvious long-range weapon was the standard gun (cannon). The earlier cannons were cast-iron (iron, carbon, silicon), and deck guns weighed anywhere from a few hundred pounds to a few tons. Most of the larger guns were mounted onto wooden carriages with wheels. This enabled the gun to smoothly recoil backward when fired (recoil is the backward jerk or jump of the heavy gun when gunpowder is ignited and the ball is forcefully propelled from the barrel), then be rolled back into position for continued firing. The longer the barrel, the greater the distance a projectile would travel in a straight line. In theory, this worked. However, if the inside bore of the muzzle had not been cut absolutely dead center (straight) or if there was too much space between the edge of the projectile and barrel, the shot (ball) would strike short of its target or fly off in an odd direction. An experienced gunner knew the idiosyncrasies of each gun aboard his ship and compensated accordingly.

Cannon on carriage.

Iron to Bronze—and the Problems with Both

Corrosion from seawater was a big problem for these early iron guns. Shot (cannon balls) often became lodged inside the gun barrel and produced a dangerous misfire. By the 1560s, the Spanish replaced the iron with bronze. Though still weighing tons, the Spanish felt the bronze could withstand the heat from repeated firings, and they didn't corrode. Unlike cast iron, when bronze guns became worn from overuse and high temperatures, they could be recast. The downside of bronze was that it required a complex process of casting, and it was expensive. Discovering the bronze cannon shattered too easily, the Spanish resumed casting in iron.

Spanish muzzles were elaborately decorated. For luck or blessings, the Spanish typically cast portraits of saints or the story of a saint's life on their cannon. The name of the ship on which the cannon was to be mounted was cast in raised letters on the cannon barrel along with the decorations.

Treasure Chest

Casting the name of the ship it was intended for onto the cannon barrel during manufacturing continued to be popular beyond the mid-eighteenth century, after the trend of elaborate decorations declined. Though the designers didn't realize it at the time, the practice of labeling and decorating would enable undersea archaeologists to better identify and date pirate shipwrecks in the twentieth and twenty-first centuries.

Guns were identified by the weight of their shot. Though the gun could be as heavy as 1,000 pounds of cast bronze, a 4-pounder meant that that particular cannon fired a cannonball weighing 4 pounds.

The swivel gun became popular in the fourteenth century. This lightweight gun normally was seated on an inverted pivoting shaped horseshoe mounted onto a ship's railing (like a rowboat oar lock). Its speed, accessibility, and lateral swiveling capability served a purpose similar to that of a modern mounted machine gun.

Firing More Than Just Cannonballs

Both pirate crews and sailors on naval vessels were ingenious when it came to the variety of deadly projectiles they shot at their prey. Chain shot was simply two cannon balls attached with a length of very heavy chain. When fired correctly, these two attached balls could easily tear down a ship's rigging or damage sails. If the chain spun and hit a sail, large holes were punctured in the canvas. If the chain remained straight when it hit the sail, it produced a razor rip along the canvas. The bar shot was shaped like a modern weightlifting barbell or a cannon ball sliced in half welded with a bar in between. It spun in flight and ripped sails. This was also intended to entangle itself in the rigging and tear the sail lines down. The blackpowder residue on the bar shot also caused fires.

A Hailstorm of Lead, Iron, and Wood

Double shot was the term used when a gun crew loaded two cannon balls and extra powder into one gun. This could also be dangerous to the crew firing the gun. If the gun became too hot from constant firing, a double shot might cause the muzzle to explode.

Case shot or canister shot consisted of a cylindrical tin case stuffed with pistol balls. Its primary function was to pepper an opposing ship's deck, killing and maiming men indiscriminately.

Grape shot was a cluster of walnut or tennis-ball–size iron balls wrapped in canvas. It cracked holes in ship hulls, tore through sails and rigging, and literally ripped men's bodies to shreds.

Langrage was a canister made of wood or iron and filled with small pieces of scrap metal. It was specifically aimed at sails and their line. The diameter of the canister was in direct relation to a particular gun's muzzle.

Refining Gunpowder Increased Firing Dependability

Gunpowder, a Chinese invention from the ninth century, forever changed the nature of warfare. The basic ingredients of sulfur, saltpeter (potassium nitrate), and charcoal are still in use today. The only changes have been the differing ratios of these elements and the technique of mixing.

Early Europeans ground these three elements into a very fine powder. Mixed, it was known as serpentine powder. There were two major disadvantages to this mixture. Loaded into a tight chamber, the powder was hard to ignite and slow to burn. Worse was the problem of transporting. When carried over any distance on land or aboard ship, the three ingredients separated. When the gunpowder was at its destination and ready to be used, it needed to be remixed, a time-consuming and dangerous proposition.

A technological breakthrough came in the fifteenth century. Sometime between 1429 and 1450, gunpowder manufacturers began to experiment and mix the powder into a granulated or "corned" state. By mixing the three elements into a paste, pressing it and drying it into a cake, it became easy to crumble in pieces. Then passing the crumbled gunpowder through a series of fine sieves, it was discovered the elements didn't separate. The finer the sieve mesh, the finer the powder. It could then be transported anywhere and in any quantity.

The Great Equalizer

Gunnis cum telar, or "guns with handles," began to be referenced in documents around 1350. This ingenious concept was developed and improved upon by weapons manufacturers throughout the civilized world. A version of this invention, the flintlock pistol, was developed in the sixteenth century and used until the end of the nineteenth. It did not require a slow match to ignite the powder as in the earlier matchlock pistol, nor did it require a two-handed aim.

Flintlock pistols were expensive but favorite weapons. Light for carrying, these weapons killed more quickly, more easily, and with more accuracy than a sword. It was far easier for a pirate to become an expert pistol marksman than a master swordsman.

Flintlocks were manufactured with long, smooth-bored barrels of 12 inches or short barrels of 9 inches, and they had a range of 3 to 4 yards. Firing such a weapon required a steady hand, a good eye, and a recognition of which direction a specific weapon might pull when fired.

Flintlock pistol.

(Photo: William Perlis)

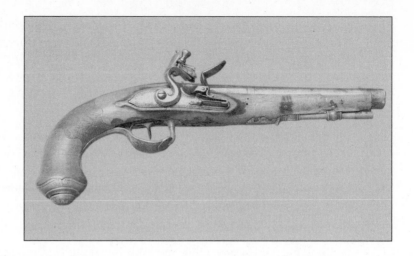

When a pirate showed exceptional bravery in the heat of battle—and if flintlocks were taken as part of the booty—the captain or quartermaster would reward the pirate with the first pick of the pistols.

Care and Wear

The salt air and probability of water dampening the powder made a loaded pistol— carried daily on a ship—unreliable when it needed to be fired. Consequently, a few smart pirates loaded them just prior to an attack.

There were a number of ways to wear pistols. The simplest way was to tuck the weapon inside one's belt or waist sash. If the pirate wore a *baldric*, he had the option of leather pistol holsters being sewn across the wide leather front. For more than one pistol on a baldric, the holsters would be positioned at a slight upward angle toward the pirate's shooting hand. If an ambidextrous shooter, the holsters were placed in alternating directions for two-handed firing.

> **Knowing the Ropes**
>
> A **baldric** was a broad strip of leather worn diagonally across the right or left shoulder that held a sword and sheath at waist or hip level. It was either ornately decorated or plain. Many featured leather holsterlike compartments or silken strings attached to the front to hold a number of pistols.

Another common way pistols were worn was as a set or pair of them tied together with a silken cord and draped around the neck. Flintlocks were single-shot weapons. After they were discharged, it was not a simple matter of slipping another bullet in the barrel like modern pistols. Reloading was far too time-consuming for hand-to-hand combat. Instead, the shooter had two options: he could release his grip on the weapon—allowing it to hang freely while he reached for another weapon—or he could use the pistol butt with its metal base as a bludgeoning weapon. Thus, it was aptly nicknamed "the skull crusher."

Loaded and Primed for Action

The flintlock used the same basic principle of loading as a cannon with some significant differences. The pistol rammer was called a "ramrod." Made from wood, it was 3 inches longer than the muzzle. A carved ring designated the 3-inch mark. This carved ring was used as a safety measure. When finished firing, if the ramrod didn't sink to the carved mark lining up with the tip of the muzzle, something—perhaps a patch or clump of gunpowder—was stuck in the barrel.

The design of the flintlock allowed the user to slip the ramrod into a secured grooved area just below the muzzle made for that very purpose. Priming the pistol was, however, different than priming a cannon. The other difference was, unlike a cannon, after a flintlock was fired, it wasn't swabbed out and cleaned immediately. Swabbing and cleaning was done after the fighting had ended. At a slight weight of 4 to 6 pounds and a compact length of 10 to 18 inches, the pistol was an easy weapon to handle.

Loading a flintlock, a pirate poured a measured amount of gunpowder into the barrel from a powder horn. Powder horns were made from animal horns, wood, or copper to prevent the powder from accidentally sparking. With a patch of cloth to keep it in place, the ball would be rammed into the muzzle to the breech (the end of the barrel holding the gunpowder charge).

At that point, the pirate was ready to prime the pistol. The firing mechanism operated on a simple system: flint striking steel, which caused a spark to ignite a bit of powder in the flash pan. This in turn ignited the gunpowder in the barrel. The exploding powder then propelled the ball.

A small piece of thin leather was sandwiched around a chunk of flint securely screwed into the jaws of the hammerlock. The flint would be whittled to a thick point. (The best flint to this day comes from Germany and England. It doesn't crumble easily, and lasts 40 to 50 firings before it becomes too worn down to be effective.)

The frizzen is a combination metal-striker and flash-pan cover. Holding the pistol, the pirate would push the frizzen forward toward the tip of the muzzle to expose the pan. The flash pan was simply a shallow trough on the top of the pistol. After the pirate poured priming powder into the flash pan, he pulled the frizzen back. This prevented the powder from spilling out. It automatically positioned the top of the frizzen, the metal striker, closer to the flint.

Flintlock mechanism.

(Artist: Gail Selinger)

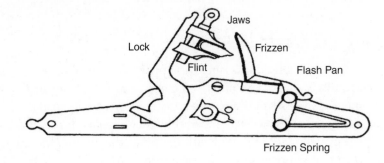

Going Off "Half-Cocked"

The inside mechanism of the flintlock engaged a tumbler that latched into one of two metal notches. If the shooter pushed the lock-cock back one notch, the pistol was at half-cocked position. When he pushed the lock-cock back again, the flintlock was at full-cocked position and ready to fire.

> **Treasure Chest**
>
> The expression a "flash in the pan" refers to a pistol's primer powder igniting in the flash pan, but the weapon failing to go off or propel the ball. Similarly, it has come to mean a person who is flamboyant or flashy but without any great substance, or a person or a venture with great albeit dashed hopes.

Half-cocked was the safety-yet-armed position. Pirates were known to walk around with their pistols loaded and notched half-cocked ready to pull the hammer to full and fire at a moment's notice. Though it was considered the safety position, if the pistol was juggled the wrong way, the flintlock could accidentally fire. Thus the term "going off half-cocked" acquired a double meaning: if someone is "going off half-cocked," then they, too, are exploding when they aren't supposed to be, or they are not as prepared as well as they might be.

Pirate Long-Arms

"Firing" weapons became equalizers. They leveled the field of warfare for the individual combatant. In conjunction with the pistol, the flintlock mechanism was employed in "longer," more accurate, firing arms known as "muskets." Like those utilizing pistols, combatants employing muskets no longer needed to be the stronger opponent to win a fight. He just had to be an accurate shooter.

The Blunderbuss

The blunderbuss—an odd cross between a flintlock pistol and musket—had a flaring muzzle and a wide bore. It could fire balls, nails, and small pieces of scrap metal. Ranging in length from 2 to 3 feet with a weight of 10 to 16 pounds, it scattered shot at close range, and thus was extremely effective in killing, maiming, and instilling fear in anyone on the receiving end.

The Muskatoon

Incredibly effective as a short-range shooting weapon before boarding, the muskatoon was a short-barreled musket, approximately the same length as a blunderbuss. It weighed between 9 and 15 pounds, and was the equivalent of the modern shotgun or police riot gun.

Weapons with an Edge

As we've mentioned, most men who went into piracy were not members of nobility. Thus they rarely had any formal training with swords. And navies or shipping companies did not permit ordinary seamen or sailors to own their own swords for fear they might turn the weapons on their officers. A cutlass was issued to crew during battle practice and locked away afterward.

So how did pirates learn to fight so well with swords? In most cases, skills were achieved by instruction from an experienced pirate who was willing to teach a junior pirate how to handle the weapon. In some cases, the junior pirate learned the hard way, by surviving a number of sword fights.

The Cutlass and the Hanger

In almost all cases, the sword of choice was either the famous cutlass or the lesser-known hanger. The reasoning was simple: the man wielding a cutlass—a hack-and-slash weapon—or a hanger did not require as much training or finesse as a man with a rapier.

The cutlass evolved from the medieval curtal axe. It became a slightly curved yard-long sword. Its wide razor-sharp blade made it the perfect hack-and-slash weapon. It cut through to the bone. The rounded hand guard was often made of brass. The blade—usually iron or steel—was sometimes painted black to protect the metal from the corrosive effects of saltwater. With its short blade, the cutlass was the sword of choice aboard ship. It was far easier to handle on a crowded deck. Longer swords, such as rapiers (a thrusting weapon), were more difficult to maneuver and often got caught on rigging.

Cutlass.

(Photo: William Perlis)

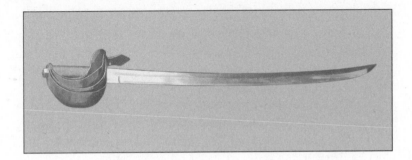

The hanger was shorter than the cutlass: its blade was approximately 24 to 27 inches in length. It was worn suspended at the waist by a simple belt. The hand guard was not as wide or curved as the cutlass.

The Dusägge

The German dusägge was another highly prized sword. Its broad double-edged, serrated, curved cutlass blade measured 30 inches long and weighed approximately 3 pounds. By the late-sixteenth century, this weapon had rightly earned a reputation as the most efficient killing weapon designed for high-seas warfare. The blade was known for its razor-sharp ability to slash, hack, and rip a man in two. The hand protector, a high seashell-patterned guard, was not just beautiful but practical. The ridges in the pattern pooled blood away from the sword hand so the owner didn't lose his grip.

Dusägge cutlass.

(Photo: William Perlis)

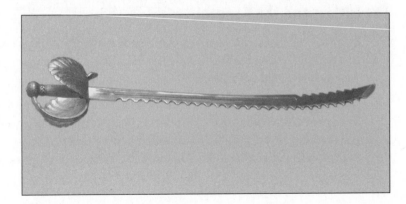

Pirates used the flat side of their swords to repeatedly strike their captives until questions concerning concealed treasure were satisfactorily answered or the cutthroats simply tired of the torturing.

The Dagger and the Dirk

A dagger could be concealed anywhere on a pirate, either inside his clothes or boots. Unlike swords, pirates usually did not favor one type of dagger over another. The choices included everything from a thin Italian stiletto blade to a stout Scottish dirk (shown here) or a curved Moorish dagger.

Dirk.

(Photo: William Perlis)

The Spanish Main gauche was a left-handed dagger used in conjunction with a right-handed sword. The stiletto blade, as long as 20 inches, was designed to puncture and cut. The triangular or sail-form knuckle guard provided significant protection for the hand. The quillon (extended cross guard) helped parry (avert) or entangle an opponent's blade.

Spanish Main gauche.

(Photo: William Perlis)

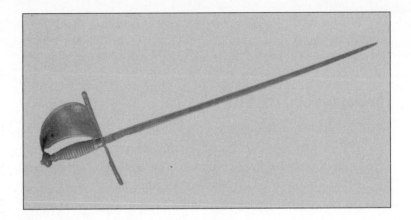

Come a Wee Bit Closer

As ships drew closer during an engagement, other weapons came into play. The granado (or grenado), the predecessor of the modern hand grenade, became a widely used weapon by 1700. Its name was a bastardization of the Spanish word *granada*, or "pomegranate." Another term for the deadly granado was "powder flask."

A granado.

(Photo: William Perlis)

Granadoes were hollowed-out cast iron balls approximately 1 to 2 ounces in weight. If the pirates didn't want to waste an iron cannon ball, they would use wood or glass. The granadoes were filled with gunpowder and capped off with a cork. A touch hole was bored into the cork with a fuse attached. Pirates would either tie it with cordage and throw it like a slingshot for more accuracy, or just lop it onto a deck. When lit, thrown, and exploded, it caused massive panic, death, and injury.

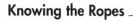

Knowing the Ropes

Asafetida is a spice first found in Iran and Afghanistan and used in cooking. Known to the French, Germans, and Swedish, they all have their own descriptive name for the spice that roughly translates into "dung of the devil."

Stinkpots were the pirate equivalent of tear gas bombs. The preferred container was a ceramic or glass handled jug. The pirates would stuff a mixture of any decaying meat they had aboard, saltpeter, limestone (calcium carbonate), and *asafetida* (a vile-smelling resin) into the jar. Tying a rope around the handles and inserting a lit fuse, they would hurl it from the topmast onto a deck or preferably into an open hatch. The ensuing chaos and nauseating illness caused by the fog created enough of a diversion to make it easier for the cutthroats to board.

Four-spiked cast iron projectiles known as caltrops, crowsfeet, or iron barbs were the bane of every barefooted seaman or sailor. The different angles of the spikes guaranteed that however the weapon landed, one of the spikes was always pointing straight up. French corsairs favored these barbs and threw handfuls of them onto decks, where unwitting men stepped on them. The resulting puncture wounds were excruciatingly painful and became dangerously infected.

Dead Men's Tales

In December 1718, Governor Lawes of Jamaica sent out two sloops to capture a pirate ship commanded by Captain Thompson .... The first sloop to reach the pirates was shocked into submission when the pirates "threw vast numbers of powder flasks, granado shells, and stinkpots into her which killed and wounded several and made others jump overboard."

—David Cordingly, *Under the Black Flag* (1995)

Makeshift Weapons

Much of a ship's maintenance equipment easily converted into effective weapons at a moment's notice. Railing attached along the bulwarks on the sides of the quarterdeck and poop, and also around the mainmast and pumps, called "pinrails" or "fiferails," held belaying pins placed within circular notches. The primary function of the belaying pins was to secure the different lines that controlled the multiple sails, which were coiled around them. Weighing 3 to 5 pounds and ranging in length from 1 to 3 feet when needed, they could instantly revert to clubs.

Belaying pin.

(Photo: William Perlis)

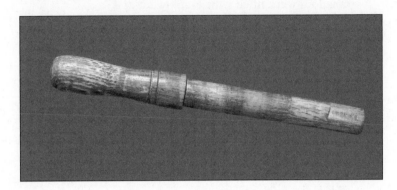

Long curved loading hooks normally used to grab, lift, or move cargo turned into slashing weapons.

The multifunctional boarding axe was an offensive or defensive weapon. Between 2 to 3 feet in length with a heft of 3 to 5 pounds, it cut down men as well as rigging, sails, and netting, all of which would disable a ship.

Boarding axe.

(Photo: William Perlis)

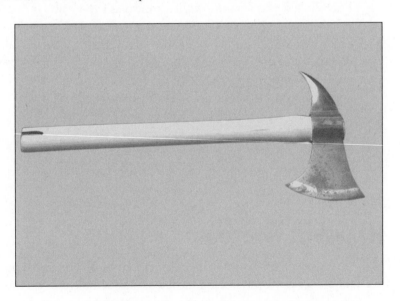

Another vital tool when sailing was the marlinespike. Similar in design to an ice pick, it had a large round wooden handle. The balled end eased the pressure on one's hand while using the tool. The round blade had an extremely sharp point. It separated the strands of the marline, essentially two lines of tarred rope, when repairs were needed. It made an excellent partially concealed weapon.

Used to bring the two ships closer for transferring cargo or stripping the ship of equipment, pirates often employed grappling hooks (also called grappling irons or grapnels). Grappling hooks looked like small anchors with four or five iron claws attached to a heavy rope. The hook was light enough in weight for a man to hurl a considerable distance. The hook's weight—10 or more pounds—was largely dependent on the class of ship. The claws would entangle the rigging or latch onto the under side of the railing and enable one to pull the two ships side by side.

Once pulled close, boarding pikes jockeyed ships right next to one another. The wooden staff—usually made from ash—ranged anywhere from 4 to 6 feet in length. The boarding-pike end had two design types. The combined straight and hooked iron spike, and the single iron spike. Weighing approximately 5 to 7 pounds, it enabled one to keep a sword a good distance away, or if aimed and thrust properly, could easily pierce a man's heart.

The Least You Need to Know

♦ Terminology changed when weapons transferred from land to sea.

♦ Guns fired many different types of projectiles. Each one was designed to do specific damage to the opposing vessel.

♦ The invention of the flintlock pistol gave an ordinary man a greater chance of surviving close combat.

♦ The cutlass came in many sizes and shapes. Other hand-to-hand weapons were portable firearms and throwing canisters that used blackpowder or spices to inflict the most damage possible.

♦ Common pieces of sailing equipment, which were employed daily aboard ship, became weapons of opportunity during times of battle.

Part 3

The Golden Age of Piracy

Here we unmask the characters employed in the sweet trade and focus on a period in history known as the "Golden Age of piracy," a period between 1692 and 1725 when the swashbuckling pirates as we know them from books and film prowled the seas and oceans in their greatest numbers. This was the time in which bloody red rags and black flags emblazoned with skulls and crossbones flew above bejeweled, boozing, and murderous crews captained by legendary skippers with names such as Blackbeard, Bonnet, Roberts, and Kidd. This was a time when crews of merchantmen and men-o'-war alike kept a watchful eye in the Atlantic and Caribbean for the infamous "Jolly Roger."

Chapter 13

Flying the Skull and Crossbones

In This Chapter

- Flags identify friend or foe
- The decision to attack or flee
- A pirate's calling card
- Rolling out the big guns
- Crossing swords with a pirate crew
- A pirate's wish list of ships

Combat aboard a pirate ship was nothing like what we today might see in an Errol Flynn or a Johnny Depp movie. After all, it is impossible for the silver screen to capture the sounds, smells, and overall feel of a ship in action. Keeping your balance on a rolling deck covered in blood and water. Ducking away from the metal fragments and wood splinters zinging toward you. Deafeningly loud explosions ringing in your ears. Iron shot whizzing overhead. The nauseating stink of sulphur and exposed human entrails. Your eyes tearing so much you can hardly make out shapes. Torn sail and tackle jumbled in heaps, mangled and groaning bodies scattered on the crowded, cramped deck making you stumble. Men screaming in utter agony. Commanders shouting inaudible orders. Desperately you try to keep your footing so you don't cut your feet on caltrops, broken pottery, or glass. All the while you're fighting for your life against a berserk pirate swinging a cutlass at your head and chest.

Crews fought gallantly to save their ships, their cargos, and—more important—their very lives. Close-quarters combat on a ship's deck was an ugly, frightening affair, especially if men weren't accustomed to that type of fighting. Merchant ships, if singled out by cutthroats, typically had untrained fighting crews and few adequate weapons.

In fact, having one's ship boarded and subsequently fighting it out was an experience many finally chose to avoid after accounts of attacks filtered back to land. By the end of the eighteenth century and throughout the nineteenth century, merchant ships, brazenly approached by pirates, usually surrendered without a fight and hoped the brutal tales of torture were false. Unfortunately, most of the tales were true.

Friend or Foe?

As a vessel drew near on the horizon, all hands aboard a pirate ship would strain over the gunwale or climb the rigging in an attempt to identify it, and to double-check its identity. Standing on the topmast crosstrees (horizontal timber spreading the shrouds on the top-most mast) or clinging to the topmast were the best vantage points from which to recognize ship design and the flag flown.

If it were a state naval man-o-war out hunting for pirate ships, the pirates were usually smart enough to know they would be outgunned in a fight. Faced with such a vessel, most pirates usually attempted to escape as fast as their own ship could find a wind.

Dissension Within the Pirate Ranks

As in any society, even a piratical one, not everyone got along. Many pirate captains had individual flags flying high on a topmast. By flag design, the ship's captain and crew would be known and identified as friend or foe.

If foes—depending upon how intense the hatred between the two pirate captains—the crews usually chose to let their captains decide their own fates by settling the matter on land whether by duel or ambush whenever they might meet. Pirates generally chose not to chance their own lives or damage the ship over a captain's personal vendetta.

Comrades in Arms

Whenever one pirate crew recognized a compatriot vessel, it was not uncommon for the two ships to anchor alongside each other and exchange greetings, current news, food, and drink. If one or the other ship had a specific objective in mind, crews might agree to join forces and share in any forthcoming treasure. Many, in fact, did so.

Whether these temporary joint forces worked out depended on the men involved. Stede Bonnet, for example, chose to sail with Blackbeard, to Bonnet's great regret (as you'll see in Chapter 17).

On the Attack

Once the decision was made by the crew to attack, it was the captain's job to come up with a battle plan. The objective was to capture, with as little damage as possible, their intended prize. Many ploys were used to lure an unsuspecting ship. As early as the fifteenth century, a common method of deception was to hoist a flag identical to that of a pirate crew's intended victims. When within firing range, the pirates would lower those colors and raise their own standard, a declaration of intent. The victim would then choose to surrender or fight.

> **Pirate Yarns**
>
> Dressing as women to lure unsuspecting ships has been a ploy used for years in countless poems, novels, and movies. However, to date there are no substantiated eyewitness accounts by survivors of such a method to a pirate attack.

Another strategy entailed dragging heavy items from the stern for hours, thus appearing to be a slower lumbering ship. Pirates would use items such as hatch covers or even their anchor during the ruse. When the unsuspecting vessel drew near, the pirate ship would simultaneously begin hauling up gear, readying the guns, and turning to attack.

I Dub Thee "Jolly Roger"

Thanks to countless books and movies, the white skull of death above (or over) a pair of white crossed bones on a black background is universally recognized as the standard emblem of pirates. This symbol was indeed used by a number of rogues sailing the seas and oceans of the world, but by no means was it the only identifying insignia on a pirate ship declaring to other ships its crew's malicious intent.

Knowing the Ropes

The term **no quarter** meant that the pirates demanded their targeted ship's crew surrender without resistance. If they did so, the pirates guaranteed the entire crew would live. However, if anyone chose to resist, there would be dire consequences, for the entire crew would be murdered when the ship was taken.

Red Flags

The original buccaneers' flag was referred to by many of their victims as "the bloody flagg" or "the red flagg." This blood-red symbol was instantly recognizable by all seafarers, naval or civilian. A red flag was particularly terrifying in that it meant *no quarter* would be given to those seized by force of arms. It has since been speculated that the red flags raised by the very first buccaneers of the 1600s were their bloodied hunting shirts or aprons.

"Pretty Red," a Tamil Pirate, or the Devil Himself?

There is no definitive explanation as to how the banner we traditionally associate with being a pirate flag became known as "the Jolly Roger" or "Old Roger." There are, however, a number of theories. Being that the largest population of early buccaneers came from France, it is believed by some historians that the name is derived from the French *joli rouge*, which literally means "pretty red." This term was later bastardized by the English to Jolly Roger. Another theory credits the English pirates sailing along the Indian Ocean. Ali Raja was a famous southern Indian Tamil pirate who flew a red flag. Based on the Englishmen's propensity for nicknames, it is believed the English began calling Ali Raja and his flag the Ally Roger or Olly Roger, eventually Jolly Roger. Roger was also an English slang word for rogue or villain; and the common slang expression for the "devil" himself was "Old Roger."

No matter which origin is accurate (and it very well could be a combination of all three), the name came to describe all pirate flags. And these images of terror worked.

Communicating Colors: What Captains Conveyed

In 1700, Captain John Cranby of the HMS *Poole* recorded what was to be the first official sighting of the now symbolic pirate flag. Chasing the French pirate Captain Emmanuel Wynne, he noted the flag was "a sable ensign with cross bones, a death's head and an hourglass."

Moreover, the black Jolly Roger seen throughout the eighteenth century became personalized. The designs and symbols held specific meanings, and their various combinations reflected the views of the captains who sailed beneath them.

Christopher Moody

Edward England

Pirate flags of Captains Moody, England, Wynne, and Worley.

(Artist: Gail Selinger)

Emmanuel Wynne

Richard Worley

Wynne's symbol of the hourglass made the point that time was running out for all who opposed him. To get *his* point across, Captain Christopher Condent flew a pennant with three skulls. Captain Walter Kennedy (whose previous life in Ireland was that of a pickpocket) flew a flag depicting himself with a sword in one hand and a tankard of ale in the other, toasting the skull of death at his side. The raised arm or hand denoted one who was not afraid to kill for gain.

Christopher Moody's dire warning of "no quarter given" was hard to miss or to misinterpret. His red flag featured a white arm raised to kill, flanked by a yellow skull and a yellow hourglass with blue wings.

Blackbeard represented himself as the horned devil with an hourglass in one hand and a death spear pointing to a captive's bleeding heart. The heart and blood droplets were stitched in red silk. A striking contrast against the black background and white skeleton, the spear warned that violent death awaited any and all opponents, and the bleeding heart proclaimed the victim's forthcoming slow and painful death.

Pirate flags of Captains Kennedy, Blackbeard, and Condent.

(Artist: Gail Selinger)

Walter Kennedy

Blackbeard

Christopher Condent

Pirate flags of Captains Tew, Avery (Every), Roberts, and Rackham.

(Artist: Gail Selinger)

Thomas Tew

Henry Every

Bartholomew Roberts

Jack Rackham

Bartholomew Roberts sailed with two flags: the first was a traditional skeleton with crossbones and an hourglass in each hand. The second flag flown sent a more specific message. It showed the captain standing with flaming sword atop two skulls. Beneath each skull were the initials ABH and AMH for "A Barbadian's Head" and "A Martinican's Head," proclaiming his hatred of and ultimate intentions for the islands of Martinique and Barbados.

"Commence Firing! Fire at Will!"

When not readied for battle, the big guns were tightly lashed (tied with rope) to thick metal eyebolts just above the closed gun ports. When "clear for quarters" or "beat to quarters" was called by the captain or master gunner—if the pirate ship had a separate gun deck—the area about the guns would be cleared for action. Because living quarters were so tight, hammocks were also slung between cannons on this deck. This meant everything not involving battle would hastily be removed.

Ropes known as gun-tackle were tied to both sides of the gun carriage to keep the gun secure. An additional heavy rope, called a breeching rope, was tied around the cascabel (knob at the rear end of a gun) and fastened to a ring on the ship's side by the gun port. This helped secure the weapon from *jumping its track* when it recoiled. When the gun was pulled inboard, the breeching rope gave only 18 inches of loading room from muzzle to gunwale.

Additional rope was tied to an eyebolt at the rear of the gun carriage below the cascabel. This was known as the train tackle, and it was used to haul the cannon inward.

A number of shots would always be seated (stored) on the shot-garland ready for instant battle. This special horizontal rack with hollowed-out semi-circles was spaced between each gun port.

> **Knowing the Ropes**
>
> **Jumping its track** was a result of the gun recoiling so forcefully that it literally snapped all the lashing ropes. This was extremely dangerous because a gun—weighing several tons and rolling around unchecked on a heaving deck—could inflict catastrophic damage on ship and crew.

Fighting as a Team

Firing a single gun was a group effort. Ideally, five men operated a weapon. A minimum of four men was needed to maneuver the heavy weapon. This was not a haphazard exercise either. Men knew which gun they were assigned to and their particular job pertaining to that gun long before any battle was initiated. If not, utter chaos might have ensued.

After the men unlashed the weapon from its secured ropes, they quickly attached the train and gun tackle and pulled the gun farther forward onto the deck for loading.

One man would open and secure the gun port; the hinged square wood flap was lifted open from the outside of the hull by a rope pulled through the rail and secured on an inside rail ring. Once opened, this allowed the gun to be rolled to the very edge of the gunwale. The muzzle would then be positioned over the water and aimed.

While gun crews laid out their equipment, fellow shipmates threw sand (if any was aboard) on the deck floors to help prevent slippage by absorbing any water or blood spilled during action.

Wooden buckets of water were set out to cool overheated guns and to soak the swabbing sponges. Meanwhile, the powder monkeys were hauling up the gunpowder in canisters or passboxes.

The Gun Captain

The gun captain would light a "slow match" or a piece of coal that hooked onto a lintstock. The slow match consisted of loosely woven hemp cord that had been boiled in saltpeter and dried. The lintstock staff measured 3 feet in length. When setting it aside during a battle, the lintstock was propped securely against the notched grooves of a sand- or water-filled bucket. This allowed any ash from the coal or slow match to fall onto a safe surface. If the bucket contained sand, additional lit matches or coal pieces were also stored in this bucket.

The Loader

The pirate designated as a "loader" cleared the touchhole vent on the top of the muzzle of any residual clumped powder, cord fuse, or quill. He used an instrument called a pick or priming iron. Approximately 9 inches in length, the pick resembled a thick sewing needle with a circular loop at the blunt end large enough to hook a finger through.

If firing loose powder, the loader used a powder ladle—a copper scooped ladle attached to a rod. The loader dipped it into the passbox and measured an amount of gunpowder approximately one third the weight of the cannon ball. If filling a cloth cartridge on deck, he used a copper powder measure. Gunners used copper because this metal would not cause gunpowder to accidentally spark and ignite.

Swabbing the Bore

On some vessels, the rammer and the swabbing sponger rods were two different pieces of equipment. Sometimes they were combined. The rammer, a long rod with a wooden head as its name implies, rammed the powder charge, the wadding, and the shot down the cannon barrel. The swabbing sponge soaked the inside of the barrel after the gun was fired to extinguish any gunpowder sparks. If combined into one tool, the man employing the rammer had to ensure that water from the wet sponge did not drip down to the wooden head on the opposite end. He couldn't chance getting the powder inside the bore damp.

The worm rod was so named because it had one or two pointed metal spirals attached to an end. This tool was used to clean out the barrel of any remaining wadding or cartridge charge. Ramming it into the muzzle, the crewman rotated the tool a few times, then withdrew it slowly from the barrel. The rod was also used to carefully dislodge shot and wadding if the cannon misfired.

Ramming Home the Shot

After measuring the loose gunpowder with the ladle, the loader had one of his mates cover the touchhole vent with his finger while he carefully poured the powder into the barrel. This prevented any gunpowder from escaping through the vent. With the wooden head of the ramrod, he gently pushed it to the back of the muzzle.

With two or three strong strokes, the loader then wedged a sizeable wad of loose hemp rope yarn against the powder. Next came the shot: once removed from the shot-garland and handed to the loader, he "put it home" or "rammed it home," seating the shot against the wadding.

To prevent the shot from rolling out of the barrel as the gun was positioned for firing, another wad was placed in the muzzle. This had to be done firmly to guarantee there was no space between the powder, the first wad, the shot, and the second wad; otherwise a misfire might occur.

"Fire in the Hole!"

The touchhole was then filled with a finer grain of gunpowder poured from a powder horn. The touchhole was located in a grooved area called the base ring. The loader continued filling the touchhole until the base ring was also filled. If using a cartridge charge, he then thrust his priming iron (pick) down the touchhole and pricked an opening in the cartridge material, which exposed the gunpowder.

Now it was time to angle the gun for firing: With brute force and the side tackles, the gun was "run out" the gun port. Pushing down with handspikes for leverage, the men leveled the barrel to the correct height. Using the quoin, a wooden wedge with angle measurements, they adjusted and secured the gun barrel.

> **Treasure Chest**
>
> Misfires were a constant danger, and the crews were always concerned about the dangers associated with overheating the guns. In a successful firing, as the shot exploded toward its target, the recoiling force propelled the gun carriage backward. The crew prayed the breeching rope held strong and would prevent the gun from breaking free.

If the gunner wished to add a fuse, he chose a hollowed quill point or corded fuse. After the gun captain was satisfied with the firing position and fuse, he reached for his linstock. Holding it below the touchhole, he blew on the slow match to produce a red flared spark, and then waited for the command to fire.

When the order was given, the gun captain warned his mates with a secondary command: "Fire in the hole!" He and his mates then moved to the side of the carriage for safety. The gunner lowered the slow match to the base ring. He did not directly ignite the powder over the touchhole, because the air escaping with the flame, known as the huff, would have then extinguished the slow match.

"Don't Lose Your Grip, Mate"

The sponger, the lucky mate who cleaned the gun, quickly took the wet swabbing sponge rod and swabbed (washed) out the bore until air or water sprouted out of the touchhole. Only then would he step aside for others to reload. As previously mentioned, with the breech rope leaving only 18 inches between the muzzle and gunwale, the sponger and rammer had to lean their arms well beyond the gun port to fit the rod into the muzzle. These men needed to be both fast and steady of hand. If either of them lost their grip and let the rammer or swabber slip, it would fall into the sea where it could not be retrieved.

Ideally, a gun crew might load and fire a gun within one minute. But this was rare. Realistically, if the firing crew was well trained, it would take them two to five minutes to load, aim, and discharge the weapon. The longer the timeframe, the fewer shots they got off, and the greater the chance their opponent had to fire at and kill them.

Broadside Was Not Always the Best Tactic

Normally, the objective was to capture a ship, not sink it. But if pirates needed to employ their big guns to obtain surrender, they did not hesitate. That said, a broadside—firing simultaneously all guns stationed along one side of their ship—wasn't the best means of achieving a pirate's goal. A broadside, if aimed properly, would shatter an opposing vessel's wooden hull. This greatly increased the possibility of sinking the prize. As an attention getter, pirates often deliberately mis-aimed their broadsides, hoping to frighten their opponent into submission. If necessary, the most effective gun barrage was a stern shot. It got the point across with minimal damage to the ship.

Shiver Me Timbers

If unwilling to surrender when pirates bore down upon them, certain death came to both ships. In action, men on either side were more likely to die from flying *shivers*—and the resulting infections—than they were from shot and shell. Shivers were created by masts, yards, bulkheads, and pieces of deck that split and splintered. Falling sails, rigging, blocks, and tackle were also dangerous.

Knowing the Ropes

A **shiver** is a wood splinter 6 inches or longer that was usually propelled from the force of shattered decking or any crashing wood forcefully landing on a deck. There are many variations to the meaning of the term *shiver me timbers*. The most literal meaning is the timbers of a ship are suddenly and surprisingly splintering. Two figurative meanings are a man's life is falling apart or a man is totally surprised over an action or information he is being given.

While the ship's musicians beat drums and blew whistles, and cutthroats shouted to disorient and unnerve their opponents, the two ships drew ever closer to one another. When positioned mere feet away, the pirates—armed to the teeth—jumped the rails and boarded their intended prize.

Down and Dirty

Close-quarters combat on a ship's deck was a nasty and frightening affair. It was particularly horrific for men who had never experienced fighting other men toe to toe and to the death.

Merchant ships, if singled out by cutthroats, were typically crewed by sailors with inadequate battle skills and few weapons. Captains were often unsure of whether they might attempt to counter an attack or passively surrender to an unknown fate. Pirates, on the other hand, were hard men. They had a variety of weapons at their disposal, and they had no qualms whatsoever about using them against other human beings.

"Take What You Want, But Let Me Live"

Along with hunting Spanish treasure galleons, pirates chose ships that appeared to have the fewest weapons aboard with the most merchandise and treasure. High atop a mast, some 100 feet above the deck, the lookout could scan as far as 100 miles in search of a ship's sail.

Trade routes along the Spanish Main, Asia, Africa, and India were constantly patrolled for likely victims. Pirates counted on their reputation as cruel and unforgiving to precede them.

An excellent example was the dreaded pirate Blackbeard. Deliberately dressed in brocade finery while sticking numerous lit slow matches in his braided hair and beard, he created the look of a madman, perhaps the devil himself. His appearance, along with his reputation for murder and mayhem, compelled ships' crews to surrender as soon as they spotted his flag.

> **Dead Men's Tales**
>
> The pirate soon came up and sent a boat on board our sloop, demanding who we were and where we were bound; to which our captain gave a direct answer ... [the pirates] demanding the name of every hand on board.
>
> —John Fillmore, great-grandfather of President Millard Fillmore and captive off the sloop *Dolphin*, 1802

In fact, by the late eighteenth century, piracy and fear of such was so great that the flag-deception trick had become unnecessary. The mere sighting of a pirate flag was enough to force a ship to raise the white flag of surrender.

Having surrendered, a crew watched helplessly as armed pirates rowed a longboat alongside, questioned their captain, and surveyed their prize. As the longboat approached, all weapons aboard the pirate vessel were trained on the victims to prevent any attempt at repelling the boarding party. Nervously, the captives waited while the pirate crew—by means of a majority vote—decided the fate of a ship, its passengers, and crew (see Chapter 10).

Swift Ships and Full Sails

If given the choice of what kind of ship they would sail, pirates naturally gravitated to the swifter shallow draft vessels capable of outrunning most anything large fielded by state navies.

By the end of the golden age of piracy, around 1725, vessels had evolved to the point that they were not only identified by their standard design, but also by the type of sails rigged onto them. No matter the rigging, specific ships were always high on a pirate's wish list: the sloop, schooner, and brigantine.

When pirates captured a ship, they often tore down its deck cabins to create more space. Cargo holds were stripped and modified for guns and men. Gun ports were created on decks to accommodate whatever size guns were acquired during a raid and added to their arsenal. A pirate ship did not have a set number of guns. It was more a matter of how many guns the pirates could acquire and how much additional weight their ship could carry without fear of capsizing.

The Least You Need to Know

- A pirate ship's flag told a great deal about who was sailing. It not only identified the captain, but also his dastardly intentions.

- Pirates would not attack a heavily armed ship, merchant or naval. And pirate crews often spent hours trailing a ship before they were able to identify it.

- Firing a ship's guns required precision teamwork. If not cautious, a gun crew could catastrophically damage its own ship. Guns had a variety of shot types to cause specific damage to their enemy.

- In combat, more men died from falling/flying wreckage and ensuing infections than from swords or guns.

- Continuous vessel redesign and the different sails used, and the ability to interchange the two, created a new era in maritime history and piracy.

The Men Who Sailed the Pirate Round

In This Chapter

◆ Pirates follow the riches east

◆ American colonies embrace illegal trade

◆ Captain Tew makes piracy attractive

◆ Henry Avery becomes a celebrity

◆ William Kidd: a ruined reputation

◆ Three observers, one major expedition

It's not that the pirates of the golden age of piracy were any nobler or more colorful than pirates prior or since, but—during that era—they did proliferate in both numbers and activity in the Caribbean. Their reputation for ferocity grew, and their blatant disregard for life and the cost to global commerce earned more space in newspapers and broadsheets than ever before.

The exotic places pirates dared travel and the impact they had on global trade created major national concerns—and ironically, a fascination—during a period when European countries were unable to remain at peace for any length of time. The way in which governments handled their countries' economies after treaties were signed and peacetime directives were issued in fact created what the public dreaded most: pirates, men who swore no loyalty to king or country.

Seafaring pirates weren't the only kind of pirates. Many unscrupulous government officials achieved great wealth by granting legal (and false) letters of marque while finding ways to divert attention from their own nefarious activities.

International Trade Boom

By the late seventeenth century, bustling seaports and trading posts had been established throughout the world. These points of commerce connected continents through a complex system of land/sea shipping routes. Governments and private companies were importing and exporting a phenomenal amount of goods and raw materials. The Spanish treasure fleets had sailed from the Spanish Main to Seville for more than two centuries.

In the 1680s, the Spanish were still storing their vast riches in treasure houses. However, by the mid-1690s, the nature of their West Indies storage and transport changed. The treasure houses were no longer used, and the treasure fleets were either accompanied by warships or themselves heavily armed. The cargoes were also changing from the enormous wealth of gold and jewels to mercantile.

Fewer treasure-laden merchant ships and increasingly powerful navies forced pirates to rethink their modus operandi. It was during this same period that seafarers were telling tales of endless riches in the East Indies, Red Sea, Asia, and Africa. Those regions of the world were said to yield vast wealth, gold and jewels in amounts similar to the great bounties that had lured men to the Spanish Main during the "good old days." And so pirates and privateers began turning their vessels eastward.

The Pirate Round: A Hazardous But Lucrative Route

The Pirate Round, as it was aptly named, covered some 22,000 miles of oceangoing highway. Commencing on the northern coast of America, ships fully loaded with cargo sailed out of a dozen ports, the biggest being Philadelphia, Newport, New York, and Boston. For such long journeys, the vessels first stopped at New Providence and Madagascar for provisions and to sell their colonial cargos to pirates living on the islands.

When their ships were restocked, the privateers and pirates sailed to and around the navigationally dangerous tip of Africa to India and Asia. On the return trip, their vessels bulged with traded and stolen goods to sell throughout the colonies.

Only the bravest of men sailed the long and hazardous ocean routes. And the prizes available to them were worth their hardships. There were East Indiamen (merchant ships owned by the various East Indian Companies) from England, Holland, Portugal, and France to plunder sailing from Asia, Ceylon, Africa, and India—not to mention the pilgrim fleets to and from Mecca.

If a pirate ship captured one good prize—and not all seized ships yielded one—each seaman could share out with as much as 2,000 pounds sterling (equivalent to $320,000, today).

Knowing the Ropes

The Pirate Round, beginning in the 1690s, refers to the pirate hunting route from North America to New Providence, on to Madagascar, the Indian Ocean, and back to North America.

American Colonies: A National Brokerage Exchange for Pirates

North America proved to be most eager to participate in the buying and selling of illegal goods. England valiantly attempted to suppress piracy, which cut into their economic profits. But along North America's eastern seaboard, colonial governors as well as common colonials often greeted pirates with open arms, provisions, and free ports.

The Trade-Stifling Navigational Acts

As the Spanish had attempted to do along the Main, England attempted an economic monopoly with her American colonies. Beginning in 1647, with amendments added in 1651 and subsequent years, the British Parliament enacted a series of Navigational Acts. These acts stated that all produced goods imported or exported from America or England must be shipped exclusively via English ships crewed by English sailors. This restriction, along with England's limited products, created an atmosphere in which the colonists began to resent their mother country's interference. Large numbers of colonists, in fact, became unabashed supporters of piracy and smuggling.

A Threat to the American Pocketbook

Most lords in Parliament cared so little for the welfare of their American colonists they agreed with Lord Sheffield's statement that "the only use of the American colonies is the monopoly of their consumption and the carriage of their produce (for the English economy)." England failed in the economic dominance of her colonies as the Spanish had failed before in theirs.

Colonial governors who were more than happy to welcome pirates for a bribe or a percentage included the following:

◆ Governor William Phipps of Massachusetts traveled to Philadelphia and campaigned among the pirates for them to relocate their bases to Boston.

◆ Governor William Markham of Pennsylvania not only welcomed pirates to his state, his daughter Jane married James Brown, a former pirate who once sailed with Henry Avery.

◆ Governor Benjamin Fletcher of New York was considered one of the biggest advocates of pirates. There wasn't a bribe he wasn't willing to take. He actively encouraged Thomas Tew to move his pirate base from Newport, Rhode Island, to New York.

The Agreeable and Companionable Thomas Tew

A native of Newport, Rhode Island, Thomas Tew (a.k.a. Thomas Too) hailed from a wealthy, respectable family. In 1690, with England and France at war, he traveled to Bermuda to become a privateer.

In 1692, Captain Tew was commissioned by the governor of Bermuda, Issac Richier, in conjunction with the British Royal African Company, to sail to the Guinea Coast of Africa and raid the French trading posts. Investing in the enterprise himself, Tew took command of the *Amity* and signed on 60 seasoned men.

At sea, Tew proposed an idea: the crew would gain more riches, he said, if they sailed not to Africa as planned, but to the Red Sea. If they failed, they would have nothing to show but the brand of pirate on their heads. If they succeeded, they would have wealth beyond their wildest dreams. The men agreed to follow Tew's proposal. They sailed for months in search of a prize. Finally, in the Straits of Bebelmandebin in the Red Sea, their patience paid off.

A Grand Treasure

Tew's crew spotted and attacked one of the tribute ships of the Grand Mogul. The vessel's 300-man crew surrendered with little resistance, few casualties, and no deaths to Tew's men. The booty transferred onto the *Amity* was impressive.

Tew's crew sailed back to Newport with £100,000 ($16,000,000) worth of gold and silver; chests of gems, pearls, spices, and elephant tusks; and hundreds of bales of silk fabric. Each man shared out between £1,200 ($192,000) to £3,000 ($480,000). Because they had raided ships belonging to "heathens," they returned home as heroes in April 1694, after 15 months at sea.

Merchants, upon hearing the news, traveled from New York and Boston to buy the cargo Tew unloaded. Not forgetting his original investors in Bermuda, Tew paid each man a considerable profit.

New York's Governor Fletcher invited him to dine at his home in New York and found the man quite "agreeable and companionable, with interesting stories to tell."

Men Eager to Cast Their Lot with Tew

After months of socializing, Tew decided to return to sea. When word got out he was sailing, the wharf in Newport was jammed with men and boys from every walk of life wanting to sail with him.

In the event they were waylaid en route by an English warship, Tew bought a letter of marque for £300 ($4,800) from Fletcher. With two other vessels commanded by Thomas Wake and William Want, they set sail in November 1694.

An Ill-Fated Voyage

Tew was killed while attacking another of the Grand Mogul's ships. Unlike the last voyage, this ship put up a fierce fight. The members of Tew's crew who survived the engagement were captured and executed.

Dead Men's Tales

In the Engagement a Shot carry'd away The Rim of Tew's Belly, who held his Bowels with his Hands some small Space.

—Charles Johnson, *A General History of Pyrates*, 1724

Henry Avery, the People's Pirate

Throughout his own lifetime, when people thought of pirates, Henry Avery was the man they envisioned. His exploits and adventures were so famous they inspired a play, "The Successful Pirate," which ran for several years in London.

Avery fired everyone's imagination, and stories relating to his exploits—real or otherwise—got a lot of printer's ink. Yet the real man behind the popular *broadsides* was a far cry from the dashing public image.

It is said Avery earned his sea legs as a boy. As a young man, the governor of Bermuda employed him as a slaver along the Guinea coast. Avery traveled under a number of different aliases. He introduced himself as John Avery, Henry Every, Long Ben, and Captain Bridgman.

Avery next signed on in 1693 with Captain Charles Gibson aboard the *Charles II* as first mate. The ship's owner, Sir James Houblon, had leased the vessel to the Spanish government in hopes of curtailing the French smugglers along the Main.

Knowing the Ropes

A **broadside,** also known as a broadsheet, was a large sheet of paper printed on one side posted for everyone to read. Everything from news, political satirical cartoons, to plain advertisements was published on broadsides. The first publications of the Declaration of Independence to be circulated throughout the 13 colonies were printed as broadsides.

After eight months at sea, the vessel sailed into the Spanish port of La Coruña intending to refit for supplies and take on passengers for the trip back to the Caribbean. Avery and the rest of the crew had their own plans. Receiving no pay when they docked—and not convinced that they would ever be paid—the crew planned to mutiny. Patiently, they waited until Captain Gibson got drunk. Then they struck.

With Avery as their leader, the crew renamed the ship *Fancy* and proceeded to attack ships from any nation. Eventually fitted with 46 guns, they set their course for Madagascar by rounding the Cape of Good Hope.

A Flair for Self-Promotion

Captain Avery docked in 1695 at the port of Johanna on the Comoros Islands northwest of Madagascar. He soon captured a French corsair, and her crew eagerly joined his fleet.

Before leaving Johanna, Avery left a letter to be delivered to the first English ship that docked. It was to be printed in a London newspaper. He stated that he had captured the *Charles II* and renamed her. He continued to proudly announce he had not harmed any Englishman or Dutchman, but his crews would if they were pursued. Though the ship's skipper, he warned if they were attacked he could not guarantee his ability to control his men's behavior.

After signing his name with a grand flourish, he added an odd postscript: he warned the English government there were 160 shipwrecked French corsairs waiting at Mohilla, another island in the Comoros chain, to capture any passing ship. The missive caused mixed reactions. Some Englishmen viewed him as patriotic. The government branded him a pirate and issued a bounty. Ships from the East India Company sailed to Mohilla and captured the Frenchmen. Avery's reputation was firmly established.

Henry Avery.

(Courtesy of the Library of Congress, Prints & Photographs Division)

A Legend Is Born

Avery had a plan. He would intercept the pilgrim fleet as it journeyed from the Indian port of Surat across the Red Sea to the cities of Mocha and Mecca. It was common knowledge among seafarers of the region that fully stocked merchant vessels traveled with the pilgrim fleet. Scouting the Red Sea for the fleet, Avery joined other pirate ships to increase their chances of success. Three of those ships—the *Pearl*, *Portsmouth Adventure*, and *Amity*—were from the American colonies. The *Pearl* and *Portsmouth Adventure* made their home port in Rhode Island. The *Amity* berthed in New York.

Avery nearly missed his greatest opportunity. During the moonless night, the pilgrim fleet of 25 ships returning from Mecca slipped by unnoticed. But a lookout spotted two other vessels lumbering in the distance.

The slower vessel belonged to the grand mogul, emperor of India. His flagship, the *Ganj-i-Sawai* (later anglicized to *Gunsway*) meaning "Exceeding Treasure," lagged behind with only one escort, the *Fath Mahmamadi*.

Eager for action, the pirates prepared to attack the swifter escort. Upon hearing gunfire, the *Ganj-i-Sawai* unfurled all sails and fled. The escort was taken with little resistance.

The Cowardly Khan

Next the pirates pursued the flagship. It was a truly impressive sight. Sixty-two guns were mounted on her decks, and 500 riflemen were aboard to protect the 600 passengers, primarily officials from the grand mogul's court. Daunting in its sheer size and firepower, no ship had previously attempted such an attack.

Terrified and unaccustomed to fighting, her captain, Ibrahim Khan, hid below. As with most non-Western forces, the Indian troops were not trained to think for themselves. Consequently, without their captain to issue combat orders, they panicked and offered little resistance. With minimal casualties, Avery and his crew boarded.

Romance Hides Reality

The capture of the grand mogul's ship was later dramatized and romanticized in many venues. Each variation of the story typically concluded with Avery marrying the mogul's daughter, who was a passenger and living the charmed life of a princess. It is a fact that a princess was aboard, the grand mogul's aunt, but that is where the truth ends. Wisely, Avery was able to keep his men away from her. The other passengers weren't that lucky. The women were savagely raped, the men slaughtered. Many women died after continuous attacks or chose to commit suicide. A week of plundering concluded, the pirates departed. With her mainmast shot off and her sails destroyed, the *Ganj-i-Sawai* could only drift back to Surat.

The Wrath of the Grand Mogul

Enraged, the grand mogul immediately ordered his army to round up the officers of the East India Company in Surat and Broach. Sixty-four men were arrested. In prison for more than a year, they were chained to walls and tortured. Many didn't survive. The prisoners gained their release only after the company could prove to the grand mogul's satisfaction that they had no involvement in the attack. The East India Company was forced to close many of their trading posts and lost millions of pounds sterling in commerce.

The Great Escape

Weighted down with booty, Avery's fleet sailed for North America. Bribing Governor Cadwallader Jones for safe harbor, the pirates docked in New Providence for provisions. The accumulated treasure seized by Avery's fleet was shared out to a staggering £1,000 ($160,000) per pirate. The estimated amount of gold and jewels totaled £600,000 ($96,000,000). The pirates were rich. But aware they were being aggressively hunted, they were unable to come to any mutual agreement on their next action. The majority voted to disband and disperse.

Avery sold the *Fancy* and purchased a sloop. By now, a combined reward between the English government and the East India Company was posted offering £1,000 ($160,000) for each individual who had participated in the attack, seizure of goods, tortures, and killings.

Changing his name to Captain Bridgman, Avery cruised the sloop up the North American coastline, surreptitiously dropping men off in small numbers to avoid suspicion. His last mate disembarked in Boston. Avery then vanished into thin air, never to be heard from again.

> **Treasure Chest**
>
> Stories abound regarding the fate of Avery. No one truly knows how he ended his days. His exploits and great escape fueled imaginations and most likely inspired men with no real future to take up the pirate trade.

Blame It on Avery

With colonial governors themselves deeply involved in the pirate trade for their own gain, it isn't surprising that Governor Benjamin Fletcher of New York was also in collusion.

Freely handing out licenses—and often under false pretenses—Fletcher knew that the licensed seafarers were attacking fleets in the Red Sea and India for their rich cargoes. To stem the corruption in New York, and as an example to others, Fletcher was removed from office. Richard Coote, the earl of Bellomont, was appointed the new governor of New York and New England. He was just as corrupt, if not more so, than Fletcher.

Avery's Attack Negatively Impacts the Efforts of Captain Kidd

As you'll see in a moment, the downfall of the famous Captain William Kidd was a direct result of the East India Company's desire to take advantage of the great trading wealth of India. Attempting for years to establish trading posts throughout the grand mogul's kingdom, negotiations were constantly stalled by the many pirate attacks within the mogul's domain. And in 1695, when Avery, financed by a merchant syndicate from New York, captured the grand mogul's personal ship, that was the last straw.

London's Lords Try to Sooth Feelings

Meeting with King William III, members of the House of Lords needed to map out a plan that would eradicate pirates, or at least placate the grand mogul. The Admiralty admitted there were not enough ships available. William suggested they consider a private venture. The men understood his meaning. A private syndicate of noblemen would finance the enterprise that would not only capture pirates, but also provide a profit to investors. That the items were stolen from someone else was not a consideration.

Nothing Up Our Sleeve

Six of the king's closet ministers were invited to join the syndicate. They included Charles Montague, first earl of Halifax, the chancellor of the Exchequer (later to become founder of the Bank of England); Charles Talbot, first duke of Shrewsbury, the secretary of state; Lord John Somers, lord keeper of the great seal; Edward Russell, first earl of Orford and at the time admiral of the fleet and treasurer of the navy. Also among the group was the new governor of New York, Richard Coote, earl of Bellomont. Now they had to find the right captain for the venture. Colonel Robert Livingston was in London attempting to get in the good graces of Bellomont. Upon hearing he was searching for a captain, Livingston offered his assistance, for he knew Captain William Kidd was in London.

The Right Place, the Wrong Time

At 50 years old, Captain Kidd owned a small fleet of trading vessels anchored in New York. Married and with a new baby girl, he was semi-retired. He was called to London that summer as a witness in a fraud investigation. Naturally curious to meet the new governor, Kidd agreed to see Bellomont. The latter approached Kidd about the expedition. Kidd didn't like the scheme or the hints that powerful men were silent partners. He didn't need the money and he didn't desire to embark on such a long voyage. Turning down the offer, Kidd quickly realized he had been trapped. Bellomont openly threatened that it would be unwise for a New York merchant to cross the governor of his home state.

Political Pirates Force Kidd to Sign Articles

When Kidd read the contract, he was appalled. The rules of agreement stated that Bellomont and his unnamed partners would put up 80 percent of the venture. Kidd and Colonel Livingston, who was now a partner in the syndicate, would supply the other 20 percent, but only receive a 15 percent profit. Bellomont would receive 60 percent, and Kidd's crew a mere 25 percent, not the standard 50 percent privateering cut.

The governor even had the audacity to ask Kidd to try to lower the crew's profit margin. Adding insult to injury, Kidd had to put up a bond of £20,000 ($3,200,000) to assure Bellomont would get his initial investment back if the venture failed.

There were in fact two commissions: France and England were again at war; consequently, Kidd's commission granted him legal authority to seize anything belonging to the king of France or his subjects. The other commission granted authority to seize any pirate vessels anywhere found. The governor was only too eager to stamp the commissions with the Great Seal of England.

Kidd didn't have to guess who was one of the silent partners.

His ship, *Adventure Galley*, was hastily built and armed with 30 guns. Edmund Harrison, director of the East India Company, assisted in selecting his crew. Harrison rejected any man who was of Scottish or American birth. He feared they would too easily turn pirate as soon as they set sail.

The ship was barely beyond English waters when the Royal Navy ship HMS *Duchess* pulled alongside and kidnapped Kidd's men through the Defense of the Realm Act. This law permitted the Royal Navy to impress men while they were at sea. Even the commission papers with the king's seal couldn't dissuade the *Duchess*'s captain from impressing his men. This forced Kidd to return to England. He was eventually required to replace the number of men the *Duchess* had kidnapped off the *Adventure Galley*. He did so with inferior crewmen.

Back in New York, Kidd had to scour the dregs of the wharfs to find an additional 150 men to round out his crew.

The Hangman's Noose

When the sails of a Dutch ship were sighted, William Moore—a seaman who had begun to voice dissent because of his overzealous eagerness to attack—threatened mutiny. Because the Netherlands was not an enemy of England, Kidd could not legally capture the ship. Convinced his crew would overpower him, Kidd's survival instincts took over. Grabbing the ship's wooden bucket, he smashed it against Moore's head. The mutiny was quashed. Moore died the following morning.

Captain William Kidd kills William Moore.

(Nineteenth-century engraving, artist unknown)

A Prize at Last

Three weeks after Moore's death, Kidd captured a French ship, the *Rouparelle*. He posted some of his men aboard her, and the little fleet sailed to Madagascar. Though his commission papers clearly stated that all treasure be sent to Boston, Kidd immediately shared out the booty with his men (knowing full well that after so much time elapsed without capturing a prize, they would never have arrived in Boston).

Kidd's Last Bit of Adventure, and Freedom

In early 1698—while operating out of sight of the *Adventure Galley*—the *Rouparelle* captured two ships. Neither was French. Nor were they pirate vessels. Technically Kidd's crew devolved from privateer to pirate. Not that it would matter at his forthcoming trial, but it was never proven Kidd himself was involved in those specific attacks and seizures.

Kidd spotted his big prize off Cochin in the East Indies. The *Quedagh Merchant* was a huge 500-ton ship with only 10 guns carrying more than £45,000 pounds ($7,200,000) of treasure. The ship itself was worth the cost of the entire voyage, and the blunt in her hold was enough to pay back everyone with a profit.

A Mutiny Spoils Everything

Knowing they did not have the firepower to counter the *Adventure Galley*'s 30 guns, the ship's master surrendered and produced her sailing papers. Kidd, to his dying day, maintained that they included French *passes*. With that proof, all the cargo was considered French property. The vessel was legally his prize. Capturing the *Quedagh Merchant* was fortuitous because the *Adventure Galley* was in such bad condition it almost floundered before they reached Madagascar.

Unfortunately for Kidd, he also met a pirate captain by the name of Culliford. What happened then would became a debatable issue during Kidd's trial. What is not disputed is the fact that on Madagascar the majority of Kidd's crew mutinied and attempted to kill him. They burned his journal and joined with Culliford.

> **Knowing the Ropes**
>
> **Passes** were safe-conduct documents issued to ships of neutral countries carrying cargo of warring nations. It assured their own countrymen would not erroneously seize the shipment.

Kidd was only able to save the *Quedagh Merchant* and some £30,000 ($4,800,000) he had carefully hidden. The ship and loyal members of the crew made it to Anguilla (a Leeward Island) in April 1699. When he sent for permission to acquire provisions, Kidd was shocked to learn he had been declared a pirate. A large naval force was scouring the sea for him. In a blanket pardon for pirates issued in 1698, it was specifically stated that Captain Kidd would *not* be pardoned.

Trusting a Business Partner Can Cost You Your Life

Kidd left the *Quedagh Merchant* with trusted friends and sailed to Long Island Sound to meet with his lawyer, James Emott. Kidd presented Emott with a letter for Bellomont. In it, Kidd explained everything, including his willingness to surrender in Boston if Bellomont would assure him a fair trial. Bellomont gave that assurance. He lied. Not completely without his wits, Kidd, en route, anchored off Gardiner's Island near Long Island. The island was a major stopping point for all illegal merchandise flowing into the area.

With his men's approval, Kidd buried some of the treasure from *Quedagh Merchant*. They didn't trust the outcome, and decided to use the booty as a bargaining chip. Before he embarked, Kidd showed John Gardiner where the treasure chests were buried, and Gardiner handed him a receipt.

The Noose Tightens

In the three years Kidd was at sea, the king's syndicate became a political nightmare. The opposition party, the Tories, uncovered the scheme. To satisfy the grand mogul, the East India Company publicly demanded Kidd's arrest and the return of the grand mogul's possessions. The king's ministers agreed that the only way to survive the scandal was to divert everyone's attention. Kidd became that diversion as he was publicly branded an "evil pirate."

Pirate or Privateer Is a Court Decision

Sent to London for trial, Kidd languished in jail for more than a year. On May 8, 1701, his trial began. Kidd was accused of two counts of murder and piracy. He wasn't allowed any legal representation. He conducted his own cross-examinations. The crew that went to Boston was also arrested. Their testimonies were dismissed because they themselves were prisoners. Their word could not be trusted. Pardons were issued to others after they testified to the atrocities Kidd allegedly performed as a pirate. During the entire trial, Kidd insisted he was no pirate. He seized the *Quedagh Merchant* because she carried French passes. When asked to produce the passes, Kidd could not. He continually maintained the Admiralty had taken all his papers. Despite numerous requests, his personal papers were never returned. When the judge questioned the Admiralty, the department always stalled for time. Captain Kidd never had a chance.

The murder charge was for the killing of William Moore. It was publicly known and an accepted fact that captains on naval and merchant vessels regularly beat or even killed crewmen to maintain discipline without any repercussions leveled against the captains. Therefore it came as quite a shock to Kidd when he was found guilty of murder. The charge carried a sentence of death.

On May 23, 1701, a huge crowd formed at Wapping on the Thames near Execution Dock clamoring for the death of the bloody pirate Captain Kidd. Still professing his innocence, the noose was placed around the doomed man's neck. When the trap door sprung, the rope snapped in two. Falling to the ground, Kidd was escorted back up the gallows. He had to experience the gruesome terror once again. The second time the trap sprung the rope held. As was the custom for pirate executions, his body was cut down and dumped in nearby backwater until the tidal muds washed over it three times. The corpse was then sent to Tilbury Point on the Thames and hung wrapped in chains in a *gibbet* for years.

> **Knowing the Ropes**
>
> **Gibbets** were metal cages hung from wooden gallows that held the body upright in full view along the water's edge. The corpse was completely covered with tar before being placed inside a gibbet, where it remained until it completely decomposed. The decomposition normally took years. It was used as a warning to other pirates and proof the government was protecting its citizens.

Three days after Kidd's execution, a special envoy was sent to the grand mogul of India informing him of Kidd's death. The grand mogul released his English prisoners and resumed trade negotiations with the East India Company.

A naval ship sailed to Anguilla to take possession of the *Quedagh Merchant*. It had vanished. The Gardiner's Island treasure was ordered by Governor Bellomont to be dug up and sent to him. John Gardiner obliged, but it has been implied he kept a portion for himself. The confiscated treasure was not returned to the Grand Mogul. Bellomont died a few months before Kidd's execution.

In 1911, Ralph D. Paine, an American historian going through the files in the Public Records Office in London, found the French passes.

Captain Kidd's body hanging from the gibbet.

(The Pirates' Own Book, *Charles Ellms, 1837)*

Explorers and Buccaneers

Ironically, the paths of three keen literate observers of man and nature crossed during a daring buccaneer raid across the Isthmus of Darien aimed at the treasure cities of El Real de Santa Maria, then Panama.

In 1680, a veritable who's who of buccaneers gathered and proposed a daring raid that began with 9 ships and 477 buccaneers. The raid and its aftermath included captains Bartholomew Sharp, Peter Harris, Richard Sawkins, John Cook, Robert Alleston (Allison), John Coxon, Edward Davis, John Watling, and Charles Swan; Mr. Jobson (a former divinity student); William Dampier (buccaneer, navigator, and writer); Basil Ringrose (buccaneer and writer); and Lionel Wafer (buccaneer, surgeon, scientist, and writer).

Upon reaching the Gulf of Darien with the help of Indian guides, the pirates hiked inland for days. The men arrived at Santa Maria to find themselves three days late. The 300 pounds of gold dust stored in the treasure house had been shipped to Panama. They continued to Panama to find their escape blocked by a Spanish fleet.

Undeterred, 5 canoes filled with the surviving 68 pirates attacked the 5 Spanish war-ships and 3 barques (small warships). After a three-hour bloody battle, the buccaneers captured the Spanish flagship and escaped to the open sea.

The published journals of Dampier, Wafer, and Ringrose reflect this adventure along with many other escapades and provide us with insights into buccaneering ways, the people they met and fought alongside, and the regions they traveled.

William Dampier

William Dampier is better known for circum-navigating the globe three times and publishing his observations than he is for piracy. In 1679, he signed on the account with Captain Bar-tholomew Sharp. It was on this trip to the Province of Darien that he seriously began recording his observations. He kept his journal dry by storing it in a "jointe of Bambo well stopt with wax at the two end." In 1697, the first of his many volumes, *A New Voyage Around the World*, was published.

> **Treasure Chest**
>
> William Dampier's detailed descriptions of the wonders he observed while traveling opened new vistas for many European readers. He was the first to describe in great detail a typhoon and its devastating effects.

Basil Ringrose

Basil Ringrose joined Bartholomew Sharp as a runaway indentured servant. After the raid on Santa Maria and Panama, he remained with Sharp for the next 18 months, sailing the western coast of South America sacking cities and seizing ships. He re-turned to England in 1681. His account, *The Dangerous Voyage and Bold Attempts of Captain Bartholomew Sharp and Others Performed Upon the Coast of the South Sea for the Space of Two Years*, was published as the second volume of Alexander Exquemelin's book. In 1684, Ringrose returned to the West Indies and resumed his pirating ways under Captain Charles Swan. Ringrose was killed in 1686 during an attack on the city of Santiago.

Lionel Wafer

In 1679, Lionel Wafer sailed from England to Jamaica as a surgeon's assistant. Wafer deserted and joined Captain Edward Cook's crew as surgeon. And so began his bucca-neering career. In 1690, Wafer settled in London. His book, *New Voyage and Description of the Isthmus of Panama*, was published nine years later. Scientists still study his observations concerning the environment and customs of the native Kuna (Cuna) Indian tribe of Darien, with whom Wafer lived for a time.

The Least You Need to Know

- When the wealth along the West Indies diminished, pirates turned their attention to the East. India, Africa, and the Red Sea regions became their prime targets.

- With the restrictive navigational laws in effect, the American colonies turned to pirates for the majority of their import and export needs.

- Thomas Tew turned from a career of privateering to piracy when the lure of eastern riches became too strong for him to ignore.

- Henry Avery captured the great ship of the grand mogul of India. The action, though romanticized in a popular play, had dire political and economic ramifications for England.

- William Kidd reluctantly sailed on his last privateering voyage with the English monarch and members of Parliament as his secret backers. He subsequently became a political pawn and a scapegoat for the monarchy.

- Pirates all, William Dampier, Basil Ringrose, and Lionel Wafer are best known for the detailed journals of their circumnavigational voyages.

Chapter 15

Pirate-Friendly Cities and Islands

In This Chapter

- ◆ Safety in paradise
- ◆ Boozing and betting
- ◆ Strutting their stuff
- ◆ Countries regulate what people wear
- ◆ Calculating coinage

Safe-haven cities, towns, and even entire islands existed in which pirates could safely stroll without fear of being stopped, questioned, or arrested by military or law-enforcement officials. Such safe havens might be found anywhere in the world. Each was very different in character than the other—from cities comprised of honest citizenry who were forced to endure the raucous behavior of pirates each time a ship docked, to havens comprised solely of individuals awaiting the sight of a black flag looming on the horizon. And there, in all these varied havens, local merchants welcomed the selling and trading opportunities created by the existence of pirates who supported their fragile economy.

No matter where pirates landed, the scene was almost always the same: a rowdy group of men disembarking, eager to lighten their load of coins and jewels, and then to get their fill of liquor and women.

The Nefarious Port Royal

Port Royal had no running water, was built on a filled sandy cay that yielded no crops, and required basic supplies shipped in daily. Yet in its heyday—the 1680s—more than 2,000 buildings and 8,000 inhabitants were jammed onto this strip of Jamaican coastline.

The city was built at the entrance to a natural harbor that easily accommodated 500 ships. Fort Charles, Fort James, and Fort Carlisle guarded the harbor entrance. Located in the center of the Caribbean, Jamaica was the ideal island for anyone who wanted to make money. First settled by the Spanish and then seized in 1655 by the English, Jamaica needed a strong naval force to protect the island against possible invasion. The solution was simple. The English invited the Spanish-hating buccaneers living on Tortuga to settle in Port Royal. In return, the citizens gladly accommodated their every need. It was a win/win situation. Port Royal became a free port, the center for trading Spanish plunder. Any and every type of merchant set up a stand or opened a store, and every cutthroat, adventurer, and lowlife followed. And they all had the run of the town.

The wharfs were busy with men loading or unloading cargo. Revenue from contraband and piracy sustained the economy. Not only did buccaneers and pirates come, but Spanish colonists unable to purchase basic supplies from Spain shopped, too. Merchants purchased items from expeditions for low sums and resold them at exorbitant prices to England, the American colonies, or back to the Spanish. Merchants of Port Royal were known to be as dishonest as the men with whom they dealt.

Not Your Typical Island Day

The city had its own unique heartbeat. Each morning, ferries brought fresh water into the city from the Rio Cobre (Copper River) six miles away. Separate markets for fish, meat, and vegetables opened for servants and slaves to begin shopping. Retail stalls and shops opened for business. Wealthy merchants built homes some four stories high with bricks imported from England. Mornings would find them arriving at the customs house to check on cargoes.

For those just stumbling out of taverns and brothels, the day was ending. Some of the 200 doctors in town, mostly quacks, were busy patching up the men wounded from fights and duels. More men died in the city from drunken encounters than in sea battles or storms.

Prisoners arrested for disorderly conduct were brought before the magistrate. There were two prisons, Marshallsea for men and Bridewell for women. The severity of a person's punishment hinged on the mood of the magistrate on that day. Punishment was either a whipping or a dunking in the public square. Both events were always well attended.

An Entire City Stops

One signal shot from Fort Charles, and Port Royal virtually shut down. Businesses closed, court trials were suspended, and the majority of its population converged on the wharf. Sails of the returning buccaneer fleet soon came into view. Excitement heightened as the flagship anchor dropped and the gangplank spread. Aboard ship the crew waited on deck, where all the plunder was stacked. Government officials boarded the ship first. They immediately took one tenth of the entire treasure, the official fee for granting the letter of marque.

After the crew disembarked, the expedition's creditors boarded and carefully watched the unloading of cargo. The ship's quartermaster auctioned off the goods at the wharf auction blocks. Between 1671 and 1679, more than 12,000 slaves were sold from those blocks. After paying off his creditors from the sale, the captain shared out the additional blunt with his crew. Then it was time to eat, get rowdy and seriously drunk, and find a woman. The business census of the day registered that one out of every four buildings in the city specifically catered to lascivious pleasures. John Starr, owner of the largest brothel in Port Royal, had 23 ladies working for him.

> **Treasure Chest**
>
> In one month, July 1661, the Council of Jamaica granted licenses to more than 40 new taverns, grog shops, and punch houses. Upon hearing this news, King Charles proclaimed a royal monopoly on the sale of liquor within the city. The revenue collected helped fortify the city battlements.

Religious Worship?

As wanton as was its reputation, the city's greatest point of pride was the impressive St. Paul's Church, financed by Sir Henry Morgan. Surprisingly, religious tolerance was observed. Along with the Church of England, there was a Presbyterian church, a

Jewish synagogue, a Roman Catholic chapel, and a Quaker meeting house. The few good and honest citizens who lived on the island were horrified by the lawlessness, but they could do nothing about it. Reverend John Taylor called Port Royal "the most wicked and sinful city in the world." A law passed in 1682 imposed a fine on any person caught drinking or gambling on the Sabbath. It was roundly ignored, and Port Royal's coffers grew.

The End of Boom Town

It happened as it always does, without warning. Between 11:00 A.M. and noon on June 7, 1692, the first of three consecutive earthquakes struck Port Royal. A devastating tidal wave washed through seconds after the third quake. Two thousand people died in the city, thousands more across the island. Only 10 acres of the city remained. Three fourths of the city literally sank beneath the tide. Forts James and Carlisle were below water, but most of Fort Charles remained intact. Port Royal never recovered, and buccaneers and pirates who survived relocated to other islands.

A Pirate's Paradise

By contrast, the island of New Providence (Nassau) had everything: fresh water, plentiful food, and a dense forest off the beaches populated by wild game. The natural harbor was ideal for seamen's needs. The waters were deep enough for the ships pirates favored, yet far too shallow for heavy men-o-war. The harbor was large enough to accommodate upward of 500 vessels, and it was ideal for careening a ship. The mouth of the harbor had two inlets created by a small island outcrop. The inlets ensured a single government ship could trap no vessel. Natural coral hills curved along the harbor providing sentries with boundless views of the horizon. White sandy beaches surrounded the island perimeter. Situated off the Florida channel, and directly in line with the sailing routes from the Spanish Main and Caribbean as well as North America and Europe, what more could a pirate hope for? Moreover, when Captain Henry Jennings and his crew first landed in the early 1700s, all that remained of previous colonial settlements were ruins and wild goats.

An Island Free-for-All

After the treaty in 1670, the increase in American colonial contraband, and the end of the War of the Spanish Succession (discussed in Chapter 16), the number of pirates preying on ships reached their greatest number. These cutthroats attacked ships of all nations. Hunted by all, a safe haven was needed. Word traveled fast, and other pirates discovered New Providence.

Tent City with a View

By 1715, the island was a pirate shantytown, occupied by more than 3,000 people. The permanent residents who greeted ships were traders, tavern owners, prostitutes, and common-law wives, accounting for roughly one third of the constantly shifting population. Shelters constructed along the beaches were primarily tents made from tattered sails, discarded oars, or broken spars. The only permanently constructed buildings were huts made of driftwood with palm-frond roofs. Empty liquor barrels served as tables. Narrow walkways separated the hundreds of tents scattered haphazardly along the sand. Discarded refuse littered the once-pristine sand or was thrown into the harbor. Sanitation was nonexistent. A stiff breeze offshore sent the island's stench of rotting garbage, filthy humans, and sour booze miles out to sea. Ship crews smelled the island before it was sighted. Here they boozed, gambled, whored, and bartered stolen items with no fear of consequence.

> **Dead Men's Tales**
>
> When a pirate slept he did not dream that he had died and gone to heaven, he dreamed that he had once again returned to New Providence.
>
> —Anonymous

Preserving the Life of Their Ship

If a vessel was severely damaged—which was a strong possibility based on a number of factors—pirates were forced to repair it on any safe island, be it inhabited or not. Tropical heat and water forced the wood seams to open, allowing water to seep into the hull. Barnacles and seaweed grew on the bottom. If not routinely scraped off, the wood would rot. The biggest plague for a ship sailing in the warm Caribbean Sea was the dreaded teredo worms that bore holes through wooden planks below the waterline. All these factors not only damaged a ship, but also actually slowed her speed and maneuverability.

The ship's carpenter directed the careening operation. Ideally, it was done three to six times a year. After scraping or replacing rotted wooden planks, the crew added several layers of coating. A heated mixture of sulfur, tallow, and tar was spread over the entire hull and when it cooled offered a hard-coat protection.

Careening a ship.

(A General History of
Pyrates, *Captain Charles
Johnson, 1724)*

The Bubble of New Providence Bursts

Pirate attacks became so frequent they dramatically impinged on the economics of not only Spain, but also England, her North American colonies, and the Dutch and French islands. England had had enough. After trying to settle the matter peacefully with little success (as you'll see in Chapter 17) in 1718, the crown sent Captain Woodes Rogers to New Providence to end piracy. By the time he sailed back to England, not a pirate remained on New Providence.

A Pirate Kingdom All Our Own

To the dissatisfaction of many pirates, looting the Spanish Main for years left little treasure. In great numbers, they set their course to the Indian Ocean and Red Sea for the wealth contained there. Indian pirates already plagued the region. Pirates from every Western country increased the danger. In the 1690s, a journey from the Red Sea to European and American ports involved a long and hazardous trip, and only the bravest attempted the journey. Safe bases in the area were required. Perim Island or Bab's Cay at the entrance to the Red Sea was the first choice. A good location, its one drawback was that it had no fresh water. Madagascar and its surrounding islets were perfect. It was a great distance to India's rich Malabar Coast or the Red Sea, but like New Providence, Madagascar provided everything a pirate could possibly need—no Europeans lived on the islands, and the natives were friendly. With this unabashed freedom from governmental interference, Madagascar reached its piratical heyday between 1695 and 1699.

Baldridge's Trading Post and Sanctuary

A dispute in 1685 resulting in murder caused Adam Baldridge to flee Jamaica. He landed on the small islet of St. Mary's (Ile Sainte Marie). Realizing it had the best defendable harbor in the Madagascar island chain, Baldridge turned entrepreneur. Building a mansion in 1691 that could be seen far offshore, he built huge warehouses and a 40-cannon battery to protect against rival pirates or warships of the East India Company. He traded with anyone and everyone.

Baldridge was an astute businessman, and he quickly saw the value in a partnership with Frederick Philipse, an international trader from New York. Pirates and colonial privateers flocked to St. Mary's to buy and sell. Pirates had to depend on Baldridge for supplies and provisions. It cost them dearly, but they paid. A bottle of rum—its normal price 1 shilling (12 pennies)—sold on the island for more than 3 pounds sterling (13.5 pieces-of-eight, 81 shillings, or 972 pennies). There was a constant stream of ships and men along the island's harbor and towns. St. Mary's harbored 500 to 1,500 men. Like Hispaniola before her, St. Mary's was the new base to outfit a ship going on the account.

A Pirate King

Taking their cue from Baldridge, other pirates settled on the smaller islets of Madagascar. Setting themselves up as kings on islets such as St. Augustine, Diego Suarez, Port Dauphin, and Mathelage, they lived the charmed lives of men in possession of everything anyone might ever dream of. Pirates housed harems of local beauties.

Most nonadventurous businessmen like Baldridge lived easy lives. They traded with merchants when necessary, and they no longer risked their lives at sea. John Pantain, briefly mentioned in ship logs, set himself up as king of Ranten Bay. Then, like so many others, he drifted into obscurity. Though a paradise for many, St. Mary's and Madagascar were unlucky, too. A number of men, penniless from nights of carousing and with no prospects of any ship in sight, lived a beggar's life or starved.

St. Malo

What was unique about the French port of St. Malo, their enclave for corsairs, was the fact that at low tide it was a city at the tip of the connecting land mass. At high tide, the waters cut it off from the peninsula, creating an island accessible only by boat. The English knew St. Malo as "that nest of wasps."

In 1693, desperate to rid themselves of the French corsairs, the Royal Navy built a "bomb ship" filled with barrels of gunpowder, incendiary bombs, and missiles. Measuring 85 feet from bow to stern, she sat high in the water so that the English fleet could sail her close to the city walls. But on the night of the attack—unbeknownst to the English sailors—their bomb ship hit a rock. Water began seeping into the hull, dampening the gunpowder. When the ship was ignited, it went off like a firecracker, not a bomb. The result was a single casualty, a cat.

The corsairs on St. Malo continued to be a force until the end of the eighteenth century. The corsairs of St. Malo were so protected and wealthy they loaned money to the French monarchy.

A Pirate's R & R

Three things were foremost on the minds of most pirates when they came ashore, anywhere: first, to fill their stomachs with food; second, to get so drunk they wouldn't be able to tell the floor from the ceiling; and, third, to find women.

Punch houses, grog shops, taverns, and alehouse proprietors were all happy to oblige. Hot vittles and fresh insect-free bread were in great demand. Men wanted their hot "belly timber" as highly spiced as possible for flavor. As long as it didn't taste like ship's fare, they'd eat whatever the shop owners had on hand. When it came to beverages, the pirate was even less demanding. Served hot or cold, the drink just needed to put him into a drunken stupor.

Pirates consumed a wide variety of concoctions. Straight rum of the day was called "kill-devil"; it was so potent many who drank it didn't survive the alcohol poisoning. Notorious throughout the West Indies, the drinks served in English colonies were mentioned in official government dispatches. A five-ingredient mixture of rum, water, sugar, lemon or

Dead Men's Tales

The Spaniards wonder much at the sickness of our people, until they knew of the strength of their drinks, but then they wondered more that they were not all dead.

—Sir Thomas Modyford, *Calendar of State Papers, 1661–1668*

lime, and sweet spices, punch or poonch was named for the land of five rivers, the Indian region of Punjab, where the drink was first encountered. Another popular—and often lethal—drink was wormwood wine. Innocuous as a brewed tea, wormwood was first used in Europe to heal stomach ailments. However, mixing wormwood leaves with alcohol released thujone, a hallucinogen that was part of the same group of active ingredients found in cannabis. It drove many who drank it insane.

Liquor transported by ship was ported in wide, squat, glass containers called onion bottles. The shape of the bottles reminded one of large onions. This design, with a wider bottom than conventional liquor bottles, made them less likely to tip over and break during a rocky sea voyage.

Onion bottles and coins.

(Photo: William Perlis)

The Games Men Play

Gambling and games of chance were the natural play after a full stomach and a night of drinking, particularly if no women were around. In addition to the games they played aboard ship (see Chapter 11), a few more complicated board games were played on land. Among the more popular were tables (a gambling form of backgammon), draughts (similar to checkers), shove ha'penny, shut the box, and noddy (a precursor to cribbage).

A Good Smoke

Smoking tobacco was a luxury done mainly ashore. With the uncertainty of wind and wave, tobacco aboard ship was chewed unless one owned a covered pipe. Clay pipes were the most commonly smoked. They were available in different stem lengths. The longest pipe stem was a 14-inch pipe called the "churchwarden." Clay pipes had one drawback: the bowl had to cool after each smoke. Regulars kept a number of pipes at their favorite punch house for just that reason. If a new patron entered the establishment, and he owned only one pipe, the proprietor would happily rent him a pipe per smoke or a few pipes for a set rate. After a rented pipe was returned, the used stem was snipped off. The pipe would then be rented again as new. By the 1750s, clay bowls with reed stems came into wide use. These pipes allowed a man the luxury of smoking one pipe for an entire evening. At the excavation of Port Royal, clay pipes from 66 different manufacturers were unearthed.

Tobacco pipes and tankards.

(Photo: William Perlis)

A Good Woman, a Good Time, and Soon Broke

Women were everywhere and eager to help men part with their money for services rendered, even if she was not working with an established brothel. A man could lose his entire share of blunt in a night of drinking, gambling, and whoring. Once sober, he'd have to go back on the account to line his pockets again.

Polly Want a Parrot?

Colorful birds of all species were prized items brought to every port. Parrots became the rage when it was discovered they could mimic speech. Small monkeys were considered exotic curiosities. So that they would survive long sea voyages, these animals were housed in large wide-barred cages with room for them to move about. Animals were sold at exorbitant prices affordable only by the extremely wealthy. Merchant seamen might own a monkey or a parrot if the ship's captain would allow it aboard.

Pirate Yarns

Pirates didn't keep parrots or monkeys as pets. True, they were seen carried on their shoulders around town, but only to advertise they were for sale.

A Very Serious Dress Code

Pirates delighted in mocking the laws of their countries and members of high society: what better slight against members of the social and political elite than dressing up as wealthy landowners and aristocratic men of property?

Sumptuary Laws

From the early fourteenth century, most European countries—particularly England and France—enacted and actively enforced sumptuary laws. Simply put, sumptuary laws were a legal means by which the ruling classes could separate themselves from commoners by regulating what the latter could wear, drink, and in some cases, even where they could live.

In England, during the reigns of King Henry VIII and Elizabeth I, the laws were exceedingly tight, separating the varying stratas of nobility and sex. Stiff monetary penalties to imprisonment in the stocks awaited any man or woman who dared to thumb their nose at the sumptuary laws.

The Fabric Ban

In France during the reign of Louis XIV (1634–1715), the importation of costly fabric was not permitted. The expression *you can tell the man by the cut of his coat, or lack thereof,* summed up the sumptuary law. One's class and social standing were immediately apparent by what a person wore. Clergymen advanced this so-called "God-given" theory by preaching that it was "heresy" to rise above one's social class in dress or living conditions. Some of the items prohibited to commoners included fabrics (silk, satin, velvet, brocade, grosgrain, taffeta, damask, lace, any gold- or silver-threaded cloth or lace, foreign wool); colors (gold, silver, purple, scarlet); adornment (pearls, gold, silver, earrings, necklaces, bracelets, gemstones); and furs (mink, sable, fox).

Dressing Up to Go to Town

Pirates did not always choose coin, gems, or weapons as booty. Clothing was in high demand. After the shares had been divided, the "auction at the mast" began. The quartermaster announced a time, and those interested gathered at the mainmast. Elaborate clothes were high-bid items, their prices rapidly escalating with fierce bidding and friendly goading from mates. Money from the auction went into the ship's common stock for supplies to be purchased at friendly ports.

Aboard ship, with few exceptions, pirates wore practical clothing. Finery came out of the sea chest after the ship docked. "Dressing up" to go into town was no different in those days than it is today. The attire might have included a shirt of fine linen, cotton, or silk with handmade lace cascading off the cuffs. White cotton or wool stockings rolled above the knee would have been held in place with ribbon or garter, and tight-weaved woolen, silk, or satin breeches would have buttoned below the knees. A heavily brocaded surcoat with long wide cuffs turned up to the elbows and a line of stamped brass buttons would have completed the suit. This was worn over a thigh-length waistcoat of intricate design or solid color, this, too, made of fine satin or brocade. The look was then topped off with a fine-linen neckstock or layered lace jabot in white. A wide-brimmed, cocked or tricorne hat with bright colorful bird plumage and broaches completed the outfit.

Dressing in this manner was premeditated. A buccaneer or pirate wanted to walk through town in full view of the upright citizens knowing they would be horrified by his appearance. Realizing they could do nothing to him only added to the pirate's amusement. More important, a pirate's dress was a statement of just how successful he was at his trade. It added to his reputation. And it was an advertisement to the towns-women that he was successful and that he had money to spend on himself and on anyone who cared to spend time with him.

Ashore, an earring was not the only item of jewelry a pirate was likely to wear. The Spanish along the Main fashioned much of their wealth into portable jewelry. The tax on jewelry entering Spain was far less than on ingots, loose gems, or coins. Yards of gold chain, jewel-encrusted pendants, rings, bracelets, and earrings crated and intended for Spain ended up in pirate hands. Some pieces that caught a man's fancy were kept and worn. The remainder, he spent.

A pirate in fancy finery.

(Photo: William Perlis)

Dressed to Kill and Fully Loaded

Dressing as a gentleman didn't mean the pirate acted like one. In isolated safe-haven cities, pirates strolled freely, haughtily, and were almost always armed. Drunken brawls and duels to the death were nightly occurrences. Fancy baldrics and flashy swords worn ashore might convince lesser men to keep their distance.

Whether in a pocket, tied to his leg, tucked in a boot, or shoved into a belt, sash, or hat brim, at least one—most likely two—knives were hidden on a pirate's person. By the 1700s, a small pocket pistol, the forerunner of the derringer, was carried.

Fancy baldric (top) and box lock pocket pistol (bottom).

(Photos: William Perlis)

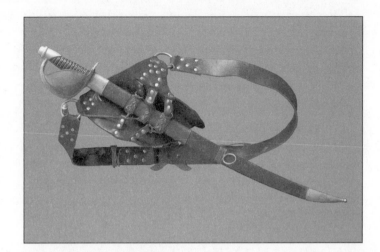

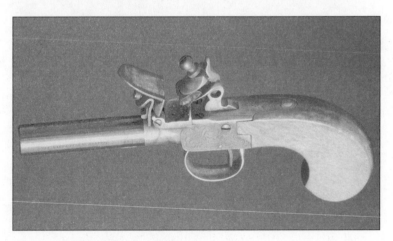

The International Currency Exchange

Merchants had to be math whizzes or have a gram weight scale behind their counter. Many did keep scales, especially in Port Royal. Why? Coinage value was based on gram weight and purity of the gold and silver. With the amount of treasure flowing throughout pirate havens, currencies from every country traded hands. The purchasing power of this money was considered 6 to 10 times greater than the actual currency amount. The U.S. modern dollar amount stated here appears to be a significant amount, when one sees that one piece-of-eight has the buying power of $30, until yearly incomes are considered.

Numerous denominations were minted in every country in the world. To make it as easy as possible to understand, only the English and Spanish currency of the 1700s is explained here. They are today known as the English shilling, penny (pence), ha'penny, and farthing.

English currency began with a coin denomination—valued even less than a penny—called a farthing. Two brass farthings were the equivalent of a copper half-penny or ha'penny. It took four farthings, or two half-pennies, to make a copper penny, also known as a pence (today worth 67 cents). The 12 pennies added up to 1 silver shilling, worth roughly $8. And 20 shillings equaled one pound sterling (silver), or $160. The pound sterling wasn't currency at the time, but a form of accounting equal to approximately four and a half pieces-of-eight.

Minimum Wages

Depending on the job, an unskilled laborer was paid 6 to 12 shillings a week. An average seaman received a monthly wage of 2 pieces-of-eight or 12 shillings. What is most important to understand is that manufactured goods were more expensive in those days. Machined items such as clothing didn't exist; therefore clothes were charged based on the materials and the labor required to produce them. For nonfarmers, food could cost up to half one's daily pay. Disposable income for a friendly drink cost a man dearly: a shilling for a bottle of rum, two shillings for a cheap bottle of wine. A watered-down pint of cheap wine cost a man one or two pennies, and a quart of ale set him back a penny. An average person had to shell out two-and-a-half weeks' wages to purchase a pound of tea. Barter for most was a significant means of acquiring essential items. With the wealth one successful pirate expedition could provide a man, it is easy to see why so many took to piracy.

> **Treasure Chest**
>
> A scam tried in many taverns throughout the world was called a "blackdog." One took a copper ha'penny and whitewashed the coin. In the dim candlelight, the ha'penny would often be accepted as a shilling.

Gold Doubloons and Pieces-of-Eight

Gold coins were not minted in cities along the Spanish Main. All gold was smelted into ingots and sent to the treasury in Seville. There, the gold was remelted and uniformly minted. The gold coin denomination was the escudo. The famous gold doubloon in today's changing foreign exchange market is worth $120. It weighed 27 grams and was 92 percent pure gold, or 22 carat gold. Gold doubloons were not commonly circulated in the Caribbean. Few people were that wealthy. The more common coinage was silver coins.

The silver piece-of-eight (or piece-o-eight) was originally minted in Spain as the eight reales or reals. Later it was renamed the *peso de ocho reales*, or the peso. The silver in a piece-of-eight had the same weight and purity as a gold doubloon. It was therefore a fairly uniform rounded shape. Minted in Spain, a Roman Catholic country, the back of the piece-of-eight was imprinted with the holy cross. When change was required, the design of the holy cross made it easier for people to cut the coin into evenly weighted two-, four-, or six-reale sections. Therefore, the piece-of-eight when cut into sections was worth the true silver gram weight of two reales each. The current market value of one piece-of-eight would be $30.

Uniform Measurements for Silver and Gold

After large veins of silver were discovered in Peru, it took too long for the Spanish treasury to receive the silver, mint the coins, and ship them back to the Main.

In 1572, the government sanctioned private contractors to produce the pieces-of-eight (eight-reale coins) for use in their colonies. To guarantee their continued purity, a government assayer inspected and placed his mark on every ingot poured.

The silver was melted and poured into long flat bars. Once checked by the assayer, captive Indians hammered the bars by hand into crude round bars. The ends of the bars were then sliced, creating coin blanks. The blank would be placed between two metal dies and hammered until the image was struck. The assayer then measured each coin, assuring consistent weight. If the hammered coin was over the silver weight, the edges were shaved until correct. Because it was the weight and not the thickness or shape of the coin that mattered, no two coins looked exactly alike. The colonial-minted eight reales or piece-of-eight was called a "cob." It was a shortened version of *cabo de barra*, meaning "end of bar." Each cob being so irregular, the sections broken off for change were called bits. With the irregular shapes, thieves found it easy to shave off additional bits of silver from a cob and then purchase items for less than their value.

Because the Spanish were mining such huge quantities of silver and gold, Spain's currency became the accepted international norm. To keep the world economic system on an even keel, all other European countries changed the weight of their coins to match that of Spain's.

> **Treasure Chest**
>
> The piece-of-eight was circulated in the American colonies and later the United States. The coin was worth one dollar and used as legal tender until demonetized in 1857. The expression *two bits' worth of change* referred to a quarter of a cob, or 25 cents.

The Least You Need to Know

- Whether a city or an island, pirates created safe bases of operation throughout the world. From these locations, they had easy access to all of the most heavily traveled shipping lanes.

- In a single night of excessive pleasures, a man could easily lose the entire share of treasure it had taken him months to acquire.

- Once ashore, many pirates dressed in gentlemanly attire. They enjoyed mocking polite society and the thumbing of their noses at the sumptuary laws while advertising their newly acquired wealth.

- Spain's currency—the fabled piece-of-eight—not only became the most widely circulated coin, but also the international monetary standard.

Chapter 16

War, Peace, and Pirates

In This Chapter

- ◆ The Piracy Act: court trials made easier
- ◆ A family feud starts a major war
- ◆ Peace breeds piracy
- ◆ A bold yet foolish plan
- ◆ Charles Vane and "Black Sam" Bellamy

The Pirate Round brought wealth to the colonies for merchants and government officials alike, inspiring ordinary men in the Americas to join piracy in the hopes of lining their own pockets.

With the increase in piracy, honest citizens pressured the English judiciary to take more a more aggressive stance against thievery on the open seas. Realizing they had to respond to the colonists' demands, the crown enacted a series of edicts to deal with increased pirate activities. The first was a pardon by King James I in 1687, which in the long run was not greatly honored. The second made it easier than it had been to prosecute and convict pirates.

In the eyes of many governments, the transition between buccaneers and privateers becoming pirates was significant. Once again, men who fought for their country during wartime were ceremoniously abandoned after peace was declared. These actions set into motion the biggest wave of piracy to engulf the world.

Miles Less Traveled for Trial: The Piracy Act

Bringing pirates to trial in London was becoming far too costly and time-consuming. Not only did the criminal have to be transported, but all witnesses were also required to appear. For that reason alone, many officials in the West Indies and England's North American colonies did not bother prosecuting those deemed to be minor offenders.

In 1699, the Piracy Act was created to change the system. Now officials in all parts of the British Empire had the authority to seize, prosecute, and execute pirates. This law did assist in greatly reducing the pirate population.

A King's Death Starts a Family Feud

During the late seventeenth century peace in European colonies was tenuous. Countries continued fighting, creating secret alliances and treaties, and fomenting open hostility until things reached a boiling point involving all of Western Europe.

The War of the Spanish Succession began as a localized dispute between Leopold I of Hapsburg (Germany) and King Louis XIV of France over who would be crowned the next Spanish king. King Charles II of Spain named Philip, duc d'Anjou, of France as his successor. Upon his death in 1700, Charles II was the last in the hereditary line of Spanish Hapsburgs. Leopold wasn't so willing to relinquish the Hapsburg family claim of Spain to France. England and the Dutch hated the idea of a combined Catholic French and Spanish throne.

Full-fledged war broke out in 1701 and waged for 13 long years. England, Portugal, Prussia, the American colonies, and Austria, with the Dutch and German principalities, were pitted against the combined forces of Spain and France.

Primarily a naval war fought in European waters, the West Indies, and the Spanish Main, vast numbers of men were needed to crew vessels. England emptied her prisons to provide seamen. Press gangs were once again dispatched in force, taking young boys along with men.

News of the war reached the West Indies in the summer of 1702. Pirates now had the opportunity to legally plunder as privateers. Once again gleefully refitting their ships, they prepared to cruise the Caribbean and West Indies for prey. Seasoned pirates in the West Indies, now owning letters of marque, attacked French and Spanish settlements and ships with impunity.

To England's amazement, few sailors or seamen answered the call to arms. As the war dragged on and casualties mounted, the crown was forced to grant huge concessions to attract private vessels to the effort.

> **Treasure Chest**
>
> The English Prize Act of 1708 withdrew the required one fifth share (20 percent) of all privateering plunder that went to the treasury. Guaranteed 100 percent of profits, merchants from both America and England began outfitting ships and contracting privateers. England's naval force swelled in numbers.

Sailors Need Not Apply

The Peace of Utrecht ended the War of the Spanish Succession with the signing of several treaties between 1713 and 1714 that ceded various territories among all the warring nations. Philip V of France was now king of Spain. Warships from every nation were ordered home. Naval ships were decommissioned, and privateers dispersed. For the first time in years, the common seaman was allowed to disembark his ship.

Fearing major desertion of their crews during the war, navies allowed only officers to disembark. When ships docked for provisions, liquor and prostitutes were brought on-board for the crew. Now with war's end, seamen were unceremoniously dumped ashore to fend for themselves. It was a repeat of the crisis that occurred after the defeat of the Armada. The Dutch were the only ones to see the potential danger in having unemployed men roaming the countryside. They kept their veteran seamen employed by creating and subsidizing herring-fishing fleets.

The Grant of Assiento

The Grant of Assiento in 1714 legally allowed the English Royal African Company to bring ivory and slaves to the settlements of the Spanish Main. The Portuguese and Dutch merchants sailed the entire world. Goods and raw materials from the American colonies were shipped to England. Pilgrim ships sailed to Mecca, and the convoys of

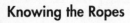

Knowing the Ropes

Craft guilds were the precursor to the modern trade union. To learn a skilled job such as printer or mason, a boy or man had to first apply and be accepted to apprentice to a master (expert). After a set number of years (different for each guild) learning the trade he would become a master and be able to earn a living.

the grand mogul cruised between the Red Sea and the Persian Gulf.

Craft Guilds

Craft guilds were unwilling to consider training a seaman. The years had not changed their attitude toward a man's ability to change his social standing or occupation. Having so many men clamoring for berths on merchant ships, captains were able to save money by cutting wages. Frustrated and angry, some 2,000 men went back to sea; this time as pirates. They felt they had nothing to lose and everything to gain.

A Fast-Growing Reputation

Not all pirate careers lasted decades. Some acquired instant fame and disappeared. Others were captured by naval and law-enforcement authorities soon after becoming pirates. Some sailed years before they were apprehended. But with each freed captive or a captain's log recounting a pirate story, the general public—for the first time—became aware of the proliferation of piracy and the pirates' deeds.

Unless recorded in trial records, little if anything is known concerning the origin of many of the famous pirates. As curious as we may be about their earlier life, many of the more colorful pirates are known only for their pirating personalities and their actual crimes.

A Respected Man

Captain Benjamin Hornigold (a.k.a. Hornygold) plied his way across the Main and West Indies from 1713 to 1719, first as a pirate and then as a pirate hunter. It is speculated he began as an English privateer during the war and later turned pirate. He also has the distinction of mentoring many famous pirates, as you will see throughout the next few chapters.

Wanting More Percentage of the Prize

In November 1703, a syndicate of Bostonians was given a letter of marque from colonial governor (of Massachusetts) Joseph Dudley for a privateering venture off the coast of Arcadia and Newfoundland to attack the French. One John Quelch was signed on to the *Charles* as quartermaster.

After the ship sailed out of Marblehead, Massachusetts, the crew mutinied, and locked the captain, one Daniel Plowman, in his cabin. Yearning for greater riches than they could find up north, the crew elected Quelch their new captain and sailed south to the West Indies. Somewhere along the journey they threw Plowman overboard. (Whether the man was dead or alive at the time has never been firmly established.) Sailing off the coast of Brazil, the *Charles* captured nine Portuguese vessels.

The seized booty was impressive, sharing out 100 pounds of gold dust, coins worth approximately £1,000 ($160,000), arms, ammunition, ship's provisions, a quantity of rum, and many bales of fine fabric.

What the crew did not know was that England and Portugal had signed a peace treaty on May 16, 1703. Notwithstanding the fact that they had murdered their captain, they might have bluffed their way past that charge, but they had in fact attacked their country's ally. They could no longer claim they were privateers. They were pirates.

The *Charles* sailed back to Marblehead, where her arrival was noted less than a year after her departure and drew great suspicion. The crew began dispersing throughout Massachusetts and Rhode Island. Quelch fabricated a story of finding a wreck in the Indies, though residents of Marblehead knew the ship was bound originally northward.

Treasure Chest

The Boston-News Letter, the first newspaper published in the providence of the Massachusetts Bay area, was only on its fifth printing when the *Charles* returned in 1704. The paper announced her arrival in the May 15–22 issue, listing Quelch as captain and the ship's arrival from "New Spain." The newspaper published every ship arrival and departure from the colony. As piracy grew bolder in the mid 1700s, the newspaper printed the names of men who departed on legitimate vessels and were forced mid-journey to join pirate crews. Other colonial newspapers began the same practice. The "forced" notice was used in court as evidence of innocence if the pirate vessel was apprehended.

Going After What's Theirs

Reading of the ship's arrival in Marblehead, two of her owners, John Coleman and William Clarke, no longer wondered what happened to their "missing" ship. They filed a complaint with the attorney general of the province claiming ownership and piracy charges. The attorney general, Paul Dudley, the son of the governor, immediately sought the capture of the pirates, and broadsheets were posted for every civil and military officer with orders to apprehend the pirates and secure the treasure. An extensive land/sea search ensued, with rewards offered to informants and customs-house officials searching outbound ships. By May 30, a week after their return to Marblehead, all but 18 of the 43 crewmen aboard the *Charles* had been apprehended.

The Trial

Governor Dudley opened the trials on June 13 in Boston's Town House, and the proceedings were closely followed by the local citizenry. The Reverend Cotton Mather, pastor of the Second North Church of Boston, attended daily. All were pronounced guilty as charged. Fifteen originally pleaded not guilty but then withdrew their pleas and fell on the mercy of the court. Two were executed as an example; the others remained in prison until 1705, when they were given a pardon to join the Royal Navy. Two men during the trial were acquitted when they were able to pay their prison fees.

One mate on the *Charles* was John Templeton. It was revealed during his trial his position aboard was that of servant. He never participated in any attacks nor did he receive a share of the booty. He was acquitted. Templeton was only 14 years old.

A Public Spectacle

The execution of the others was set for Friday, June 30, 1704. Forty musketeers and all the town constables guarded the condemned pirates. The hangings were a huge public affair. The Reverend Mather, who went to every public execution, presented a sermon at their hanging that he later published as "Faithful Warnings to Prevent Fearful Judgments." As was the custom, Quelch was permitted to say a few last words. He warned the public of the double standard involved in how money and goods were brought into the colonies.

Vane, Bellamy, and Two Destiny-Altering Storms

Captain Charles Vane began the better part of his piratical career as one of the many who joined Captain Henry Jennings. In 1714, Captain Jennings—later known as "he who lifted the Spanish plate"—took the *wracking trade* and turned it into one of the world's most lucrative operations. He stole the retrieved treasure of a sunken Spanish plate fleet (near Florida) straight from the Spanish salvagers. Vane realizing the advantage of this operation, followed Jennings's example. When another galleon sank in 1716, Vane sailed to the spot. Instead of engaging in an attack, he waited until recovery was complete and then captured the salvage ship.

On the way to New Providence to enjoy the fruits of their labors, Vane and his crew continued to seize ships. They settled in New Providence for a time, until an official edict changed everything (see Chapter 17).

> **Knowing the Ropes**
>
> The *wracking trade*, or diving for sunken treasure and cargo, began in Port Royal as a treasure-hunting business for sunken ships. Escaped pearl divers from the Spanish fisheries off Venezuela were hired out from Port Royal. Able to dive to great depths for long periods using no diving apparatus, these men were in great demand. Captains hired the divers and sailed to the last-known region in which any ship might have sunk.

"Black Sam"

With his friend Paul Williams, Samuel Bellamy began his career in the wracking trade. Having no luck, they decided to go on the account, and in 1715 both joined a pirate fleet. They found themselves aboard a vessel captained by Benjamin Hornigold sailing with the French pirate Oliver Le Bouche (a.k.a. Louis la Bouse, or Oliver de la Bour).

After many treasures were taken, a dispute erupted between the men. Hornigold and other English pirates refused to attack English ships. In 1716, the fleet decided they would part company on friendly terms. Hornigold sailed off on a prize sloop with 26 men; the remaining pirates elected Bellamy captain of their ship.

Williams was given command of a fleet ship, *Sultana*. With the remaining fleet, Williams and Bellamy sailed across the West Indies. On December 19, 1716, the pirates captured a ship, the *St. Michael*, bound for Jamaica. The *Sultana*'s crew stripped the ship of provisions and forced four men into piracy. One of the men was Thomas Davis, a 21-year-old carpenter from Wales. So distressed was Davis that Bellamy promised him his freedom when they next captured a ship. In early January 1717, Bellamy and Le Bouche parted company near the island of St. Croix.

Charles Vane.

(Courtesy of the Library of Congress, Prints & Photographs Division)

The *Whydah*

Sailing once again near Jamaica toward the end of February 1717, the watch on the *Sultana* spotted the *Whydah* (a.k.a. *Whidaw*), an 18-gunner with a crew of 50, commanded by Lawrence Price. The *Whydah* was a slaver sailing to England with a rich cargo of African tusks, gold dust, slave profits in the amount of £20,000 ($3,200,000), and sugar and indigo from the Caribbean.

Bellamy's fleet chased the *Whydah* for three days. As soon as they were close enough, Bellamy demanded the ship's surrender. Price obliged. Bellamy and his crew transferred to the larger *Whydah* and added 10 guns to her 18. As a reward for a quick surrender, Bellamy gave Price the *Sultana* and the freedom of his crew with the exception of John Julian, a Cape Cod Indian serving as navigator. He also permitted Price to load the *Sultana* with cargo the pirates did not want.

Before Price departed, Bellamy handed him £20 ($3,200) in silver and gold "to bear his charges." Davis then approached Bellamy about his promise to set him free. Bellamy called for a vote, but the rest of the pirates voted no. They would not sail without a carpenter. Dejected, Davis remained on the *Whydah* as she sailed to the American Northeast.

The Virginia Storm

A sudden storm caught the pirate fleet off the coast of Virginia. All vessels were severely battered, so Bellamy sailed toward Green Island in Maine. There he hoped to careen the fleet.

On Friday, April 26, 1717, near Nantucket, they captured Captain Crumpstey's pink (a small square-rigged ship), the *Mary Anne*, with a cargo of wine from Madeira. Because Crumpstey was familiar with the area waters, Bellamy ordered him to navigate the lead ship while the pirates took turns on the *Mary Anne* enjoying his cargo.

A Wrecking Nor'easter

Around 10 in the evening of the 26th, just off Cape Cod, a nor'easter struck. The ships in Bellamy's fleet were badly damaged. The pirates who managed to get ashore were arrested and sent to Boston for trial.

The *Whydah* wrecked on a sandbar near Wellfleet, Massachusetts (on Cape Cod), and broke apart. Of the 145 men aboard, only Thomas Davis and John Julian survived. At the court hearing, Davis was able to produce evidence that he had been forced into piracy. At the age of 22, he was acquitted and set free. John Julian was never sent to trial. His name disappeared from all records, and his fate remains unknown.

Pirate Yarns

Cape Cod lore states Samuel Bellamy was sailing east to see his love, Maria Hallett of Eastham, Massachusetts. He left her in 1715 to seek his fortune and prove to her parents he could support their daughter. When the wracking business failed, he refused to return empty-handed and instead turned pirate. With the wealth of the *Whydah* and other prizes, he was returning to ask for her hand in marriage.

The wreckage of the *Whydah* was scattered over four miles. Citizens of the area rushed to the site to salvage whatever riches they could. Upon hearing of the wreck and treasure, Governor Samuel Shute dispatched Captain Cyprian Southack to the wreck site to supervise the underwater recovery of the *Whydah*'s cargo. The weather was so bad and the waves so fierce the mission had to be abandoned. (In 1984, off the deep waters of Cape Cod, treasure hunter Barry Clifford rediscovered the wreck of the *Whydah*. The artifacts are on display in Provincetown, on Cape Cod.)

Pirates Make Better Sailors

With the navies of Europe now manned by green officers and raw recruits on fewer warships patrolling an enormous ocean, the tactical advantage went to the pirates. The old hands knew the waters of the Americas and the West Indies, and they willingly taught their new mates all the tricks of the trade. They knew the best vessels to seize; they also knew where the best cays, inlets, and islands were to hide, the towns that welcomed them, the islands that protected them, and the cities that continually accumulated riches to plunder.

Not one pirate ship was captured in 1715 or 1716, and only one was captured in 1717, although its crew managed to escape. By 1717, the exploits of pirates surged as never before.

The Least You Need to Know

♦ With the time and expense of transporting every suspected pirate and their witnesses to London for trial, the English crown changed the law. Any English colony or island could now set up court and try the accused.

♦ The War of the Spanish Succession involved all of Western Europe and lasted 13 years. Navies swelled, and pirates found themselves on the right side of the law for the first time.

♦ After the war in 1588, countries decommissioned their warships and navies. Without regard for the livelihood of their naval veterans, countries were flooded with unemployed sailors. With no other alternatives, these men turned to piracy.

♦ No longer willing to work for little profit, men from the American colonies, such as John Quelch, joined the pirate trade.

♦ Samuel Bellamy was a successful pirate. His place in history was assured by the artifacts unearthed around his watery grave.

Chapter 17

Hunting the Scourge of the Seven Seas

In This Chapter

- ◆ Retire or die
- ◆ The right man for the job
- ◆ A comfortable life no more
- ◆ Blackbeard: the devil incarnate or an ordinary man?

Believing there was no way to stem the rise of piracy and its overall cost to Britain, King George I issued a broad edict: all pirates, who came forward and confessed their misdeeds would be pardoned. Those pirates savvy enough to realize the political tide was turning accepted the pardon. There were, however, those men who believed they could outsmart the law and continue in their black trade.

To shut down the unrepentant, the crown took a different approach: they hired an ex-privateer by the name of Woodes Rogers.

This Time the War Is on Pirates

So astronomical were the insurance rates for sailing merchants, the entire shipping business nearly collapsed.

By 1715, New Providence had become the home of a dangerous pirate population, so notorious it was referred to as a "nest of infamous rascals" by the governor of Bermuda. In an attempt to address the problem, George I issued three major orders: Three warships were to be sent to the Caribbean, a proclamation of amnesty would be issued to all pirates, and a governor of the Bahamas would be appointed who could handle the cutthroats and clean out "the nest of pirates."

Choosing an incorruptible governor who could fearlessly stand up to pirates took some serious thought. But the king and parliament ultimately chose the right man, Woodes Rogers, whom we return to in a moment.

On September 5, 1717, George issued a proclamation "for Suppressing of Pyrates." The proclamation gave every pirate until September 5, 1718 to surrender to an English official to receive a full pardon for all crimes, including murder. A reward was offered for every pirate who refused the pardon from £100 ($16,000) for the ship's top crew down to £20 ($3,200) for "every pirate man." The proclamation was printed and dispersed throughout every known pirate haven and watering hole.

On February 23, 1718, Captain Vincent Pearce of the HMS *Phoenix*—his orders being quite clear—faced down a mob on New Providence and read the document. Initially, no one accepted the offer. Determined, Pearce returned three more times to convince the men to take the pardon. Before Pearce returned to New York on April 6, 209 pirates surrendered.

A New Governor Sails into Port

On July 26, 1718, Rogers sailed into New Providence with six ships—three Royal Navy warships and three of his own vessels—and a company of marines. His orders were to offer the pirates the King's pardon, fortify the island, and suppress piracy. The pirates had heard of Rogers as he was by then a wealthy and famous privateer.

Pirate Strategy: The Welcome Deception

Upon learning that a new governor was en route, the pirate captains held a war council. Captains Henry Jennings and Benjamin Hornigold—two of the older, more-respected pirates on the island—came up with a plan. They knew they'd lose in any open confrontation. Therefore, all the pirates would graciously welcome Rogers and appear to accept the pardons. After a short while, they would—as they had done with all other governors—simply cut him in for a percentage. Jennings figured the men would lose only a few weeks of sailing profit. And so it was that when Rogers landed, only one pirate, Charles Vane, gave his answer to the pardon by turning a captured brigantine into a fire ship aimed straight for one of the English war ships sailing out of the harbor.

To Rogers's astonishment, the pirate community rolled out the red carpet for him. He announced he was ready to accept anyone's pledge. Every pirate on the island lined up to sign the pardoning documents. But Rogers was no one's fool. He knew he was being set up, and soon he was proven correct. After a number of refused bribes, the pirates realized Rogers was an honest man who could not be bought, and they were not at all happy.

But Rogers was smarter than Jennings realized, and he was an astute judge of character to boot. He, in fact, had plans the pirates never could have imagined.

Early Land Reform and a Bit of Trickery

Rogers announced that anyone willing to clear land and build a shelter would receive 120 square feet of real estate. Rogers had impressive highly decorative documents drawn up for each willing individual. Most thought it a ridiculous proposal. But because they were *giving* the land away, why not? The men didn't grasp the significance of it right away, but for the first time in their lives they were legal landowners. It was something that would never have occurred in their homelands.

Rogers's next move was to restore the crumbled fortress back to a viable defensive bastion, and he had to do it fast. Unknown to the other pirates, Charles Vane had sent Rogers a warning note. He was waiting for Stede Bonnet (whom we'll meet later in this chapter) to join him, and together they would retake New Providence. Rogers knew the pirates wouldn't defend the island against a colleague. But he did know they would defend it against the hated Spanish.

Rogers let it be known that he received a dispatch that a Spanish fleet was heading to New Providence to capture it again. That was all the men needed to hear. Not only were they not going to let the Spanish take over their territory, they now each had a personal stake in defending the island: their own legal plot of land. They quickly set about repairing the fort. Though their enthusiasm waned at times, they did manage to rebuild it.

Rogers's ruse turned out to be real. He soon received word that a Spanish fleet had sailed into Havana with an officer claiming he had orders to retake New Providence.

Rogers first had to deal with Vane.

Pirates and Privateers Turn Pirate Hunters

In a stroke of genius, Rogers convinced Jennings and Hornigold that if Vane and Bonnet did attack, they would probably level the rebuilt fort and leave everyone defenseless against the Spanish.

Hornigold asked whether it would make a difference which ships went after Vane. Hornigold suggested if Rogers could see his way clear to make them legal privateers, they could go after the pirates who now threatened their homes. Rogers agreed, insisting that under the commission as privateers they could attack only pirate and Spanish ships. The men agreed. Rogers had accomplished the unthinkable. He had convinced one of the original pirates of the Caribbean to willingly hunt down fellow pirates.

Though unsuccessful in catching Vane, a precedence was set. More pirates turned privateers. They used their old ships with their same crews, receiving a percentage of any Spanish or pirate prize, and became zealots in hunting down their former mates.

The Gentleman Pirate

Captain Stede Bonnet was an atypical pirate. A retired major in the British army, he was married and owned a large plantation on the island of Barbados. He was one of the social elite and influential in his church. A rarity among pirates, he was the only one known to have purchased his ship. Under the guise of outfitting a trading vessel, he armed her with 10 guns and recruited 70 men. He named her the *Revenge*.

Without informing his wife, Bonnet left his mansion one evening in 1717, met his crew, and sailed away. He didn't know the first thing about sailing, but his years in the army had taught him a thing or two about command and discipline.

A Fighter, But No Sailor

Those who personally crossed Bonnet quickly discovered he was an accomplished swordsman; however, aboard ship he was out of his element. He was prone to massive bouts of seasickness. And he must have looked quite out of place aboard his own ship, dressed as he would at home—a short, fat man wearing a white powdered wig, silk waistcoat, white breeches, stockings, and shoes.

In the first few weeks, sailing toward Virginia, Bonnet captured four prizes. With his plunder, he sailed to Gardiner's Island off Long Island, New York, and there sold the lot. The Carolinas were his next destination.

By this time Bonnet's crew could no longer ignore the fact he was an amateur seaman. And only a few mates had any sailing experience themselves. Bonnet also hated what he considered to be roughhousing leading to unnecessary violence. Consequently, he managed to constrain his crew with hard work and discipline. Disgruntled mumblings soon began throughout the ranks.

Then, when a promising prize sailed into view, Bonnet—sensing the crew's gray mood—began to express emotional exuberance. But as the two ships closed with one another, Bonnet determined his prize was bristling with more than 40 guns. Wisely, he prepared to run. But when a pirate flag was spotted on the mast, he decided to meet the captain. It was a good idea, but the wrong pirate.

> **Treasure Chest**
>
> Stede Bonnet never revealed to anyone his reasons for suddenly turning pirate. Captain Johnson relates his friends and neighbors believed he left because his marriage was a shambles and he had enough of living with a shrewish wife. Others believed he simply went insane.

The Odd Couple

Invited aboard the *Queen Anne's Revenge*, the first meeting of the pirate captains couldn't have appeared odder. Here was the short stocky gentlemanly dressed Bonnet coming face to face with the tall bizarre-looking Edward Teach, better known as Blackbeard.

Bonnet proposed they join forces. Teach readily accepted. But after a time, Teach realized Bonnet was not a competent seaman and seized his ship. Bonnet was virtually a prisoner aboard Teach's vessel. He could only watch as Teach hunted for prizes between the Carolinas and the West Indies and blockaded Charlestown.

For reasons unknown, Teach chose to accept the king's pardon. He released Bonnet and returned the *Revenge* with no booty or provisions aboard. Appalled by Teach's brutality and treachery, Bonnet sailed to Bath Town, North Carolina, and accepted the pardon.

Captain Stede Bonnet.

(Courtesy of the Library of Congress, Prints & Photographs Division)

Couldn't Stay Honest

A free man, Bonnet's next move was inexplicable. Upon learning of yet another war, he received permission from Governor Eden to sail to St. Thomas and receive a privateer's commission to attack the Spanish. But he didn't go to St. Thomas. He changed his name to Thomas and renamed his ship the *Royal James*. Then he cruised from Delaware to Cape Fear; some historians have suggested that he was hunting for Teach. Whatever his motives, Bonnet began attacking merchants and amassing a small fleet and fortune. News reached Charleston that a fleet commanded by one Captain Thomas was careening off Cape Fear.

Colonel William Rhett requested permission from Governor Robert Johnson to arm warships and pursue. He discovered Bonnet's fleet at night on September 26, 1718, and waited until light. Trapped on the Cape Fear River, Bonnet determined that his only chance would be to ride the morning tide out into the ocean.

Rhett realized what Bonnet was about to do.

Battling on the Bar

With the newly named *Royal James* being the only seaworthy vessel, Bonnet attempted to sail across the bay, but he ran aground on a sandbar. His luck still holding, his pursuers also grounded in nearby shallows. The hull of the *Royal James* rolled away from the *Henry* while the *Henry* listed toward the *Royal James*.

For six long hours the two officers battled it out on ships stuck in the mud. It came down to whose luck would hold and become the first vessel to float. It wasn't Bonnet. Raising the white flag, he had one more trick up his sleeve. His crew realized his intention to blow up the ship as soon as Rhett boarded and overpowered him. Rhett was thrilled to discover he hadn't captured a Captain Thomas at all, but the infamous Stede Bonnet.

Captured, Recaptured, and Hanged

Bonnet and his navigator, David Harriot (who had captained the *Adventure*), were then confined to the marshal's house in Charlestown with only two guards. Perhaps it was believed that a gentleman such as Bonnet would quietly resign himself to capture. If so, he was misjudged. On October 24, before his trial, Bonnet and Harriot escaped and stole a small boat. Amid public outcry over lax security and bribery, Governor Johnson sent out search parties and issued a £700 bounty on Bonnet, dead or alive.

Bonnet's luck finally ran out. Bad weather forced them back to a small cove near Charlestown Harbor. Waiting for the weather to clear, Bonnet was discovered. Rhett went after him. He killed Harriot and again captured Bonnet.

> **Treasure Chest**
>
> On November 10, 1718, Bonnet went to court 2 days after 22 of his crewmen were hanged at White Point in Charlestown. Even the judge questioned why Bonnet, with all his advantages of birth, went on a course of pirating. He received no reply. Because he had attacked 11 ships and killed 18 seamen after accepting the king's pardon, Bonnet was hanged that same day.

The Infamous Blackbeard

Blackbeard! His background is so shrouded in mystery, historians can't even agree on his real name. Though his reign of terror lasted less than two years, his notoriety and horrific deeds have made him one of the most infamous characters in history.

For an educated criminal who could read and write, it would make perfect sense that he would use an alias—or aliases—to protect the reputation of his respected family. That's exactly what Blackbeard did.

Believed to be born Edward Teach (a.k.a. Thatch or Tache) in Bristol, England, around 1680, the future pirate captain sailed on a merchantman to the Caribbean. He drifted to New Providence in 1715 and signed on with Captain Benjamin Hornigold's crew. Hornigold held the respect of every pirate who sailed. He was shrewd and considered to be one of the fiercest members of their profession. Early on, Hornigold recognized Teach's qualities and took him under his wing.

Natural-Born Killer

Teach was an expert marksman and a master of intrigue, and he had a near-insatiable thirst for blood and combat. By 1717, Teach had proven his worth, and Hornigold consequently awarded him command of the captured French ship *Concord*. When amnesty was announced, Hornigold accepted the pardon and departed on friendly terms. Teach renamed the *Concord* the *Queen Anne's Revenge* and added 40 guns. As his infamy spread, Teach's crew swelled to some 300 men, each man dreaming of great wealth.

A Self-Created Legend

Teach was a physically powerful man. Over 6 feet tall and with broad shoulders, he was known by the brethren as a man who could handle excessive amounts of liquor and still fight and win in battle. Teach himself realized that image and reputation held as much sway over mates as they did victims. Beards were not the norm in that era, but Teach stopped shaving or cutting his hair. His coal-black beard grew coarse and wild, extending down to the middle of his broad chest. Braiding his beard in numerous rows, he tied them off with colorful ribbons. Two pigtails stood straight out from under his broad hat. He had eyebrows as wild and bushy as his beard. And he gave himself the now-well-known nom d'guerre "Blackbeard."

Though he frequently dressed in all-black clothes with knee-high leather boots, Blackbeard occasionally appeared in a surcoat of bright colors made of silk or velvet, gaudy-colored breeches, and buckled shoes.

In combat, Blackbeard wore a brace of three or more pistols, and he stuffed as many additional pistols and daggers around his waist as he could fit. His weapon of choice was an oversized cutlass. Before going into battle, he tucked thin cannon fuses of hemp cord under his hat and in his beard. Having been previously dipped in a mixture of saltpeter and limewater, the fuses burned at a slow rate of 12 inches an hour. The mixture produced heavy curling smoke that framed his face and gave him an even more frightening appearance. His ploy to intimidate worked; even his compatriots considered him the devil incarnate.

Edward "Blackbeard" Teach.

(A General History of Pyrates, Second Edition, *Charles Johnson, 1726*)

Cruel to His Crew

Blackbeard didn't exclusively reserve his antics and wild behavior for his enemies. His crew never knew what evil joke he would play on them to show his superiority. Charles Johnson retells how a drunken Blackbeard decided to play a game with some mates to see how long they would be able to bear living in hell. Going down to the ship's hole, they closed the hatches and lit several pots of brimstone and other combustibles. They remained below until they almost suffocated. It wasn't until the other men cried out for air that Blackbeard opened the hatches and gloated at having held out the longest.

The Ultimate Pirate Captain

No records indicate that Blackbeard murdered anyone who immediately surrendered. All he took was their cargo and perhaps their ship. If they resisted, however, he was without mercy. Consequently, poorly paid seamen and sailors who faced Blackbeard preferred to surrender rather than risk almost certain death for someone else's benefit.

Blackbeard's reputation was enhanced when he repelled an attack by the HMS *Scarborough*, a 30-gun man-o'-war out of Barbados with direct orders to capture the infamous pirate captain.

Blackbeard sailed from the West Indies up along the North American coastline taking ship after ship. He sold his plunder at the pirate-friendly harbor towns in the Americas. Like many others, Charles Eden, the governor of North Carolina, was unable to control the pirates in his state and so decided to profit from them.

On the Prowl for Prizes

Blackbeard was known for his clever diplomacy as well as his fighting ability. He not only sought wealth, but ships. While sailing with Stede Bonnet, they anchored at Turneffe Island, off the coast of British Honduras, for fresh water. Upon sighting a sloop, the *Adventure*, coming into the harbor, they hoisted their individual black flags. Her captain, David Harriot, was smart enough not to fight. Blackbeard invited Harriot aboard the *Queen Anne's Revenge* and invited him and his crew to join his fleet. They readily accepted. (Whether they were really keen to join Blackbeard's crew or just feared for their lives if they refused is not known.) Israel Hands (a.k.a. Hezekiah Hands, a.k.a. Basilica Hands), Blackbeard's first mate, commanded the *Adventure*, and Blackbeard instructed half of each crew to switch ships.

Sailing to the Bay of Honduras as a lesson to Bostonians, Blackbeard's fleet captured, plundered, and burned the *Protestant Caesar* out of Boston. Boston had recently tried and hanged a group of pirates. Of the remaining ships, Blackbeard burned a sloop when her captain protested the plundering of his vessel. The others he released after his crew

Dead Men's Tales

Such a day, rum all out: - Our company somewhat sober: - A damned confusion amongst us! - Rouges a-plotting: - Great talk of separation - so I looked for a sharp prize: - Such a day took one, with a great deal of liquor on board, so kept the company hot, damned hot; then all things went well again.

—Blackbeard, from the ship's log found aboard the *Adventure*, 1718 ransacked the ships, taking everything they could. As Blackbeard headed toward the eastern seaboard, he continued to seize vessels, adding to his fleet. Cleverly, Blackbeard knew he had to keep his men occupied and satisfied to prevent any discord.

Blockading Charlestown

With his fleet of 7 ships and 300 men (60 of whom were black), Blackbeard headed straight to Charlestown, South Carolina. In May 1718, he stopped just outside Charlestown Harbor.

One of the busiest and wealthiest cities on the eastern seaboard, Charlestown was a prime target for the likes of Blackbeard, who wasted no time spreading out his fleet and blockading the port. Quickly he captured nine ships. He found his best bargaining chip on the last ship, the *Crowley*. Bound for London, the *Crowley* carried Samuel Wraggs, a member of the governor's council, and his 4-year-old son, William. Blackbeard sent Mr. Marks, one of the passengers, with a ransom note to the governor. The pirate's demand was simple: a full chest of medicine was to be delivered, or the people he'd taken hostage aboard the nine ships would all die a slow and painful death.

Why medicine was demanded and not money has been a question asked over the centuries. After all, a fully stocked medicine chest was worth only £300 ($48,000) to £400 ($64,000). It has since been speculated that Blackbeard was either a drug addict who needed the laudanum or he needed the mercurial preparations to help him or his mates fight venereal disease. True to his word, as soon as the medicines were delivered, the pirate ships released the prisoners unharmed and sailed away.

Deceit at Topsail Inlet

Soon after leaving Charleston Harbor, Blackbeard decided to accept the king's pardon. Having enjoyed his many trips to North Carolina and being on friendly terms with Governor Charles Eden, he planned to receive his pardon there and retire. But before doing so he had to disband his fleet and divide their large booty.

Blackbeard had no intention of sharing with 300 men. An accomplished navigator, he devised a plan to keep the treasure among only 40 of his closest and most-trusted mates. Secretly, Blackbeard had the very best of the swag transferred to the *Adventure*.

In June 1718, under the pretense of careening the ships, the fleet eased into Topsail Inlet (Beaufort Inlet) on the North Carolina coast. Making it look like an accident,

Blackbeard deliberately ran the *Queen Anne's Revenge* onto a sandbar. He then hailed the *Adventure* and ordered her to help pull his flagship off the bar. His first mate, Israel Hands, who was in on the plan, boarded one of the sloops from the *Adventure*.

Throwing towlines over, Hands made a great show of extricating the ship off the sandbar. What he was really doing, according to plan, was pulling the sloop onto the bar and damaging both ships beyond repair. The crews abandoned the two ships as they sank. Before anyone realized what was happening, Blackbeard boarded the *Adventure* and sailed out of the inlet, leaving the men of his fleet to fend for themselves.

To make his treachery worse, when 25 of his crew discovered his intent, Blackbeard marooned them on a small, uninhabited island without shot, arms, or water. By chance, Stede Bonnet, having just been released by Blackbeard, sailed past the island and saved them.

A Pardon, Then Back to Piracy

Heading for familiar territory, Blackbeard sailed through Ocracoke Inlet, North Carolina, into Pamlico Sound, and then into Bath Town. With his remaining crew, he accepted the king's pardon from Governor Eden. He then purchased a home at Plum Point on the eastern side of Bath Creek, across from the governor's home. Having received royal pardons, he and his men went freely about town. Blackbeard, now a celebrity, entertained and was entertained by the social elite.

> **Pirate Yarns** _____
>
> One of the many legends surrounding Blackbeard was his unsuccessful courting of Governor Eden's daughter. She rejected Blackbeard's offer of marriage (because she was already engaged). Jealous, Blackbeard captured and killed her young fiancé, cutting off his hands and dumping him into the ocean. Blackbeard sent the severed hands to her in a jeweled casket to prove no one else could have her. Legend has it she died from anguish and a broken heart. The primary flaw in this yarn, however, is that Charles Eden died childless.

Blackbeard and his men did not remain landlubbers for long. Blackbeard officially registered the *Adventure* as a trading vessel and stated his intent to sail to St. Thomas. The registration document and his pardon were placed in safekeeping in his ship's cabin. He sailed first to Philadelphia, but upon his arrival learned the city no longer welcomed pirates. Soldiers were actually out looking for them, so they quickly departed.

Following his pardon, Blackbeard is known to have captured only one French vessel. It seems as if he was content to just sail around for some time and then anchor at his favorite spot, some 30 miles southwest of Cape Hatteras, on Ocracoke Inlet, known by the locals as *Teach's Hole*. In September, Charles Vane and his crew sailed into the channel and proceeded to have the largest pirate gathering on the American mainland.

Knowing the Ropes

Teach's Hole was Blackbeard's favorite spot to anchor. It was located on the narrow channel of Ocracoke Inlet to the extreme right on the Atlantic side south of Springer's Point. From the dunes, a sentry with a glass (telescope) had an unobstructed view of passing ships.

"Enough Is Enough!"

Pirates were overrunning cities in the colonies. Officials who once entertained them were now issuing arrest warrants. Governor Alexander Spotswood of Virginia, one of a few incorruptible men, had had enough of pirates and Blackbeard in particular. He did not trust Eden or his ability to control the pirates. He hated the fact that many of Blackbeard's crew had migrated to Virginia. He also hated that Blackbeard had settled in Bath Town.

Upon learning of the gathering of pirates and the rumor that Blackbeard was intent on establishing "another Madagascar," Spotswood acted. Spies were dispatched to North Carolina. They returned with navigators who knew the waterways. Even better, William Howard, once a quartermaster on the *Queen Anne's Revenge*, was seen in Virginia. Spotswood arrested him on charges of piracy. Fortunately for Howard, the night before his execution the king's declaration of pardon arrived at the state house in Virginia and he was freed. Spotswood didn't mind "losing a pirate to the hangman" because Howard had revealed information about Blackbeard's fighting tactics, his hideouts, and how many men served aboard his ship.

Organizing the Hunt

Spotswood then called a secret war council with his top officers. He didn't want spies to alert Teach of his intentions. Heavily armed warships being too heavy for the shallow Intracoastal Waterway, the Virginia governor authorized two sloops to be readied for action. He personally financed the expedition. To encourage the men, Spotswood put a bounty on every pirate they captured.

On November 17, 1718, Lieutenant Robert Maynard, with 35 men on *his* sloop—and 25 men on the other sloop, captained by a Mr. Hyde—quietly slipped out of the harbor. Captain Ellis Brand, commander of the man-o'-war *Lyme*, took a troop of men overland to Bath Town to attack Blackbeard as part of a two-pronged maneuver.

Blackbeard's Last Betrayal

The night before the arrival of Maynard and Hyde, Blackbeard was in his cabin on the *Adventure* drinking heavily with Israel Hands and another mate. Suddenly Blackbeard drew out two pistols from his baldric and cocked them under the table. Knowing that anything could happen when Blackbeard got drunk and surly, the mate quickly fled the cabin. Before Hands could react, Blackbeard crossed his hands, blew out the candles, and fired. One pistol misfired. The other ball shattered Hands's knee, crippling him for life. Questioned by his crew, Blackbeard simply cursed and stated offhand "if he did not now and then kill one of them, they would forget who he was." Hands was taken ashore by friends to have his wound tended. Paradoxically, Blackbeard's cruel antic would save Hands's life.

Surprise!

Maynard reached Ocracoke the night of November 21, 1718, and blockaded the inlet. Because Blackbeard had accepted the pardon, most of his men had left. Spotswood's report states that only 18 men were aboard Blackbeard's ship. Being warned so many times before of impending attacks, Blackbeard did what he had always done while hidden and anchored. He stacked weapons and ammunition on the deck, and then went below to party.

The following morning, November 22, Maynard sent out a rowboat to check the shoals. The pirates sighted the rowboat, and the battle commenced. When Maynard sailed into the fray, Blackbeard was ready. Maynard swung his ships to his bow and stern to avoid being struck broadside. Blackbeard sailed straight across a channel that he knew had a hidden sandbar. Both Maynard and Hyde took the bait, and their sloops ran aground. Blackbeard then turned in for the kill. The pirate guns fired, sending chain, grapeshot, and spikes tearing through Hyde's ship. Then as they were turning to finish off Maynard, the winds died, and Blackbeard's ship, the *Adventure*, wedged into the sandbar. Seconds later, the wind picked up again. Maynard was ready. While Blackbeard had been attacking Hyde, Maynard had ordered his vessel lightened. Everything except weapons had been tossed overboard. The tactic worked. Maynard ordered his ship to head straight for Blackbeard's. The pirates fired a broadside at the oncoming vessel, but Maynard kept coming. A second broadside was ordered, but then canceled. Seeing only two men on the deck of the sloop, the helmsman and an officer, Blackbeard ordered his men to board. With grappling hooks and pikes, they jumped aboard and rushed to the wheel.

Hard to Kill

As the pirates rushed toward him, Maynard shouted orders. Thirty men came rushing from the hatches. A bloodbath ensued. Blackbeard's men, though armed with cutlasses, were not accustomed to fighting in close quarters. Their opponents were handpicked veterans. Maynard's men quickly got the upper hand. The pirates called for quarter (mercy). All surrendered but Blackbeard.

Cutlass in hand, the great pirate captain charged straight for Maynard. Swinging his weapon, he broke Maynard's sword blade in half. Throwing the handle at Blackbeard, Maynard pulled his pistol and fired directly at the pirate's chest. Blackbeard kept coming. Maynard dove for a discarded rapier. Blackbeard, hovering over him, made a fatal mistake: he paused. Behind him a seaman hefted a boarding pike and struck Blackbeard twice across the neck and head. Miraculously still alive, Blackbeard staggered around the deck, swinging his cutlass. Maynard's men went in for the kill. Although he was repeatedly being slashed with pikes and swords, Blackbeard continued to fight them off.

Blackbeard's head on the bowsprit.

(The Pirates' Own Book, *Charles Ellms, 1837*)

Then at last, his great bulk stiffened, swayed, and toppled. Captain Edward "Blackbeard" Teach was dead. Upon examination of his lifeless body, Maynard counted 25 wounds, 5 of them from pistol shots.

A Gruesome Announcement of Success

Maynard wished to bring Blackbeard's corpse triumphantly back to Virginia. He wanted assurance he and his crew had undisputed proof so that they could collect the £100 ($16,000) bounty on Blackbeard. His decision changed when the stench from the decomposing body worsened. Maynard ordered Blackbeard's head severed from his body and hung on the ship's bowsprit for all to see. The pirate's headless body was then unceremoniously dumped overboard.

Treasure Chest

In 1996, Mike Daniels was diving over a wreck in Beaufort, North Carolina. Noticing a large pile of encrusted pipes, he swam closer to investigate. They weren't pipes, but cannon. Twenty feet below him lay what is believed to be the wreckage of the *Queen Anne's Revenge*. With many wrecks in the vicinity, nothing to date has provided any concrete evidence it is Blackbeard's ship. Underwater excavation of the site is ongoing.

The Least You Need to Know

- To stem the rising tide of piracy, King George I of England issued a broad pardon to any pirate willing to stop.

- Woodes Rogers was appointed governor of the Bahamas. He devised an ingenious plan that successfully curtailed piracy.

- A wealthy plantation owner with no nautical skills, Stede Bonnet became a successful pirate.

- With a reign of terror lasting less than two years, Edward "Blackbeard" Teach became the most feared and notorious pirate in history.

Chapter 18

A Colorful Cast of Characters

In This Chapter

- An unusual way to make friends
- No soft-hearted souls allowed
- Living up to a murky reputation
- A tea-sipping pirate
- Catching up with Taylor and Le Bouche

Pirates operating during the period 1716 to 1725 seem bolder, more flamboyant, vicious, and—in many ways—far more interesting than most of their predecessors. Whether this is actually true is up for debate. Certainly those operating centuries earlier in the North Atlantic, the Mediterranean, and along the Asian Pacific and Indian Ocean coastlines were regarded with both fear and fascination. But with the advent of broadsheets and newspapers in Western Europe and the American colonies, pirate activities and tales of the same began reaching a far broader public than ever before. And the pirates of the period were indeed a fascinating collection of rogues.

In the next few chapters, you will notice the interaction between many individual pirates. This was not a coincidence. They were not merely contemporaries; many were actually compatriots. They had entered the brotherhood willingly, some with friends, or as captives who eventually turned whole-heartedly to the business of "the sweet trade." These pirates rose through the ranks to their own captaincies by crew votes or the honor of being handed a seized vessel, as Benjamin Hornigold did with Edward Teach.

Starting a Chain Reaction

From the scraps of information available, we know that Captain Christopher Winter was captured by pirates and then decided to throw in with them. His name appears on the roster of pirates at New Providence when Woodes Rogers arrived (see Chapter 17), but Winter did not accept the pardon offered. Along with other disgruntled Englishmen and Irishmen, he traveled to Cuba.

Winter surrendered to the Spanish and received their pardon. He converted to Catholicism and worked as a "coast guard" for the Spanish through 1723. Under this guise of protecting Spanish property and lives, and holding a Spanish commission, Winter attacked English ships and raided the settlements along the Jamaican coast for slaves, receiving a percentage for every slave sent back to Cuba.

Winter was accused of piracy in 1722, and the governor of Jamaica, Sir Nicholas Lawes, dispatched the HMS *Happy* under Lieutenant Joseph Lawes to Cuba demanding the surrender and arrest of Winter. The government of Cuba ignored the request.

Winter Initiates Another Pirate Captain

Winter is best known for his capture of Irish-born Edward Seegar off a merchant ship bound for Jamaica. Like Winter, Seegar decided to throw in with the pirates, but not before changing his name to Edward England.

Traveling with Winter to New Providence, England, Seegar was given command of his first captured vessel. He refused to sign the king's pardon and sailed to Africa, plundering ships along the way.

Off the coast of Africa, England took a sloop, the *Pearl*, outfitted her with guns, and, as many other pirates before him, christened her the *Royal James*. He then embarked on a quest for merchantmen and slavers, hunting them along the Azores and Cape de Verde Islands.

Edward England.

(A General History of Pyrates, *Captain Charles Johnson, 1724)*

Joining Forces with Captains Le Bouche and Taylor

Though a successful sailing pirate, Englad's merciful nature would lead to his downfall. After meeting up with French pirate Le Bouche (a.k.a. Louis La Bouse) at the harbor at Whydah, Africa, the two captains joined forces. The two crews careened their ships and spent time with the native women. Back at sea, the combined pirate force rounded the Cape of Good Hope and soon took more than a dozen vessels, including a captured prize they renamed the *Victory*. Joining with the two captains was pirate John Taylor.

En route to India from Madagascar, England scuttled the *Royal James* for the 34-gunner *Fancy*, and returned to Madagascar hoping to meet up with Henry Avery.

Just missing Avery, England and Taylor set out together while Le Bouche went his separate way.

A Difficult Prize to Take

On July 25, 1720, England and Taylor entered the harbor at Johanna (an island off Madagascar) and spotted three merchant ships loaded with cargo ready to sail to the Netherlands and England. Upon spotting the pirates, the Dutch ship slipped the harbor and ran for safety. The *Greenwich* did the same with Taylor in hot pursuit. England cornered the third ship, *Cassandra*. Unexpectedly, she was heavily armed and her captain, James Mackra (a.k.a. Macrae), fought back. The battle raged for four hours.

Realizing he could not possibly win, Mackra grounded the *Cassandra*, and with his surviving crew abandoned ship and fled ashore into nearby woods. England and his men boarded and found a rich cargo worth £75,000 ($12,000,000). But the prize did not come without a price. Though the *Cassandra*'s casualties numbered 37 men, England had lost 90. His surviving crew members were not at all pleased.

Barely Surviving

Mackra, suffering from a severe head wound, led his men 25 miles inland to King's Town. By the time they arrived they discovered the pirates, enraged by the death of their mates, were offering £10,000 ($1,600,000) for Mackra's capture. Because he dealt with the residents of King's Town on a regular basis, and was known as a fair man, no one turned him in for the reward. However, as the days went by and Mackra began to heal, he began to contemplate his predicament. Another ship of the East India Company was not due for months. They virtually had no way off the island. After 10 long days, Mackra felt he was well enough to travel. He hoped the time lag and treasure would make the pirates more inclined toward mercy. Accepting the risk, Mackra returned to the *Cassandra* to negotiate a surrender.

Kindness or Weakness?

With a promise of safety while negotiating, Mackra was relieved to find men who previously sailed with him onboard. They voted to let him live. However, John Taylor and the majority of pirates wanted revenge. After hours of persuasive oratory and a great deal of rum, England convinced Taylor and the others that their booty was sufficient. Mackra should be permitted to leave. Begrudgingly, the crew gave Mackra and his remaining crew of 43 the badly listing *Fancy*.

Once at sea, the crew of the *Victory*—convinced England was too weak to remain captain—elected John Taylor as their new skipper. England and three other pirates who had voted for leniency for Mackra were marooned on the island of Mauritius.

Using wood and other debris that washed ashore, the four stranded pirates built a small boat and set sail. In early 1721, they landed at St. Augustine's Bay, Madagascar. Penniless, England was reduced to begging and living off the kindness of strangers. A broken man, he died not long after landing in Madagascar.

"I May Be a Slaver, But No Pirate"

Welshman Howell Davis had spent his boyhood on the water. So when he was old enough to go to sea in 1718, he signed on to the slaver *Cadogan* (operating between Bristol and Africa) as chief mate. At Sierra Leone, the ship was seized by Edward England, and the ship's captain was killed for not immediately surrendering.

Noted for being both clever and charming, Davis so impressed England that the latter handed him the captaincy of the *Cadogan* and its cargo, and suggested Davis turn pirate and sell the cargo in Brazil. When Davis proposed the idea to his mates, they refused. They chose to continue sailing to their original destination of Barbados. Upon arrival, the crew turned Davis over to the authorities. He languished in jail for three months until his trial. When no proof could be presented that he was indeed a pirate, he was freed.

Captain Howell Davis.

(Courtesy of the Library of Congress, Prints & Photographs Division)

If *Branded* a Pirate, Why Not *Be* a Pirate?

Though acquitted on charges of piracy, the "pirate" brand followed Davis. So when he was unable to find honest employment, he decided to become what everyone believed he was anyway.

Sailing with a crew to New Providence just after Woodes Rogers landed, Davis signed the pardon papers. Rogers, in an attempt to provide the pirates with an honest trade, outfitted two sloops, the *Buck* and *Mumvil Trader.* Their destinations were the French and Spanish settlements along the Caribbean. At Martinique, Davis organized a mutiny. After they stripped the *Mumvil Trader* of everything Davis thought they might possibly need, he gave the vessel to those who were inclined to remain honest. Wisely, not just assuming he'd be chosen as captain, Davis put the captaincy of the *Buck* to a crew vote and was himself awarded the position.

A Clever Strategy

On their way to Hispaniola for provisions, they sighted a large French vessel with 12 guns. Though outclassed, the pirates easily took the ship. As Davis sent 12 mates over to man their newly won prize, they sighted another sail. From the detained French captain, Davis learned that it was a second French ship, this one a 24-gun ship with more than 60 sailors aboard.

Davis proposed taking her as his flagship. His men initially objected because they only numbered 36 and the odds did not seem in their favor. Davis assured them he had a plan in mind that would not only guarantee them the ship, but also no loss of life. The men agreed.

Davis Hoists the Black Flag

Maneuvering close to the French 24-gunner, Davis hoisted his black flag demanding their surrender. Surprised by his audacity, the Frenchmen replied by ordering Davis to do the same. Davis then calmly informed them he intended to remain on their trail until his consort ship came about to deal with them. If they didn't surrender, there would be no quarter given. To emphasize his point, Davis ordered a broadside, which the French quickly returned. At that point, the captured ship drew near, filled with screaming pirates, guns blazing. Terrified at the sight of the larger pirate ship, the French surrendered. The pirates then stripped the vessels of everything they could possibly need. Only then did Davis reveal his ruse to the French captain of the 24-gunner.

Using a filthy darkened tarp as a black flag, he had the French prisoners stripped to their shirts and breeches, disguising them as pirates while his men fired the guns. Davis released the two vessels and went hunting for another prize.

Playing the Role of a Gentleman

The *Buck* entered the harbor of the Portuguese-held island of St. Jago (part of Cape de Verde Archipelago), under the guise and flag of an English privateer. With as much charm and gentlemanly manner he could exude, the pirate captain presented himself to the governor. Suspicious of Davis, the governor bluntly stated he thought him a pirate, not a hunter of one. Davis politely took his leave. His crew did not take kindly to the man's treatment of Davis and decided it was an insult that could not be ignored. That night the pirates mounted a surprise attack on the fort, taking as much plunder as they could carry.

To Gambia!

Davis now set his sights on the fort on St. James Island, in Gambia, Africa. It was a trading settlement of the Royal African Company and an English military garrison. Aware that the castle stored much of the treasure and gold ingots of the company, Davis presented a similar plan to his mates. They all agreed. Undaunted by his failure to convince the Portuguese he was a successful English privateer, Davis dressed once again in his finery. He introduced himself as a Liverpool trader on his way for resin and tusk in Senegal (Africa). This time he pulled it off. Impressed, Davis and his first mate and ship's surgeon were invited to dine at the castle.

Upon arriving for dinner, Davis presented the governor with an expensive bottle of wine and then proceeded to point a flintlock at his chest. While Davis held the governor hostage, the crew overran the castle, disarmed the soldiers, and stripped the treasure house of all the gold ingots and ivory.

Meeting Other Cutthroats

Preparing to leave Gambia, the *Buck*'s lookout spotted a ship bearing down on them under full sail. Davis quickly ordered the anchor up and guns to the ready. As the vessel closed with the *Buck*, her guns blazing, a black flag was hoisted aloft. Davis followed suit.

When the smoke cleared, the French pirate Oliver Le Bouche hailed Davis as a brother. As was their tradition upon meeting a fellow tradesman on the open sea, the ships hoisted flags of truce. Both captains went out in long boats to greet each other. Le Bouche told Davis his vessel carried 14 guns and a crew of 64, half French, half black. They were in search of a better ship. It was decided they would join crews. Davis kindly offered Le Bouche the first prize that was to his liking.

Paradoxically, the first vessel they attacked was that of another pirate, Thomas Cocklyn. All three chose to sail as a fleet down the coast raiding ships and settlements. They voted Davis as their commander, with their ultimate destination being Sierra Leone.

Treasure Chest

Many of the pirates who chose not to take King George's pardon set up their own secret slave-trading settlement in 1719 at the Sierra Leone River Delta in Africa. The region was an ideal place to spend the winter months. It was also close to the trading center of the Royal African Company. Indignant that the government had granted the company exclusive rights to the slave-trading business, the pirates raided the settlement as often as possible.

And Now a Famous Captive

Captain William Snelgrave, of the slaver *Bird*, sailed out of London in April 1719. Shortly before reaching the Royal African trading post the *Bird* was captured by Thomas Cocklyn. For the month following, Snelgrave and his mates were held captive. Of the three pirate crews, Snelgrave found Cocklyn and his men the cruelest, whereas Davis seemed the more generous and caring to their many captives. In 1734, Snelgrave published a book about his experiences as a slaver and pirate captive titled *A New Account of Some Parts of Guinea and the Slave Trade*.

The Setup That Backfired

It wasn't long before the three separate personalities of the pirate captains and crews clashed. Deciding to part company while still on tolerable terms, Davis continued successfully capturing ships. He abandoned the *Buck* for an impressive 32-gun Dutch merchantman he named the *Rover*. In late 1719, he sailed the *Rover* to the Portuguese Principe Island (Prince's Island), playing his usual character of an English privateer. To impress the governor, Davis had his men seize a French ship just entering the harbor, claiming them to be pirates.

As before, Davis was invited to dine with the governor. But this time his luck ran out. An escaped captive from the *Rover* revealed the pirate's attack plan. Davis walked into a trap. Taking five shots to the stomach, Davis killed two men before he died. Making sure he was not "playing dead," the Portuguese cut his throat. Upon hearing of their captain's death, the *Rover* quickly left the harbor. They did not get far.

A Successful Dandy

In terms of the sheer number of ships captured, Captain Bartholomew Roberts must be considered the most successful pirate. It is reported he plundered more than 400 ships in less than four years. He seems quite the atypical pirate when one considers he drank only tea, held to Sunday observances aboard ship, and was a strict disciplinarian.

Roberts always dressed his best before a battle. A tall, dark Welshman, he wore a rich red-crimson damask waistcoat and matching breeches with silk hose and center-buckled shoes. A bright red feather adorned his tricorne hat, and a large diamond-encrusted cross on a long gold chain hung around his neck. Also hanging from his neck were a pair of flintlocks secured by a silken cord. He carried a cutlass, his weapon of choice.

Like many before him, Roberts began as an honest merchant sailor. In 1719, at the age of 36, he signed on to the *Princess* as second mate sailing from London to Anamaboe, Guinea, for slaves. Off the west coast of Africa, his ship was seized by Howell Davis. It is unclear whether Roberts was forced or not, but either way he became part of Davis's crew.

The Great *Pyrate* Roberts

Upon hearing of Davis's death, the crew of the *Rover* elected Roberts captain. Davis must have made a tremendous impression on Roberts; for after being with him for just a mere six weeks, Roberts went on a vengeful rampage against the Portuguese. Leading the fleet back into the harbor, Roberts leveled the fort, torched the settlement, and sank two ships in the harbor.

Next he set his sights on Brazil. Sailing into the Bay of Bahia, Roberts was ecstatic to find a fleet of 42 treasure ships fully loaded and ready to sail for Lisbon. Boldly he sailed straight for the biggest vessel, the vice-admiral's 40-gunner. Taking the Portuguese by surprise, Roberts and his men boarded, and while some were engaged in close combat, others raided the ship's hold. Roberts disembarked before the convoy's warship could give chase. The booty·contained tobacco, sugar, hides, gold, jewels, silver, coins worth £80,000, and a diamond-studded cross made for the king of Portugal. Roberts returned to Devil's Island off Guinea, where he and his men celebrated their success.

In 1720, after seizing whatever ships were unfortunate enough to cross his path, Roberts sailed back to the Caribbean. When the Royal Navy patrols and island militia impeded their success, Roberts headed north, capturing ships and selling them and their cargo in New England. Roberts headed toward Newfoundland, capturing more than 170 ships. In Newfoundland, men eagerly signed on the account, finding piracy more to their liking than splitting and drying cod.

Royal Fortune

Roberts and his men cruised to the Caribbean, this time plundering the New England coast as they went. His reputation for boldness in action inspired colonists to sign on, too. Roberts continually upgraded or changed his flagship, renaming each new ship the *Royal Fortune*.

A pirate frigate.

(Artist: Ron Druett)

Provisioning the *Royal Fortune* in the West Indies, he sailed for West Africa. But the winds blew them off course. Realizing their error, Roberts was forced to turn back toward the Caribbean to catch the prevailing winds. Logging 2,000 miles without sighting land, the *Royal Fortune*'s water barrel was practically empty. One mouthful of water a day was all his crew of 124 men was allowed. Desperate, some drank seawater, but the salt only increased their thirst. Before reaching land, many died of fever or succumbed to madness. The barrel went dry mere days before they landed off the Maroni River in Dutch Guiana, South America.

Pirate Rampage and Vendetta

Roberts continued his relentless attacks along the Caribbean. Using the island of St. Lucia as his base, it was reported that in 4 days his fleet sank more than 16 ships. He went on a plundering and killing spree. His crew's propensity for torture was so horrific the French governor of Martinique asked for help not only from the French governor of the Lesser Antilles Island but also from the English governor of Barbados.

Treasure Chest

So enraged that the governors of Martinique and Barbados dared send a squadron out to capture him, Roberts designed his second pirate flag. The design showed an image of him atop two skulls, clearly stating his intention. Roberts was able to fulfill one of his threats: attacking Martinique, he captured a 52-gun frigate. Unfortunately for the governor of Martinique, he was aboard the captured vessel. Roberts hanged the man off his own ship's yardarm. Seizing the frigate as his prize, Roberts renamed her the *Royal Fortune*.

A Fitful End Over Breakfast

Having their fill of terrorizing the West Indies, Roberts and his men sailed again to Africa. Anchoring off Parrot Island, Cape Lopez (Guinea), in January 1722, Roberts began restocking his fleet. Unbeknownst to Roberts, for the past six months two English men-o'-war—the HMS *Swallow* and HMS *Weymouth*—had been hunting for his fleet. The *Swallow*, under the command of Captain Chaloner Ogle, spotted the pirate fleet. Mistaking the *Swallow* for a Portuguese merchant ship, Roberts sent the *Great Ranger* after her. Ogle sailed out of sight of the *Royal Fortune* and attacked the *Great Ranger*, capturing the pirate ship. He then returned for Roberts.

On February 10, 1722, Ogle again sighted the *Royal Fortune*. But fortune itself was not to be on Roberts's side. Roberts was eating breakfast while most of his men were sleeping off a drunken stupor. The *Swallow* approached, flying a French flag. She was ignored until Ogle set a course straight for the *Royal Fortune*. A deserter from the *Swallow* recognized the ship and raised the alarm. Aware that his men were too drunk to fight, Roberts's first order was to cut the anchor cable and make a run for safety. But for some unknown reason, the pirate captain changed his mind and ordered his helmsman to steer straight for the *Swallow*. Once in range, Ogle ordered a broadside. Roberts returned fire. After fierce fighting, those of Roberts's crew who were sober enough realized their captain was laying on the deck in a bloody heap, his throat ripped open by a blast of grapeshot. Obeying Roberts's final dying order, the men dumped him overboard in all his finery and with most of his weapons still strapped to him. At 40 years old, Roberts preferred the sharks to being hanged in a gibbet.

A pirate chase.

(Artist: Ron Druett)

So Whatever Happened to Taylor and Le Bouche?

After marooning Edward England, John Taylor and mates sailed the *Cassandra* and *Victory* to St. Mary's Island. There they met up with Le Bouche. Taylor gave him the command of the *Victory*, and together they cruised to Réunion Island, located southwest of Mauritius, anchoring in April 1721.

In the harbor for repairs was a badly damaged Portuguese carrack carrying the retired viceroy of Goa. Overrunning the helpless vessel, the pirates plundered his incredible swag of diamonds worth £500,000 ($80,000,000) and rare oriental treasures valued at £375,000 ($60,000,000). The *Cassandra* and *Victory* returned to St. Mary's to share out all the accumulated booty they had aboard. It totaled a cool million pounds. In all, 240 pirates received a pouch containing 42 diamonds and additional plunder. Taylor and Le Bouche went their separate ways in December 1721.

There are two possible scenarios to the end of Le Bouche's life. One has him remaining on Madagascar. The other has him settling on Réunion Island, where it is said he was hanged some years later.

Upon learning that an English squadron was sailing to Madagascar to wipe out any pirates they encountered, Taylor and crew settled in Africa until December 1722. Having waited out their time in luxury for more than a year, the men felt it safe to go their separate ways. Some returned to Madagascar. Taylor and 140 of his mates chose to retire from pirating and sailed the *Cassandra* to Porto Bello. Arriving in 1723, the pirates turned the *Cassandra* over to the governor in return for pardons.

Receiving full pardons just prior to the British authorities discovering their whereabouts (Royal Navy officers arriving in Porto Bello were unable to arrest them on charges of piracy), all of the pirates were free men.

Not content to stay on land, Taylor became a captain in the Spanish coast guard.

It is said Thomas Cocklyn ended his days on the gallows.

The Least You Need to Know

◆ Little is known concerning the life of Christopher Winter. He is credited with starting the interesting chain of captive men who later became famous pirates in their own right.

◆ Edward England could not abide mistreatment of captives. He continuously fought his crew over their brutal actions. Considering him too weak to sail on—much less command—a pirate ship, the crew marooned him.

◆ Howell Davis enjoyed using creative plans to attack towns and ships rather than sailing in with guns blazing. He was very successful with that strategy, until it backfired.

◆ He may have been a teetotaler who dressed like a dandy, but Bartholomew Roberts is credited with capturing more ships than any other pirate of his time.

◆ Though many of the pirates had performed despicable atrocities for sheer profit and excitement, the majority of men who had sailed with England, Davis, and Roberts ended their lives as free men.

Part 4

The End of Piracy? Think Again

Piracy continues beyond the Golden Age, and far beyond the islands of the Caribbean and the shores of the Eastern Seaboard. A new nation, largely built on the sweet trade, confronts piracy in the Mediterranean. The new United States Navy and Marine Corps cut their teeth on the Barbary corsairs. We also look at Asian piracy and pirates of the modern world.

Chapter **19**

The End Draws Near

In This Chapter

- ◆ Vane's end
- ◆ The exploits of Calico Jack and his lady pirates
- ◆ George Lowther's predicament
- ◆ Murderous Ned Low

A number of factors contributed to the end of the golden age of piracy. By 1725, the percentage of men aboard pirate ships who were taken by force was greater than ever before. The American colonies were building their own ships, and merchant syndicates were hiring more experienced men to hunt down pirates. And the pirates themselves had no inkling that their reign of terror would end so soon and so abruptly.

No Prey, No Pay

Sobering up from their month-long revelry on Ocracoke Inlet in 1718 with Blackbeard, Charles Vane and crew continued their coastal attacks. Near New Jersey, they spotted a ship they thought would quickly surrender once the Jolly Roger was hoisted. To Vane's surprise, he received an answering broadside. As his targeted ship raised her colors, the pirate captain saw that she was a French man-o'-war. Though most of his crewmembers were eager to fight, Vane realized the odds were against them. Consequently, he reminded his mates of their signed articles and the fact that prior to and during an attack, a captain had absolute command authority.

Frustrated, the pirates withdrew from the engagement. The following day, Vane—under those same articles—stood before the crew and a vote. He was branded a coward. Vane and those who voted for him were given a prize sloop and permitted to sail away. The remaining crew voted Vane's quartermaster, John Rackham, to the post of captain.

Near the coast of Honduras, Vane's sloop encountered sudden gale-force winds and was wrecked. Washed ashore on a deserted island, Vane, the only survivor, foraged as best he could.

Eventually sighting and hailing a ship, Vane was thrilled to learn that her captain was an old buccaneer cohort, Captain Holiford (a.k.a. Holford). Vane's excitement soon turned to horror when Holiford, who had accepted the king's pardon, refused to take him aboard. Despite Vane's promise not to attempt a mutiny or murder, Holiford did not trust him. As luck would have it, another ship soon approached the island for fresh water. Vane, not wanting to be recognized, posed as a shipwrecked sailor. Taken aboard the ship, he thought he was home free.

Unfortunately for Vane, Holiford himself made contact with the ship Vane now sailed as an ordinary crewman. A friend of the captain, Holiford went aboard to dine. Glancing down into the hold, he recognized Vane. Placing him in irons, Holiford brought him back to Jamaica in 1719, where he was hanged three months later.

Calico Jack and the Lady Pirates

Captain John Rackham (nicknamed "Calico Jack" because of his fondness for striped calico breeches) was confident he'd make a great sea captain. His chance finally came when Vane was ousted. But he proved to be a mediocre captain at best.

Gold riches were in Rackham's dreams, but not his reality. He considered his base to be Cuba and would land there whenever possible. He attacked mainly local merchant ships and fishing vessels. After two years sailing the West Indies, he made one of his largest hauls: "50 rolls of tobacco and 9 bags of piemento." With little luck and government pirate hunters roaming the sea, Rackham returned to New Providence in April 1719 to accept the king's pardon. It was but a mere few months before Rackham had the need to go pirating again. But Calico Jack's true claim to fame was based on two members of his crew.

Captain "Calico Jack" Rackham.

(Courtesy of the Library of Congress, Prints & Photographs Division)

The Pirate Anne Bonny

Rackham picked up Anne Bonny in New Providence. The illegitimate daughter of one William Cormac, esquire, and the family maid, Mary Brennan, Bonny (a.k.a. Anne Bonn, a.k.a. Ann Fulford) was born 1698 in Kinsale, County Cork, Ireland. After the indiscretion was discovered, Cormac took both mother and daughter to South Carolina. He started anew, becoming a prominent rice planter. Her father's social standing would have virtually guaranteed that Anne would receive the best training for a girl of the period. Attired in the latest fashions, she would have attended teas and other social events for the inevitable social triumph, a suitable marriage proposal. Yet it seems Anne was not cut from the same cloth as the other girls of her age or class.

Many legends abound concerning Anne's wild childhood, although none can be proven. It is known she did not leave home until 1718, when in her 20s she married James Bonny. Definitely not one of her father's favored suitors, the couple sailed to New Providence before the marriage could be annulled. Little—beyond a few tales—is known of James Bonny. The most common is that he became a pirate bounty hunter on New Providence to support himself.

Rackham's appeal lay in his charm and good looks. And by the spring of 1719, Anne Bonny had left her husband for Rackham. Bonny joined him, boarding his ship openly in woman's attire. Women were generally forbidden on vessels because of superstition and the sexual tension their presence created. Interestingly, Rackham's crew allowed Bonny to remain. She became quite skilled in the use of flintlock, boarding axe, and sword while acquiring a reputation within the pirate community for being fearless and headstrong in battle. Preparing for an attack, Anne would change into men's garments, allowing her greater mobility during a battle.

Mark Read Unmasked

Unlike Anne Bonny, Mary Read, posing as Mark Read, preferred to keep her gender concealed throughout most of her lifetime.

Mary's mother lived with her in-laws while her husband, a seaman, was away on a voyage when Mary was conceived. She abruptly moved to the country when she discovered her pregnancy. After Mary's birth her mother concocted an elaborate charade presenting Mary to the grandmother as her brother. Her grandmother, completely fooled, wanted the "boy" to live with her. When Mary's mother pleaded heartbreak if "he" was taken from her, the grandmother sent money every week to help support "her grandson."

To continue receiving child support, her mother clothed and raised her as a boy. When the ruse was discovered and the money ceased, Read's mother hired her out as a male page to a wealthy Frenchwoman. Enjoying the freedom her disguise allowed, Mary continued her life as Mark Read whenever it suited her needs.

When the War of the Spanish Succession (1701) broke out, Read continued her disguise and signed on an English man-o'-war. Later resigning from the navy, she traveled to Flanders (western Belgium, southwest Netherlands, and northern France), where she enlisted in the infantry and then transferred to the dragoons (mounted infantry). Read fell in love with her bunkmate and revealed her true identity. They planned to be married. Distinguishing herself in battle, her regiment was shocked when she revealed her gender and announced her marriage plans. After the initial shock wore off, the officers were so amused at this discovery they pooled their money for Mary and her lover to open a tavern.

Forced from Maternal Tradition

Upon marrying, Read and her new husband (whose name is still unknown) bought a tavern, the Three Horseshoes, near Castle Breda in the Netherlands. Military clients helped the tavern prosper. For the first time, Read did not have to conceal her gender.

But two unfortunate events were to change Read's life. Shortly after purchasing the tavern, her husband died. At the same time, the Peace of Utrecht (1713–1714) began to create a financial problem. With the military gone, local customers were not enough to keep the tavern in business. Selling the business for less than it was worth, Read's money soon ran out. She was left with few options.

Read Signs On with Calico Jack

Once again donning her male attire, Read signed on a Dutch merchant ship headed for the West Indies. The ship was captured by Captain Vane, and Read, passing as a boy, was encouraged to sign their articles and join the pirate ranks. When Vane's ship reached New Providence, Read—like many other pirates—accepted the king's pardon. Little is known beyond this until Mary, still posing as Mark Read, is found crewing on another Dutch merchantman.

Rackham captured the Dutch ship in 1720 and persuaded many of her crew to sign his articles. Here, fate came into play. Rackham recognized one of the crew as Mark Read, a young man who had once sailed with Captain Vane. He was thrilled when Read eagerly signed. What no one knew at the time was that Mark Read was in fact Mary Read. According to legend it was Anne Bonny who first discovered the ruse. Afterward, Rackham and his crew were informed and readily accepted her as a crewmember.

Mary and Her Man

Having spent years in various branches of the military service, Mary was a confident and accomplished fighter. And as bloodthirsty a pirate as she was, there was a romantic side to her.

Mary fell in love again, this time with a pirate aboard Rackham's ship. Her lover was known for his temper. He started a fight with another crewman. Rackham ordered them to save their dispute until they could go ashore. As stated in the articles, ashore their differences could be resolved with a duel to the death.

Killing for Love

Mary, however, feared for her man, who was a far better lover than fighter. So she came up with a plan that would not only save him, but guarantee he would not gain the reputation of a milksop (a weak sissy). Mary, who was a better swordsman than her lover, purposely picked a fight with her lover's opponent. The shipmate, being new to the crew, did not know her gender or her fighting skill She cleverly scheduled her duel two hours before the two men were slated to fight. The result: Mary killed her lover's opponent.

Mary Read killing fellow pirate.

(The Pirates Own Book, *Charles Ellms, 1837)*

Calico Jack's Hellcats

What is so historically significant about Rackham's crew is not that there were women pirates on board, but that there would be official documentation of that fact. Again, stories abound about how Anne, infatuated by this young man Mark Read, pursued him only to discover the truth of gender; and how Rackham's jealousy nearly caused a fight between the three until the women revealed Read's secret. What is known is that during the two years Anne Bonny and Mary Read sailed with Rackham, all of their crewmates *knew* they were women and accepted them as equals. Accounts of fighting side by side with their shipmates were recounted by former captives who came forward during their trial. Everyone around New Providence was aware of their gender, too. According to French captives, Mary and Anne were seen aboard ship wearing women's clothing. Their gender was also widely known throughout the island of New Providence.

On August 22, 1720, Rackham stole the ship *William* from Nassau Harbor. For Governor Rogers, it was the last straw. On September 5, he issued a proclamation of piracy specifically listing Rackham and all of his crew, including "two women, by name, Ann Fulford, alias Bonny and Mary Read."

The Legend of Rackham, Bonny, and Read Grows

Cruising his favorite hunting grounds along Jamaica's coast, Rackham attacked several ships and settlements. Outraged, the citizens demanded Sir Nicholas Lawes apprehend the fiends. Governor Lawes outfitted a sloop-of-war and commissioned Captain Jonathan Barnet, a privateer, to capture the *William*.

October 22, 1720 began as a successful day for Rackham and crew. Toward evening, near Negril Bay (Long Bay) on the southwest side of Jamaica, they captured a turtle-fishing boat with a large cache of rum. By 10 P.M., most of the crew were passed out in the hold. When Barnet came alongside and hailed the captain, Rackham identified himself. Barnet immediately ordered the pirates to surrender. Drunk, Rackham defiantly fired a swivel gun at Barnet's ship. Barnet retaliated with a broadside. Disabling the ship, he and his men boarded. Drunk to a man, the pirate crew could not fight. Rackham surrendered. Only two members stood against Barnet and his men, Anne Bonny and Mary Read. At their trial, Barnet testified they screamed, swore at their shipmates to attack, and attempted to repel Barnet's men with pistols and cutlasses. Unaware they were women, it allegedly required many men to subdue the two female pirates.

One Sensational Set of Trials

The next morning at Davis's Cove, Rackham and his crew were handed over to Major Richard James of the island militia and sent to St. Jago de la Vega for trial. On November 16 and 17, Rackham and crew were tried at the admiralty court. Governor Lawes presided. Those who could not prove they were forced to serve with Rackham were condemned. The hangings were set for November 17 at Gallows Point near Port Royal and November 18 in Kingston.

Rackham was one of the first to be executed. His final request was to see his lover, Anne Bonny, one last time. He may have hoped for a tearful parting. It was not to be. Chained in her cell, Anne purportedly shouted, "I'm sorry to see you so, but if you'd fought like a man, you need not have been hanged like a dog." Their bodies were hung in gibbets along the shore: Rackham at Plum Point (a.k.a. Deadman's Cay, today known as Rackham's Cay), the other men at Bush Cay and Gun Cay.

Anne Bonny and Mary Read's trial was held on November 28, 1720. Governor Lawes again presided. The courthouse was packed with onlookers. Though both women pleaded innocent, the prosecutor had many witnesses. Each had detailed accounts of the women's actions aboard ship, proving they were direct participants in piracy. The most damaging evidence against them came from Dorothy Thomas, who was captured by Rackham's crew off Jamaica. For everyone curious, the trial transcripts were printed in the pamphlet "The Tryals of Captain John Rackham and Other Pirates, Viz. ... as also the Tryals of Mary Read and Anne Bonny, alias Bonn ..." in 1721 by Robert Baldwin in Jamaica.

> **Dead Men's Tales**
>
> ... That Two Women, Prisoners at the Bar, were then on Board the said Sloop, and wore Mens Jackets, and long Trouzers, and Handkerchiefs tied about their Heads; and that each of them had a Machet and Pistol in their Hands, and curse and swore at the Men ... (she stated) ... That the Reason of knowing and believing them to be Women then was, by the largeness of their Breasts.
>
> —Dorothy Thomas, witness at trial, November 28, 1720

They Plead Their Bellies

When Governor Lawes announced they were sentenced to hang that day, both women calmly announced to the court "they were quick with child" (pregnant). Shock filled the courtroom, so much so that they were required to repeat their statements. Because her common-law husband had been forced aboard ship, Mary refused to reveal his name. Conversely, he did not reveal himself. Once proven by a medical examination, the women's sentences were reprieved until after the birth of their children.

Mary died in prison on April 28, 1721, reportedly from fever. However, there is speculation she died from complications during childbirth. She was buried in St. Catherine's Cemetery. Criminals were not customarily given proper burials, but innocent babies were buried on sanctified church property. Could a pirate mother be buried there with her innocent child?

And what of Anne Bonny? Before her child's birth, she vanished into thin air. Though there is yet no proof to this theory, many believe her father became aware of his daughter's fate either through correspondence with Anne or from the sensationalism of the trial itself. Being a man of wealth and influence in the Carolinas, it is not inconceivable that he was able to quietly arrange for her release with a large contribution to someone's bank account—perhaps even to Governor Lawes himself.

Just Wanting What Was Promised

After Howell Davis destroyed the Royal African Company's trading settlement on St. James Island on the Gambian River, a company of soldiers, under army captain John Massey, was sent to Fort James to provide additional protection. Sailing aboard the *Gambia Castle*, Captain Russell's ship, was second mate George Lowther.

Arriving in May 1721, Massey was taken aback over the substandard provisions and living conditions provided for himself and his men. Before departing for Africa, he was assured quality accommodations if the assignment was accepted. With veiled threats, Massey strongly urged the citizens to honor their promise or he'd take matters into his own hands.

The new governor, having arrived that same day, also was not pleased with his reception and threatened to return to England. Massey held an audience with the governor to resolve the issue because open mutiny looked imminent.

The Moment That Changed Everything

The crew of the *Gambia Castle*, having been told the identical story, did not fare better. When Lowther pressed Russell over their conditions, Russell ordered him flogged. The crew refused to permit the punishment. Fearing for his life, Lowther locked Russell in his cabin and sent a note to Massey for help.

The governor refused to assist Massey and decided not to resign. Receiving Lowther's note, Massey approached his soldiers with a proposition. If they wished to return to England, this was their chance. Agreeing wholeheartedly, the soldiers broke into the provision stores. Massey dismantled the fort's cannon they had brought with them. Taking 11 pipes (casks) of wine, they all boarded the *Gambia Castle*. Sending Russell ashore, they sailed for England.

At sea, Lowther realized his actions' consequences. Gathering everyone on deck, he explained their predicament. Because many of the shareholders of the Royal African Company were government officials, returning to England would only result in the crew's imprisonment or death. Lowther impressed on the men that the only option was to turn pirate. Those not so inclined would be set ashore at a destination guaranteeing their safe return home. All 50 men aboard agreed. Renaming the ship the *Happy Delivery*, they drew up articles (see Chapter 7) and headed to the West Indies.

Soldier Turned Pirate

Off Hispaniola, Lowther's men sighted and hailed a French sloop. Discovering her cargo hold filled with 30 casks of brandy and 5 of wine, Massey went aboard posing as a merchant. Calmly aiming his weapon at the captain, he informed the captain that he would take it all. His crew transferred the cargo and £70 ($11,200) in coin. Before departing, Lowther gave the Frenchman £5 ($800) for his graciousness in entertaining Massey.

> **Treasure Chest**
>
> Though insisting he was only acting in the best interests of his men while on St. James, army captain John Massey was sent to England for trial. He was convicted of mutiny and hanged on July 26, 1723.

Being soldiers and not sailors, Massey was discontent with the life at sea. So despite Lowther's warning, Massey and 10 soldiers took the next prize and sailed to Jamaica to plead their case.

Meanwhile, Back in the Caribbean

Lowther continued raiding any ship he encountered. During one of these incidents, Charles Harris joined his crew. At the Grand Cayman Islands (northwest of Jamaica), Lowther met pirate Ned Low, who just lost his ship. Low and crew boarded the *Happy Delivery*. Lowther appointed Low his lieutenant. But their methods and personalities clashed. On May 28, 1722, they parted company. Harris and Francis Farrington Spriggs, an original crewman of the *Gambia Castle*, chose to sail with Low. Lowther's men continued on as before.

One More Journey

In the spring of 1723, they sailed to Newfoundland to rob the towns and merchants. En route to the Caribbean and in dire need of careening, Lowther chose to land on Blanco Island, near Tortuga. Captain Walter Moore of the sloop *Eagle* could not believe his luck when he saw the vessel beached on the island. As recounted in Chapter 7, Lowther never left the island.

In 17 months, Lowther is credited with capturing 37 vessels.

A Bad Seed from Birth

Edward "Ned" Low (a.k.a. Lowe, a.k.a. Loe) was a delinquent boy in England and grew up to become a sadistic man. Landing in Boston with a brother, he became a ship rigger, married, fathered a daughter (a son died in childbirth), and later lost his wife. Low sailed the Bay of Honduras to join one of the notorious illegal log-cutting gangs. Always short-tempered, he got into an argument with a ship's captain, attempted to shoot him, missed, and killed a sailor. Seizing a ship, he and a few other companions decided to turn to piracy.

Low met Lowther in the Cayman Islands, where the pirates gathered to hunt turtles, and the two men joined forces. Low learned his torture technique from watching Lowther. Captain Lowther's specialty was ramming splinters down victims' fingernails, setting them alight, and then watching them burn until his captive divulged the whereabouts of the captured ship's strongbox.

After parting with Lowther in May 1722, Low drew up ship's articles, proceeded to create a fleet, named his flagship the *Fortune*, and began a killing spree. Harris took command of the *Rover*, and Spriggs, the *Delight*.

Cruelty with a Quirk

Low's favorite tactic involved sailing into port and attacking anchored ships. Though he did not sail with the red flag of "no quarter," if the crew resisted he killed everyone, and then stripped and burned the ship. He also imprisoned (aboard) common seamen, whom he delighted in abusing on a daily basis.

> **Treasure Chest**
>
> When a prize was taken, the first question Low asked each man was his marital status. If married, Low set them free. So adamant was he on this issue, Low had it written into the ship's articles.

A Well-Deserved Reputation

Low's preferred hunting grounds were the eastern shores of North America and the Gulf of Honduras. He quickly acquired a reputation for cruelty. For some unknown reason, he despised the Portuguese and focused most of his sadism on their captains.

One captured crewman recounted an incident in which a Portuguese captain threw a pouch of 1,100 gold coins overboard to prevent Low from seizing the money. It was a fatal error. In his rage, Low tied the captain to the mainmast. Then with his cutlass, he cut off the captain's lips, cooked them over a fire, and forced his first mate to eat them. Low then disemboweled or decapitated the entire 32-man crew. When a colonial warship captured one of his ships in 1723, Low focused his tortures on colonial crews. His brutality only increased. Capturing a whaling ship off Newfoundland Banks, Low cut off a man's ears and then made him eat them, seasoned with pepper and salt.

His True Colors

Near the coast of Rhode Island on June 10, 1723, the HMS *Greyhound* challenged Low's fleet. Spotting the warship first, Low ordered his men on the *Fortune* to run, abandoning a co-captain, Charles Harris, who was in charge of the *Rover*, to face the man-o'-war alone. Her captain, Peter Solgard, called for Harris's surrender. He reluctantly complied. The ensuing trial was held in Newport. Of the 48 crewmen on trial, 23 were able to prove they were forced and didn't participate in any attacks or take any share of booty. They were acquitted. On July 19, Harris and 25 others were hanged.

Low continued to cut a bloody swathe from North America to Honduras until the end of 1724, when he was not heard from again. Three scenarios may explain the sudden end to his infamy. First, his ship sank with no survivors. Second, he settled in Brazil. Third, the one most circulated, is that he had a fight with his quartermaster and killed him while the man slept. Though the booty he acquired for his crew was substantial, they had had enough of his behavior and set him adrift with two others. A French ship picked them up. Low was recognized, sent to Martinique, and hanged. In 20 months, he had captured more than 140 ships.

Another Split in the Ranks

Not long after deserting Captain Charles Harris in 1723, one of Low's men killed a shipmate aboard ship.

Because their articles declared that death was punishment for a killing aboard ship, another co-captain, Francis Farrington Spriggs of the *Delight*, pressed the issue. Without any explanation, Low refused to have the man punished, let alone killed. That night, manning the *Delight*, Spriggs and a small crew sailed off on their own. He built a fleet of five ships and sailed Low's old route until May 1725, when—fate unknown—his name was last recorded in a ship's log.

Spriggs and a mate, Shipton, were ousted and set adrift by the crew. Hunting for the two, a Lieutenant Bridge, commanding the sloop *Diamond*, heard the men were living with Miskito (Mosquito a.k.a. Musketto) Indians in Honduras. Engaging an Indian guide, Bridge and a party of 50 sailors and marines surprised Shipton in bed (sleeping or otherwise occupied not noted).

End of an Era

With the demise of Ned Low and with Bartholomew Roberts's crew's quick surrender—instead of engaging in a glorious battle to the death—the Golden Age of piracy was at an end.

The Least You Need to Know

- Captain Vane thought he could stand behind his ship's articles to justify his actions. However, his crew used his identical argument of abiding by the articles to oust him.

- Anne Bonny could not stand the thought of a staid life and sailed off for adventure.

- Mary Read spent most of her life hiding behind a male persona. She was a sailor, infantryman, dragoon, and pirate.

- Captain "Calico Jack" Rackham dreamed of being a great pirate captain. He was in fact a mediocre leader whose ship was easily apprehended.

- George Lowther and shipmates unwillingly turned pirate when circumstances forced their hand.

- Ned Low was one of the more sadistic pirates of his time. Even his own pirate crew could no longer sail with him.

20

Barbary Corsairs Spread Terror

In This Chapter

♦ The Knights of Malta versus the Barbary corsairs

♦ Corsairs rule the waterway

♦ East meets West in constant battle

♦ Spain vies for control

♦ Sultan tries also using the corsairs

♦ Europe forced to concede

After piracy had been all but eradicated in the West Indies, by the 1730s economic focus shifted to the Mediterranean. Despite centuries of bloodshed and political intrigue, most Westerners were unaware of the many political rivalries and Muslim dynasties that vied for control of the area. Nor did most Europeans or colonists care until their economy was greatly impacted.

The grand period of the Muslim corsairs is considered 1492, when the Spanish expelled the Moors from Granada, until the death of the Great Ali Basha in 1580. This is the time when great men sailed and fought over control of the Barbary coastline.

Thinking they no longer needed to fear pirate attacks on their merchant fleets, European countries turned their full attention to the abundant economic possibilities offered in the region. But to their horror, Europeans faced a completely different kind of pirate: one who preferred capturing human beings (of any race and nationality) as opposed to just seizing gold and cargo—a tradition dating back centuries.

Call It What You Will, You're Still a Pirate

During the Crusades, the Knights of the Order of St. John of Jerusalem began as a group dedicated to providing hostels for pilgrims on their way to the Holy Land. They tended the sick and wounded who waged war against Islam. Acquiring land and wealth, the order eventually became a powerful military force.

The Fortress of Rhodes

Occupying Rhodes (in the Aegean) in 1309, the order turned it into an island fortress. They defended the island against attack for 200 years. From Rhodes their ships embarked, crewed by knights from Spain, France, and Italy. Their purpose was to curb the "infidel incursion." The Turks captured Rhodes in 1523 and Emperor Charles V awarded the order the island of Malta. From this base of operation, they became known as the Knights of Malta.

Though they had begun with the pure intent of protecting Christianity and Christians, by the time the Turks captured Rhodes in 1523, the men of the Knights of the Order of St. John were, for all intents and purposes, pirates.

The Base at Malta

Located in the middle of the Mediterranean Sea, Malta gave the Europeans a strategic advantage. Because of Malta's position between Sicily and Tripoli, Muslim ships could not safely sail without being detected and attacked. The Maltese corsairs (as the Knights of Malta were locally called) sailed the eastern Mediterranean and Indian Ocean. Undeterred, the Barbary corsairs—from the early 1500s—simply operated in the western Mediterranean and Atlantic Ocean. Under Muslim control, Morocco, Algiers, Tunis, and Tripoli were known as the states of the Barbary Coast. Soon Barbary corsairs and the Knights of Malta operated as private armies for the rulers of their respective countries.

Galley of the Knights of Malta.

(Sea Wolves of the Mediterranean, *Cmd. E. Hamilton Currey, R.N., 1910*)

The Fighting Ships of the Knights of Malta

The fighting galeasse of the Knights of Malta was a low galley. With a length of 180 feet and a beam of 19 feet, the depth of her hold was a mere 7.6 feet. She was built with a large forecastle and a stern castle rising some 6 feet above the rowers. When the wind was in their favor, and for additional speed, the sailors would furl the lateen sails on the two masts. However, the galeasse's primary propulsion was generated by her human rowers. With mounted guns, the galeasse became a far heavier ship, ranging upward to 1,000 tons, far heavier than that used by the Barbary corsairs. And the number of men needed to operate the vessel was close to 1,000.

Dead Men's Tales

Her crew consisted of 452 rowers, 350 soldiers, 60 Marines, 12 steermen, 40 ordinary seaman, 36 cannoneers, 12 petty officers, 4 boatswains' mates, 3 pilots, 2 sub-pilots, 4 counsellors (priests), 2 surgeons, 4 writers, 2 sergeants, 2 carpenters, 2 caulkers, 2 coopers, 2 bakers, 10 servants, a captain, a lieutenant, a purser. In all just under a thousand men, or about the same number a crew of a three-decker of a later date.

—*The Readable Treaties of Adm. Jurien de la Gravière, 1886*

Treasure and Their Cut

So equipped, the galeasse and smaller oared galleys would send out their fleets for years at a time. With their heavier vessels, they did not need to wait out the winter.

The knights sold their booty in the Christian-held ports of Acre (a.k.a. Akko, northeast of Haifa) and Joppa (southeastern coast of Palestine), and under a white flag of truce, they traded in Tunis and Tripoli. After giving a percentage to each port ruler (the amount dependent on where they anchored), 10 percent of all profits were allocated to the order for provisions. Five percent went toward the maintenance of captives. The captain received 11 percent. The crew evenly shared out the remaining profits. In addition to their personal shares, the cook received all cooking items, and the surgeon all medical items.

Hand Weapons of Choice

The soldiers aboard the Malta galleys wore armor. The helmet, called a morion, was crested and featured a curved side designed to deflect sword blows. A solid curved full-chest plate protected the wearer from Turkish arrows. During hand-to-hand combat, the soldiers wielded a full-cupped, thin-blade rapier etched with the eight-pointed Maltese cross.

Galleys manned by captives (usually, prisoners of war) were the primary mode of transportation in the Italian city-states and France. Therefore, expanding this mode of transportation into fighting ships for "the grace of God" using heathen rowers left few people outraged.

The Ships of the Barbary Corsairs

The galley of the Barbary corsair was designed specifically for the calmer waters of the Mediterranean. As for the first ships of this region, though it had two masts and sails, it was essentially an oared vessel. The galley was typically 165 feet long with a 13-foot beam and an 8-foot hold. Some 300 rowers powered the ship. With a low prow and sides, the ship was slow to maneuver. The advantage to her design was a rammer that rose high over the deck. With the oarsmen pulling, she had short bursts of extreme speed. The galley would broadside their enemy using the rammer to crash into the ship and then as a gangway to board their prey. The ship was so streamlined and spaces so tight that the men had to be well disciplined, with everyone working in unison with one another. Each man knew exactly where to stand or sit while sailing or during battle preparation. This exactness on the part of the ship's company was imperative if the vessel was to remain steady and so as not to impede the rhythm of the oar strokes.

Barbary corsair galley.

(Sea Wolves of the Mediterranean, Cmd. E. Hamilton Currey, R.N., 1910)

The Galley Crew

The hierarchy used is similar to that of privateers in the West. The ship owner or shareholders chose the captain (*rais*). The crew and soldiers received no wages, but were allowed a percentage of whatever they captured.

The janissaries were the famed fighting Barbary soldiers. Between 100 and 200 janissaries sailed on each galley. Their commander (*aga*) took charge of the vessel just before the battle, and during a boarding attack. A scribe was aboard to inventory prizes, treasure, and slaves. The ruler of each port received 10 percent of all profits.

Janissary Weaponry

Well into the 1700s, the janissaries' long-range weapon was the bow and arrow. Their close-combat weapons were the intricately etched *nimcha* swords or the old scimitar used during the Crusades.

Corsair dagger and sheath.

(Photo: William Perlis)

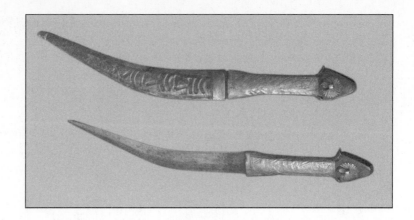

Knowing the Ropes

A **nimcha** sword was an Arabic saber used during the sixteenth century. The etched blade was approximately 37 inches long, very wide, and only slightly curved. The grip was made from a single piece of wood, or buffalo or rhino horn. The pommel was a one-sided square carved to represent a lion's head, with a curved neck that one gripped with the little finger. The scabbard for a nimcha was wood covered in velvet, leather, or (if the soldier was wealthy) etched silver.

The Manpower of the Galeasse and Galley

Enemy captives provided the manpower that pulled the oars for both these vessels. With few variations their conditions were frighteningly similar. Men who rowed the galleys did so for six-month stretches unless they were ransomed beforehand or died. Those unfortunate men on the galeasse also had either ransom or death to look forward to.

Men were shackled together by their ankles to their position at the oar. Seven men sat to a wooden oar (50 feet in length), their bench only 10 feet long and 4 feet wide. Stark naked, they sat on woolen-filled sacks. A sheepskin covered the entire length of the bench, but it was not for the comfort of the rower. It was discovered the sheepskin helped create an easier rhythm when the men rocked back and forth pulling and pushing the heavy oars continually in and out of the water.

Rowers pulled an average of 10 to 20 hours nonstop. Two brutish overseers strolled a wooden bridge between the two lines of rowers. The overseers whipped the men if they dared slacken the pace. With no room to lie flat, the slaves slept curled over their oars or against each other.

The overseers never allowed the rowers to stop for their meals. The boatswains stuffed pieces of wine-soaked bread into the men's mouths as they rowed so as not to slacken the pace of the ship. When not at a required speed, or if stopped for any length of time, the men received a biscuit soaked in oil, vinegar, and water. On a good day, a thin gruel or soup would be served. The overseers did not concern themselves with keeping their oarsmen alive.

> **Treasure Chest**
>
> The oarsmen on Christian ships were chained to their oars naked, without even a loincloth to cover their genitalia. As infidels, they were not looked upon as human and therefore did not deserve any consideration of personal decency.

They were captured "infidels" or "dogs." And if one died at the oar, there were other captives in the vessel's hold waiting to take his place, as well as replacements on future captured prizes.

Venturing Out

The corsairs refrained from sailing between mid-December and mid-March. In spring, they sailed the northern Aegean. In summer, they cruised around Cyprus. In late summer, they headed toward Syria. By autumn, they were back in the northern Aegean. Their targets were any ships crewed by Turkish "infidels." Though captives were their main commodities, they also searched for coffee, sugar, rice, and lentils. Their biggest score would be capturing a cargo of wood. Wood was extremely scarce in all the Greek, Turkish, and Barbary ports, and therefore the market price was astronomically high.

Converts to Islam

The nationality of the Barbary crews changed with the times. Before the mid-1500s most corsairs were Turkish Muslims. As European pirates began leaving the Spanish Main and West Indies, many migrated to the Berber states, converted to Islam, and were therefore treated as equals. These men from England, Sicily, Calabria (southern Italy), Venice, France, and the Netherlands brought with them valuable European navigational skills, charts, and sailing instruments. The Barbary corsairs were quick learners and grew bolder, widening their sailing routes in search of slaves for galleys, harems, and merchants.

The Corsair Routes

With the information provided by their newly converted zealots, the Barbary corsairs expanded their sailing routes, remaining at sea for five to seven months at a time. They sailed the entire western Mediterranean, the Atlantic Ocean to the Azores, and the cold north, raiding and plundering as they went. During the period 1569 to 1616, corsairs captured more than 466 men, women, and children from the British Isles. They traveled far inland on night raids into the isolated hamlets of western England. In 1627, sailing from Algiers, a corsair fleet attacked Reykjavik, the capital of Iceland. The number of captives, depending on whose report you read, ranged from 400 to 800. The Barbary corsairs well deserved the name "the scourge of Christendom." When they required provisioning or a haven, the Turks found safety on the islands of Forementara (an island of the Spanish coast), Corsica, Stomboli, or Lipari in the Mediterranean.

The Barbary corsairs did not blockade the trade routes between Europe and the Orient. Their galleys would lay hidden, patiently waiting for vessels to dare the crossing. Then they attacked.

Their Time in the Limelight

So who were these men, these dreaded Barbary corsairs who as recently as the twentieth century caused elderly fisherman to post guards around their towns in Iceland, ready to sound the alarm if an oared galley was sighted?

The Legendary Corsair Brothers

Uruj (a.k.a. Aruja) and Khizr (a.k.a. Horuk), the famous Barbarossa brothers, were not Turks. They were born of Albanian and Greek Christian ancestors. Like his father, Uruj became a sailor. But on his first raiding trip, his ship sailed too close to the island of Rhodes (settled at that time by the Knights of St. John of Jerusalem) and was sighted by the Christian knight ship *Our Lady of the Conception*. Unable to escape the 52-oared vessel, Uruj and his shipmates were captured and thrown into the hold until such time as another rower was needed. Though the other oarsmen were Muslim, and Uruj was a Christian, the knights did not release him.

Shackled with a defective bolt, Uruj broke free and—during a raging gale—slipped over the side and swam for the nearest shore. Yes, Uruj could swim, as could his brother, Khizr.

The Barbarossa brothers.

(Sea Wolves of the Mediterranean, *Cmd. E. Hamilton Currey, R.N., 1910)*

HORUSCE und HAREADEN BARBAROSSA
Könige von Tunis und Algiers und ober See Admiralen

Uruj established a corsair base on the island of Jerba off the eastern coast of Tunis, attacking any ship that did not bear the crescent of Islam, and waited for his brother Khizr to arrive. Khizr, by this time, had established himself as a fierce corsair in his own right.

When the brothers were reunited, they approached the sultan of Tunis. They requested Jerba as their official base from which to attack Spain and Venice, and Tunis as the port in which to sell their booty. Delighted, the sultan granted their requests and, agreeing to one fifth of all their spoils, provided them with additional ships and men.

Barbarossa Becomes a Much-Feared Name

In 1504, the Barbarossa fleet spotted two large galleys sailing in convoy. They purposely sailed miles apart to provide safe maneuverability. The galleys were the treasure-laden vessels belonging to Pope Julius II on their journey from Genoa to Civita Vecchia and finally Rome. The corsairs attacked the first galley. The pope's sailors, shocked that someone would dare such a sin, offered almost no resistance, and the brothers easily captured the ship.

Forcing the men to strip, the corsairs dressed in their enemy's clothes and had the oarsmen row more slowly until the second galley was almost alongside. They captured the second treasure ship with equal ease. The profits from the sale of goods, slaves, and ransom were enormous. Europeans later adapted this ruse of changing clothes and using captive vessels against corsairs.

Those who were returned to their various Italian city-states spoke in horror of the fierce Barbary corsair Barbarossa. The name translated from Italian is Red Beard. Later the Grand Turk, impressed by the valor shown by Khizr, conferred upon him the title of Kheyr-ed-Din (a.k.a. Khair-ad-Din), "The Protector of Religion." During both their lifetimes, Uruj and Khizr were known among their enemies as the Barbarossa brothers. Only after the death of his brother Uruj did Kheyr-ed-Din allow himself to be addressed by peers or compatriots as Kheyr-ed-Din Barbarossa. He added the name as homage to his brother.

Knowing the Ropes

The most common titles of the rulers on the Barbary Coast were …

- ◆ **Aga.** Leader of the janissaries, the elite Muslim soldiers.
- ◆ **Bashaw.** A Turkish head of government and top military commander.
- ◆ **Bey.** A governor or an official of equal rank to a governor.
- ◆ **Dey.** Commanding officer of all military troops.
- ◆ **Pasha.** Muslim (non-Turkish) head of government and top military commander.
- ◆ **Sultan.** Sovereign (supreme leader) of any Islamic country; also called the Grand Turk.

Spain Makes Her Move

Piracy along the Barbary Coast grew with the success of the Barbarossa brothers. Spain was vying for control of the Mediterranean, as was the great Italian city-state of Venice. And with the increasing frequency of corsair attacks on Spanish towns and shipping, the Spanish crown was demanding their heads.

In 1492, as Christopher Columbus was sailing for the New World, King Ferdinand and Queen Isabella were declaring the expulsion of all Moors and Jews living in Spain. While the Jews scattered across various countries, the Spanish Moors, all but for a few, settled en masse in Algiers, directly across from their former homes.

Adding Insult to Injury

Count Pedro Navarro seized Algiers in 1510 in the name of Spain. Navarro built a tall towering stronghold to intimidate the population from any thoughts of rebellion. For the Moors, who had been thrown out of their place of birth a mere 18 years earlier, to again be under Spanish rule was unacceptable.

Though they tried, after six long years of Spanish occupation, the Moors were unable to rid the town of their invaders. Desperate, they sent word to Uruj Barbarossa for help. Uruj set out by land with his men, meeting up with 18 galleys and 3 *barca-longas* filled with provisions. With a force of some 6,000 corsairs, Uruj attacked and seized Algiers, laying siege to the tower for 20 days without success.

> **Knowing the Ropes**
>
> **Barca-longas** (or barques) were large ships of two or three masts with lengths up to 70 feet. They used lugsails secured to the yards, which were two thirds the length of a normal sail, so the sail furled on a slant.

Uruj believed the Berber chieftains (the local tribesmen of Morocco and Algiers) and a few of their Berber corsairs had become spies for the Spanish. Enraged, Uruj had them assassinated. When it was learned that their Berber cohorts were murdered, Fray Francisco Ximenes, the cardinal archbishop of Toledo, was furious that mere pirates could flaunt themselves at the might of imperial Spain. He sent Don Diego de Vera with 15,000 soldiers to Algiers in September 1516 to rout "the pirate rabble."

Keep the Fort, We'll Keep the Town

Though successful in routing the Spanish fleet, the Spanish still held the fort (until 1529), but the brothers controlled Algiers. Uruj became sultan of Algiers. Now with his corsairs, he proceeded to sack the towns along the province of Algeria. Thus Uruj and his corsairs easily took the city of Tlemcen in 1518.

Barbarossa Loses His Head

The city of Tlemcen was located a mere 170 miles from the city of Oran, site of a large Spanish garrison. The Spanish sent a large force to both garrison the city and blockade Tlemcen until the cutthroat Barbarossa surrendered or died.

To add insult to injury, Uruj led sorties out of the city against the Spanish. During one surprise raid, Lieutenant Garzia de Tineo mortally wounded the great Barbarossa with a pike. To ensure the fallen pirate was truly dead, Garzia de Tineo cut off his head. Though the Spanish crown may have been delighted with the news of Uruj's death, they in no way had quashed the corsair menace along the Barbary Coast.

One Brother Down, the Other Rises to Glory

With the death of Barbarossa, Kheyr-ed-Din became the unofficial ruler of Algiers. Unlike his brother, Kheyr-ed-Din was a diplomat and knew he could not sustain his power base without the assistance of the Grand Turk Selim I. Kheyr-ed-Din humbly petitioned his leader for assistance. He was subsequently granted the title and power of governor-general of Algiers, with orders to wipe all "non-believers from the land and seas."

Kheyr-ed-Din.

(Sea Wolves of the Mediterranean, *Cmd. E. Hamilton Currey, R.N., 1910)*

Backroom Treaties

European heads of state continued to jockey for territories, making and breaking treaties and behind-the-scene alliances. While they were bickering and plotting among themselves, in 1534 Kheyr-ed-Din and his corsair fleet ravaged southern Italy and Spain, returning triumphantly with thousands of slaves.

Andrea Doria Sent to Destroy the Sultan's Fleet

By 1538, combined European naval forces under Admiral Andrea Doria were sent to crush the corsair fleet of the sultan. However, Emperor Charles V, who controlled the European squadrons, refused to allocate all naval power available. Unbeknownst to Doria, Charles V—up until the eve of battle—was in secret negotiations with Kheyr-ed-Din. Charles hoped to persuade the Algerian leader to ally himself with Spain and Venice and abandon the sultan. Kheyr-ed-Din refused.

Corsairs in French Rivers

The corsairs now controlled the majority of waterways along the Mediterranean for the next 30 years. The French government, realizing the futility of battling these "fierce sea-wolves," negotiated a treaty with the sultan. To guarantee safe passage of their ships, the French paid an annual tribute. Now allies, it was not an unusual sight to see a corsair galley sailing up the Seine.

Kheyr-ed-Din Barbarossa died in Constantinople in 1548. It was not the end of the Barbary corsairs, because his second in command did him proud.

The Student as Powerful as His Mentor

While Kheyr-ed-Din Barbarossa's son Hasan Pasha ruled Algiers, Dragut Reis (a.k.a. Turgut, a.k.a. Torghud) became the commander of the corsairs. He was the Muslim equivalent of Sir Henry Morgan for his ingenious battle tactics. Though he, too, was born in Greece, he turned pirate at a very early age, converted to Islam, and sailed under Kheyr-ed-Din.

Having been captured in 1540 during a skirmish, Dragut became a galley slave on Andrea Doria's ship for four years. In 1544, Kheyr-ed-Din paid Doria 3,000 gold ducats ($180,000) to secure his release. With the tactical and strategic knowledge Dragut obtained during his four brutal years on the oars, the corsairs were unstoppable.

Down But Not Out

His quest for power never ending, Dragut attacked the island of Elba and sacked Corsica in 1522. He desired to capture all of Africa and place it under the control of his corsairs. But palace intrigue in 1556 forced him from his position as admiral of the corsairs, and he settled in Tripoli as governor. Italy being his favorite hunting grounds, in 1558 Dragut and his men captured and enslaved almost the entire population of Reggio, Italy.

The Siege of Malta

Whereas some historians view the Ottoman corsair raid on the island of Malta as an attack to weaken European supremacy, others believe that it was more an attempt to rid the region of the Christian pirates called the Knights of Malta.

On May 18, 1565, one of the bloodiest and most-brutal sieges against what both groups considered the "infidel" pirates began. It did not end until September 8, four months later. Though recorded in history as a holy war, there was nothing holy about it. It was simply two groups of savage pirates fighting over turf. Drinking wells were poisoned. The heads of their dead enemies were either used as demoralizing cannon shot or paraded on spikes. Underwater pikes and knife fighting was common. Men were burned with hot oil. Period reports, if accurate, suggest that as many as 8,000 Christians and some 30,000 Muslims died.

As the Ottoman corsairs were about to overrun the siege walls and finally slaughter the remaining 600 knights, a false rumor of additional corsair troops began circulating among the Muslims. They pulled back to wait for the reinforcements that never materialized. However, some 7,000 Spanish soldiers arrived from Sicily and drove the Turks from the island. Dragut Reis was not one of the men who left the island alive.

Following in Dad's Footsteps

When his father Suleiman the Magnificent (Selim I) died in 1566, Sultan Selim II continued the tradition of employing corsairs. Selim II, desiring a legacy as great as his father's, chose to conquer the Venetian island of Cyprus. Through spies hearing of the attack, the city-state of Venice, Pope Pius V, and King Philip II of Spain created "the Holy League" to defend the island.

Battle of Lepanto

In 1571, the battle of Lepanto off the Greek coast demonstrated to Europe that the corsairs and the Ottoman Empire could be defeated at sea. The losses on both sides were horrible, 5,000 Christians and some 30,000 Turks. The numbers of captured men on both sides were also in the thousands.

Treasure Chest

Miguel Cervantes de Saavedra and his brother Rodrigo survived the battle of Lepanto. Returning to Spain, they were captured by corsairs. Both sold into slavery, ransom demands were sent to their father. Diligently saving every peso, Señor Cervantes could only save one son. The corsairs chose Rodrigo. After five years in captivity and failed escape attempts, a Trinitarian priest negotiated Miguel's freedom for a £100 ($16,000) ransom. Miguel Cervantes returned home and turned to writing. His play "El Trato de Argel," written in 1784, dealt with the life of a Christian slave trying to survive captivity in Algiers. He is better known for *El Ingenioso Hidalgo Don Quijote de la Mancha* (or *Don Quixote de la Mancha*).

Though they were unable to capture Cyprus, the territorial lines of control for the next 250 years were clearly established. European governments controlled the land from the Straits of Gibraltar to the northern shores of Dalmatia (Croatia). The Muslims held the Mediterranean from Albania to the south Atlantic shores.

Forced to Deal

Realizing that the trade routes to the Near East and the Orient were still controlled by corsairs—and as much as it hurt their dignity—the European governments were forced to deal with the Ottoman sultan. Spain was the first to sign a treaty in 1580 and pay tribute. England and the Netherlands followed suit. The large-scale corsair raids once felt in the Aegean and Adriatic shifted in the 1600s to Morocco, Algiers, Tripoli, and Tunis.

The Least You Need to Know

- Even after the Crusades ended, European Christians and Turkish Muslims continued to fight over territory.

- The Knights of Malta considered themselves the protectors of Christianity. The Islamic population considered them pirates.

◆ The Barbarossa brothers led the Barbary corsairs to legendary victories. They thwarted Emperor Charles V's dream of greater territorial control.

◆ Spain's expulsion of the Moors in 1492 forced them to settle in Algiers. When Spain decided to conquer Algiers, the Moors turned to the Barbarossa brothers for help.

◆ Dragut Reis succeeded the Barbarossa brothers. A brilliant strategist, he kept the European powers on the defensive.

Chapter 21

A New Nation's Privateers Help Topple Corsairs

In This Chapter

- A new nation of privateers
- "Great American pirate" John Paul Jones
- Independence has its problems
- America builds a navy
- One final hurrah
- Jean and Pierre Lafitte

Despite peace treaties with—and tribute from—European governments, the Barbary corsairs (operating from western North Africa, from Egypt to the Atlantic Ocean) continued to attack and seize merchant vessels.

In fact, no nation seemed capable of stopping these pirates until a relative newcomer on the world stage decided she'd had enough and would tolerate no more attacks on her ships. That newcomer was the fledgling United States of America.

A Nation Built on Privateering Goods and Profits

The war for the American colonies' independence from England was fought not only on land, but at sea. The newly formed Continental Congress in 1775 had barely enough money in its war chest to commission a small number of ships and thus establish an official American navy. And with the superiority in numbers, size, and quality of England's warships, fielding a Continental navy that could effectively counter the dominant Royal Navy seemed a daunting, if not impossible, task. To even the odds, colonial privateersmen were asked to step up to the plate.

Colonial Sailors

Colonial sailors were veterans of the continual European wars. They were expert at evading warships when outmatched. They knew how to launch lightning strikes against larger, more-powerful ships, and just as quickly withdraw if it appeared their opponent was about to get the upper hand. Colonial sailors were also adept at smuggling and dismissing laws that hindered their ability to trade whatever cargo they chose. Consequently, patriotism, mixed with a healthy dose of personal pride and a yearning for profit, spurred the sailors to accept commissions as privateers for the struggling nation.

Aware they were no match for the ships of the Royal Navy, the American privateersmen concentrated on English merchant ships transporting supplies to enemy forces. They also prevented colonial goods from reaching English ports. In addition to absconding with English goods, privateersmen provided the Continental Army with much of the armaments and provisions originally intended for English troops.

No Pay, But Adventure and Treasure

Like those from other nations and previous periods in history, American privateersmen did not earn wages. Any profit a seaman received was gained from a successful excursion. Fortunately, they were indeed successful. It has been estimated that by war's end, more than 3,000 English merchant ships were successfully brought into American ports.

The larger ships concentrated their efforts in the Atlantic Ocean and the Caribbean Sea. The smaller schooners and sloops disrupted the fishing fleets off Newfoundland. The French, hoping to weaken the British army and navy, allied themselves with the colonies. They opened all their ports as safe havens to American privateers.

Colonial sailor.

(Photo: William Perlis)

Taking the Fight to the Source

Not all naval battles between America and England happened along the shores of the American coastline. Though they were keenly aware that if they were captured they would be tried as pirates, the colonial privateersmen and sailing men of the Continental Navy chose to sail to the safety of France and then engage in battle along England's shoreline.

The Great John Paul Jones

John Paul was born in Scotland in 1747, and went to sea at age 12 as a cabin boy. Eventually earning the rank of captain, he sailed the merchant ship *Betsy* from London to the West Indies. In 1773, John Paul faced down a mutiny and killed the ring leader. Accused of murder, he fled and like many men before him, changed his name, becoming John Paul Jones.

At the outbreak of the American Revolution in 1775, Jones traveled to Philadelphia and joined the newly formed Continental Navy. With his experience he was immediately commissioned a lieutenant. By 1778, after several successful naval battles, Congress rewarded him with the command of the 18-gun *Ranger* with immediate orders to sail to France and from there engage the Royal Navy in her own waters. He was so successful in 1779 he was promoted to commodore.

On September 23, 1779, off the northeast English coast at Flamborough Head, Jones, in command of the *Bonhomme Richard* (so named by him in honor of Benjamin Franklin), and his fleet confronted a convoy of 41 merchant ships escorted by the HMS *Serapis* and the armed merchant ship *Countess of Scarborough*. Jones steered to intercept the *Serapis*, a 44-gun, fifth-rate frigate. The *Richard*'s consort, the 32-gun *Pallas*, set her course for the *Countess of Scarborough*.

At 7:15 P.M., with less than 50 yards between them, the *Serapis* and *Bonhomme Richard* engaged in the battle with simultaneous broadsides. After just 30 minutes, the *Richard* had seven holes along her waterline. Wreckage littering the deck intermingled with 60 dead and many more wounded.

Not willing to claim defeat, Jones ordered his men to grapple the *Richard* to the *Serapis* as her guns set the *Richard* on fire. With only two guns operational, Jones reciprocated until both ships were ablaze.

To deliberately strike one's colors (lower the flag) would have been a sign of surrender, which the defiant Jones had no intention of doing. The flag was shot from its mast, but was down only temporarily. To avoid any more casualties, Captain Pearson struck his colors at 10:00 P.M. After he surrendered the *Serapis*, Jones invited Pearson into what remained of his cabin to share a glass of wine.

> **Dead Men's Tales**
>
> According to legend, with the *Richard* on the verge of sinking, Captain Richard Pearson of the *Serapis* called out to Jones asking if he was ready to surrender. Jones replied, "I have not yet begun to fight." His actual reply was "No, I'll sink, but damned if I'll strike."

Jones quickly became a French national hero. Upon returning to France, King Louis XVI honored him with a gold sword and the Order of Military Merit. A popular ballad of the time hailed Jones as "a great American pirate." John Paul Jones is today remembered as the father of the United States Navy.

A New Nation Forced to Deal with Piracy

Though the Barbary corsairs lost a great deal of power after the siege of Malta, European governments under the agreed-upon treaties continued paying tribute to the sultan. When America gained her independence from England, the corsairs no longer considered them part of England's treaty and therefore a legitimate target.

The *Betsy*

In 1784, a year after the United States officially became a nation, the *Betsy* (*Betsey*), an American merchant ship, was captured off Morocco. It was the first time an American flag had been seen off the North African coast.

The American crew was imprisoned in Tangiers for six months while a treaty with Morocco was completed. It cost the United States $10,000 for their release.

In 1785, within a week of each other, Algerian corsairs captured the *Maria* off Cape St. Vincent and the *Dauphine* off Cádiz. As was their custom, the corsairs then encouraged their American captives to write letters home to raise ransoms for their release.

A Blue-Water Navy

While negotiating for the release of the crews, Thomas Jefferson was attempting to build a *blue-water* U.S. navy. Congress did not see the need to waste money on a venture they believed was no longer necessary. They thought it was far cheaper to pay the ransom tributes than finance a navy.

> **Knowing the Ropes**
>
> A **blue-water** navy is one that has the ships, weaponry, manpower, and supporting resources to project a nation's naval power far from its shores. This is usually assumed to mean that the navy has the capability of projecting sea power worldwide.

A Constitution and Peace Treaty Create a U.S. Navy

In 1787, Congress adopted the Constitution, finally making it legal and possible for the United States to act against kidnappers and blackmail.

Toward the end of 1793, corsairs had seized a dozen U.S. ships. Portugal had a strong blockade at the entrance to the Straits of Gibraltar. They prevented the Algerian corsairs from passing into the Atlantic. Portugal had agreed to send out warships as convoy escorts for American merchant ships, but Portugal's efforts were less than stellar. As hard as he tried, Jefferson still could not convince Congress to build a navy.

A Bit Too Eager

As negotiations were initiated to secure the release of the Americans, a strange turn of events began. Charles Logie, the English consul in Algiers, heard rumors that the foreign minister of Portugal, Louiz Pinto de Souza, was interested in pursuing a treaty with Algiers. Jumping at the chance of being the man to negotiate such an important treaty, Logie took it upon himself to arrange a one-year cease-fire. What Logie didn't do was notify Pinto de Souza of his plan or ask the foreign minister whether there were any provisions that should be included.

The Portuguese first became aware of the truce when a Portuguese warship stopped a Barbary galley sailing through the Straits of Gibraltar and was shown a copy of the treaty. The Atlantic was now open to the corsairs.

In March 1794, Congress voted on a two-prong law: sue for peace with Algiers and at the same time allocate money to build a navy. President George Washington was given approval to build six frigates.

Ships of the Line

To expedite the building of the ships, and to avoid any bad blood between states, Washington had all six frigates built in different shipyards down the coast:

- **U.S.S. *United States*.** 44 guns; Philadelphia, PA
- **U.S.S. *Constitution*.** 44 guns; Boston, MA
- **U.S.S. *President*.** 44 guns; New York, NY
- **U.S.S. *Constellation*.** 36 guns; Baltimore, MD
- **U.S.S. *Chesapeake*.** 36 guns; Norfolk, VA
- **U.S.S. *Congress*.** 36 guns; Portsmouth, NH

On September 5, 1795, before the ships were completed, the United States agreed to a crippling peace. It was agreed the first tribute payment would be sent in the actual cash value in 1795 of $642,000. Future annual payments of $21,600 would be payable in wood, cordage, and ammunition. The trouble now was that the United States had to come up with cash it didn't have. Scrambling to find the money, the fledgling Bank of the United States sent certificates to London banks, but they had difficulty finding countries that had confidence in an IOU certificate from a newly formed country, even if 6 percent interest was attached.

The dey of Algiers was growing impatient. To buy more time, the United States offered the dey a 36-gun frigate until the money could be raised. The treaty was upheld, and after 13 years the captives (83 out of the original 119 men) finally returned home. Following the treaty with the Algerians, treaties were signed with Tripoli and Tunis. At last, America had unfettered access for her shipping. Or so it was believed.

A Nation's First War

Convinced that six frigates were not enough, naval planners had three other ships built with private funding. They were the *Philadelphia*, *New York*, and *Essex*.

The pasha of Tripoli, Yusuf Karamanli, decided in 1801 to increase his tribute demand. He felt he was receiving an insultingly low amount for his exalted position compared to his neighboring countries. When the American government refused his demands, Tripoli declared war on the United States. The pasha hoped to receive a far greater profit through a war with the young country.

Ready for action, the ships of the new American Navy set sail with orders to blockade the Tripolitan harbor.

A Run for Supplies Catches a Warship

For two years the citizens of Tripoli endured the U.S. Navy's blockade, which prevented provisions from entering their city. The corsairs made many attempts to get supplies through with little success.

On October 31, 1803, a corsair galley attempted to run the blockade. Aware of the many shoals that dotted the harbor entrance and that the American ship had a deeper draft than the shallow galley, the corsair sailed in from the east and hugged the coastline.

A Barbary barca-longa.

(Sea Wolves of the
Mediterranean, *Cmd, E.
Hamilton Currey R.N., 1910)*

Treasure Chest

In captivity Bainbridge was allowed visits by the Danish consul in Tripoli, Nicholas Nissen. He passed personal letters of his well-being to Nissen. On the back of the letters was strategic information intended for Preble regarding ship movements written in invisible ink made from lemon juice (the ink became visible when heated).

William Bainbridge, commanding the *Philadelphia*, made his move. Bainbridge sailed after the galley hoping to stop her, but the galley made it safely beneath the fort's guns. Bainbridge then turned back toward the open sea, quickly grounding the *Philadelphia* on shoals close to the fort.

News spread quickly, and corsairs in rowboats sailed out to their enemy's ship and quickly captured the American crew. Through the sheer manpower of numerous slaves, the pirates managed to raise her from the shoals and tow her under the shore batteries. The entire city was thrilled. The pasha was overjoyed. Not only did he have captives to ransom, he now also owned a brand new frigate.

A Daring Mission

Tightening the blockade, Commodore Edward Preble began negotiations for the release of Bainbridge and his crew. Not wanting to leave the *Philadelphia* in the hands of the corsairs, a daring mission to destroy her was launched.

On the night of February 16, 1804, Lieutenant Stephen Decatur and a handful of volunteers disguised as North Africans sailed the *Intrepid*, a renamed captured corsair ketch into the harbor.

Sliding alongside the *Philadelphia*, Decatur's men caught the Tripolitans completely by surprise. The Americans torched her and barely escaped before the *Philadelphia* went up in an enormous blaze. The corsairs on shore could only watch helplessly as their prize burned.

Serious About Peace

With negotiations dragging, Morocco was becoming furious over the continual blockade and their inability to trade freely with Tripoli. They began threatening to war with the United States and applied pressure on the pasha.

U.S.S. Constitution.

The Shores of Tripoli

On April 16, 1805, a force of U.S. Marines and Arab mercenaries attacking across the desert from Egypt—and supported by warships firing from Tripoli's harbor—captured the fortress town of Derna on the eastern side of Tripoli. It was the first time in history that the American flag was raised in the "Old World."

With the Americans closing in and Tripoli's economic losses affecting his lavish life style, the concerned pasha made the decision to get serious regarding peace negotiations. On June 4, Pasha Yusuf Karamanli signed the peace treaty and released his captives. The American Navy and Marine Corps proved to the world they were a force to be reckoned with. And the iron grip of the Barbary corsairs began to crack.

Maneuvering Room

In the early nineteenth century, as Napoleon was cutting a swathe across the European continent, the corsairs again rallied. Taking full advantage of the situation in Europe, they actively hunted the supply ships and merchants that took the longer routes around numerous blockades. The corsairs again attacked cities and enslaved citizens.

With the close of the Napoleonic wars in 1815, the European nations—now with far more advanced weaponry—refocused on the Barbary pirates. In 1816, a combined Anglo-Dutch force sailed to Algiers and bombarded the city until the pasha surrendered the city. The Europeans freed some 3,000 captives. After 300 years of pirating, the power of the Barbary corsairs was breaking. With the occupation of Algiers in 1830 by the French, the Barbary corsairs were eradicated.

A Profitable Business Opportunity

While the newly established United States Navy and Marine Corps were dealing with the Barbary corsairs, a new threat was emerging closer to home.

Since its discovery, control of Florida and the Louisiana territory frequently changed between France and Spain. In 1796, both regions were controlled by Spain. During that year the slave population on San Domingue (present-day Haiti) rebelled, sending its French population fleeing to Cuba and the Louisiana Territory. Pierre Lafitte was one such refugee who settled in New Orleans.

With the Treaty of Madrid in 1801, Napoleon Bonaparte reclaimed the territory for France. With his constant need of funding for his various adventures in the eastern hemisphere, Napoleon in turn sold the area to the United States. Between the Louisiana Territory and the rest of the United States lay the parishes of Spanish West Florida, which included Pensacola, Baton Rouge, and Mobile.

On December 20, 1803, President Thomas Jefferson appointed William C. Claiborne as territorial governor. Claiborne now presided over a diverse population of French, Spanish, Germans, Free Blacks, European Creoles, Cajuns, and slaves. To assure peace, Jefferson sent gunboats to New Orleans with the assurance that the only change in government would be federally appointed customs officials. However, distrust of Americans ran high as merchants and opportunists from all over the United States flooded into the territory.

Brothers Become Partners

After numerous failed business attempts, Lafitte found success in 1805 by selling slaves through private transactions. How he acquired these first few slaves is unknown, but by 1808 there was no doubt how he was obtaining his human merchandise.

President Jefferson and Congress passed a number of laws they hoped would curb smuggling and the influx of foreign slaves. In December 1807, Congress enacted an embargo making it unlawful to trade with other nations, and on January 1, 1808, enacted the Abolition of America's African Slave Trade law. It was now illegal to bring slaves from Africa for sale within the United States. Smuggling through the Gulf of Mexico intensified.

That same year, Napoleon unknowingly assisted Lafitte with his new enterprise. When Napoleon occupied Madrid, he placed his brother Joseph on the throne of Spain. A Frenchman on the Spanish throne was too great an insult even for the Spaniards of Cuba. All French refugees who had settled in Cuba after the San Domingue revolt were forced to leave. They fled to the United States. Within one year, more than 9,000 French, free blacks, and slaves from Cuba had settled in New Orleans; among them, Pierre Lafitte's brother, Jean.

In New Orleans, many refugees were forced to sell their slaves for cash. Pierre was eager to oblige, buying low and selling high. Not satisfied with the limited availability of slaves in New Orleans, Pierre devised plans for a broader smuggling and privateering operation. He approached Jean with a business proposition, and the latter readily accepted.

Smuggler, Privateer, and Pirate

Little is known of Jean Lafitte's early years, before he joined his brother in 1808. Considered a handsome man, he stood more than 6 feet tall. He wore his hair long with his sideburns whiskers stopping just under his chin. Though a sailor most of his life, he had a pale complexion that created an appealing contrast to his dark hair, and large dark hazel eyes. What was often remarked of him (and Pierre as well) in contemporary writings was his "brilliantly white teeth," an unusual occurrence in those years.

Pirate Yarns

Lord Byron's hero in his poem "The Corsair," published on February 1, 1814, has been stated by numerous authors to be fashioned after Jean Lafitte, but this is highly unlikely. Lafitte was not widely known outside the Louisiana and Florida area until the Battle of New Orleans, almost a year after the poem's publication.

A literate man, he spoke four languages: French, Spanish, Italian, and English. Always stylishly dressed with impeccable manners, he was called by the locals of New Orleans "the gentleman Lafitte."

A Base of Operations

By 1805, Pierre Lafitte had established a thriving blacksmith business in New Orleans as one of his many covers to hide his smuggling operations. Pierre handled all the business affairs and contacts. Jean settled their base of operations on Barataria Bay on Grand Terre, situated just south of New Orleans. Like New Providence, it was ideally suited for their needs. The waterway into the bay was far too shallow for warships. The bay extended only 18 miles before it entered into the numerous bayous. Many weed- and marsh-grass–covered islands dotted the bay. Grand Isle and Cat Island were used as additional bases.

Grand Terre Island was a mere six miles long, and at its widest was three miles. The southerly winds kept the mosquito population to a minimum. The Mississippi River deposited large piles of driftwood along the coast as its waters flowed down to the gulf, making passage on the bay treacherous for large ships that didn't know the territory.

The Lafittes built huts for clients and crew and a large barracón (slave barracks) on the island. Jean's trading vessels were flat-bottomed pirogues, canoes carved from cypress tree trunks. The boats' only shelters were canvas-covered poles framed to shade the captain. They were manned by as many oarsmen as could fit each boat. The larger pirogues carried up to 100 barrels of goods and traveled up to 18 miles a day if the wind was not against them. They were also used to ferry clients to Barataria and back to New Orleans for slave and cargo auctions.

A Successful Enterprise

It was a perfect setup. Privateers landed their illegal cargoes on Barataria. Jean transported the goods to New Orleans. Pierre dealt with buyers. Large auctions of goods and slaves were regular occurrences on the island. So successful was their enterprise, privateers and smugglers sought out Jean to arrange sales of their captured goods. When life on land became too monotonous, Jean set sail on his own privateering excursions.

Because the Lafittes provided much-needed commodities that were no longer lawfully bought or sold in the territory, the majority of the populace and judiciary secretly sided with the smugglers. Despite Claiborne's continual attempts to end

smuggling, and especially the Lafittes' enter-
prises, Judge Dominic Hall's court continually
acquitted captured privateers.

In 1812, Louisiana officially became a state and
Claiborne its first elected state governor. Now
he seriously went after the Lafittes. Though it is
doubtful the Lafittes arranged all privateering,
slave sales, and smuggling flowing through New
Orleans, most citizens and Claiborne himself
attributed all the transgressions to the brothers.

> **Treasure Chest**
>
> On November 24, 1813,
> Claiborne issued a $500 reward
> for Jean Lafitte's capture. In
> response, Lafitte had a broadside
> printed and posted throughout
> the city offering $1,000 for the
> capture and delivery to him of
> Claiborne. It concluded, "only
> jesting and desired that no one
> would do violence to his Excel-
> lency."

Debts and a Murder Bring the Law

Though he was able to stay out of federal court, Pierre's extravagant living and
indebtedness constantly brought him into the civil courts. Debt judgments in New
Orleans were considered far more serious than acts of smuggling. After numerous
failed court-appointed debt payments and court appearances, a warrant was issued for
Pierre's arrest for nonpayment.

On January 16, 1814, a bungled smuggling arrest attempt resulted in the wounding of
two officers and the murder of revenue inspector John B. Stout. Whether the Lafitte
brothers were really at the scene is not known; there was no corroborating evidence.
What is known is Claiborne used the incident as an excuse to issue warrants for suspected murder. On July 8, Pierre was arrested during a visit with his common-law
wife. Because there was no real evidence that he had a hand in Stout's murder, he was
charged with failure to pay $12,514.52 in outstanding debts. Knowing the Lafitte his-
tory of making bail and disappearing, Claiborne succeeded in getting bail denied.
Pierre, known in the city far better than Jean (and many people constantly confusing
the two), the newspapers proclaimed the authorities had finally captured the
"Emperor of Barataria" and the "King of Smugglers."

Jean focused on releasing his brother from jail. Though he had enough supporters
and privateers willing to storm the jail, he preferred conventional means. National
politics and war provided his solution.

Offers and Threats

Distressed over England's maritime practices against American shipping during the
Napoleonic wars, war broke out in 1812 between England and the United States. For

the Lafitte brothers, the war meant increased business and great profits as blockades and embargos increased along the East Coast.

On September 3, with Pierre still in jail, Jean sighted a British warship at the mouth of the pass between Grand Terre and Grand Isle. When they lowered a pinnace with a white flag and began to row to shore, Lafitte went out to meet the boat. Captain Nicholas Lockyer of the HMS *Sophie* handed him a packet. Enclosed were official documents from various governmental and military leaders that offered a variety of promises and threats:

♦ England enlisting the aid of all true Louisianans to overthrow the American presence in their state with gracious rewards after victory.

♦ An offer of a captaincy in the British army, $500, and a permanent army position after Lafitte dissolved his current enterprise.

♦ Pardons for his men, land rewards, and army careers for all.

♦ A formal request to use Lafitte's compound on Grand Isle as a base of operation.

The last letter threatened Lafitte and his men if they did not side with Britain. They had to remain neutral during the upcoming military operations or they would be annihilated.

Nothing in the offers interested Lafitte, nor did he appreciate the language used in the letters. He asked for 15 days, saying that he needed the time to discuss the offers with his men. Lockyer reluctantly agreed.

Forced to Choose

The brothers had remained neutral during the war, but now Jean was forced to choose. He was astute enough to realize whichever side won the war, their empire on Barataria would not survive. As much as he disliked many Americans, he hated the English and saw his solution for freeing Pierre. Through an intermediary, Lafitte sent Claiborne the English packet and a letter of his own. Jean offered to block the British army from entering New Orleans by defending the city from his position on Grand Terre and Grand Isle under the condition that all privateers in jail, including his brother Pierre, be released. Jean did not know Pierre had been "mysteriously" freed the same day he sent the packet to Claiborne.

Preparations for Battle

Commodore Daniel Tod Patterson had orders from President James Madison to destroy Barataria. Claiborne was afraid the attack would turn the privateers straight into the British camp, but he had no authority to stop the raid. Claiborne had to wait. Patterson's raid destroyed the compound of Barataria and Grand Isle, and those who survived fled into the bayou.

Claiborne approached the American general Andrew Jackson with the British packet and Lafitte's letter. Jackson did not want to include men in his army who would be yanked from the battle line and returned to jail or arrested. Judge Hall and Claiborne came up with a solution. On December 18, the legislature suspended all pending or new civil suits for 120 days.

Jackson was in desperate need of supplies, especially gunflints. Edward Livingston, a friend of the Lafittes, informed Jackson of the privateers' huge munitions stock. He assured Jackson they would be willing to turn it over to the general for full pardons. Jackson agreed.

Claiborne had the news circulated throughout Louisiana, while Livingston forwarded the news to the privateers. Any man currently in jail or who engaged in any criminal acts would receive a full pardon if he joined the army and took an active roll in the war.

The Battle of New Orleans

On December 22, the Lafittes entered New Orleans and received safe-conduct passes. Jean issued the order, and guns, black powder, shot, and more than 7,500 gunflints flowed into New Orleans, along with 400 privateers and smugglers. Jean was sent with Major Michael Reynolds and 50 men to Temple, just south of Lake Salvadore near Baton Rouge. Pierre remained with Jackson, advising him on the bayou and plantation routes and canals. Fifty Baratarian privateers manned three cannons, making up Battery Number Three.

On January 8, 1815, 3,000 British troops attacked. Dense fog, military mismanagement, and exacting salvoes from Battery Three cut the Brits to pieces. Within half an hour, more than two thirds of the British forces were either dead or wounded. The battle was over. The formerly despised privateers were now hailed as heroes.

Next Stop, Galveston

On February 6, President Madison granted full pardons to all who participated in the battle. Whereas many former privateers retired from the profession, the Lafittes sailed to Galveston, Texas, and resumed their successful privateering and smuggling operation. By 1817, their fleet comprised 20 ships. More brazen than ever, Jean and his men sailed along the gulf attacking Spanish and American ships. In 1820, the U.S. Navy was again dispatched to destroy their operation. The brothers again escaped capture.

Legend and Death

Here is where the legend of Jean Lafitte grows even stronger. Rumors began to circulate as to the fate of the Lafittes. Some men swore they saw Jean in Texas and Louisiana. Other men boasted that they themselves were the privateer Jean Lafitte.

In fact, the brothers joined Simon Bolívar's revolutionary forces in South America. For the first time, Jean had a legitimate commission. His was a private armed vessel in the service of the Columbian navy. Pierre worked his brother's privateering enterprise throughout South America.

In 1821, Pierre died from fever and wounds inflicted during a battle with a British warship. According to the newspaper *Gaceta de Colombia*, dated April 20, 1823, Jean Lafitte died on February 5 in an armed engagement in the Gulf of Honduras.

The Least You Need to Know

- With little money for a navy, the Continental Congress commissioned experienced privateers to attack English ships.

- John Paul Jones was sent to England to fight the enemy on its own turf. Against incredible odds, Jones's fleet managed to capture two British warships.

- When the United States became an independent nation, American ships were no longer part of England's treaty with the Barbary corsairs. Therefore, American ships were seized, and Thomas Jefferson lobbied for a strong American navy.

- An ambitious British consul negotiated a treaty between Portugal and Algiers that Portugal did not approve. Because of his rash actions, Barbary corsairs once again prowled the Atlantic.

◆ The Napoleonic wars shifted the focus from the North African coast to the European continent. Thus corsair raids again flourished, but it was to be their last gasp.

◆ Jean and Pierre Lafitte played major roles in helping defeat the British in the famous Battle of New Orleans.

Chapter 22

Cutthroats of the South Seas

In This Chapter

- ◆ Not willing to share
- ◆ The family home, a pirate junk
- ◆ All in the family
- ◆ Technology and customs
- ◆ Female pirates, a cultural tradition
- ◆ Modern-day accounts of piracy

Long before Europeans were aware of the existence of the oceans and coastlines of the Far East, Asian pirates were sailing the western Pacific coastline, the Sea of Japan, the Yellow Sea (connecting northeast China and the Korean Peninsula), the China seas, and the various straits. Chinese and Japanese pirates constantly preyed on ships and settlements. They did so both as a means of projecting power and gaining a political upper hand, and for reasons that have always compelled pirates to do what they do: they were thieves.

Chinese pirates held a firm grip on the economy and trade of the area until the East India Company became stiff competition in the late seventeenth century. Then they turned their attention to the European merchant ships.

Surprised by their ferocity, Europeans had as hard a time suppressing piracy in Southeast Asia as they did throughout the rest of the world.

When the Europeans arrived and began lucrative trading companies in that specific region of the eastern hemisphere, the local pirate warlords did not take kindly to them. The pirates viewed the Europeans as interlopers horning in on their turf. And they proceeded to make that sentiment quite clear.

First on the Scene

Portuguese traders in the 1500s were the first to settle on the Malacca Straits (connecting the Indian Ocean and the South China Sea). By 1516, Captain General Alfonso de Albuquerque sent a trading *junk* through the straits to Canton, China, to open up trade negotiations. Trading became a serious enterprise between the Chinese and Portuguese that simply accelerated regional coastal piracy.

Chinese pirates traveled in small fleets attacking ships that sailed through the Straits of Malacca between Sumatra and Malaysia. As with pirates throughout the rest of the world, the Chinese targeted ships and settlements. They sought goods, treasure, slaves, and prominent people they hoped to ransom.

> **Knowing the Ropes**
>
> **Junk** is the bastardization of the Portuguese word *junco*, which they used to describe Chinese trading vessels. The word originated from the Indonesian *djong*, meaning a "vessel."

The pirates hid in the numerous mangrove swamps that dotted the area's coastlines. From there, they launched their attacks on unsuspecting victims. The pirates were swift and ruthless.

By the late sixteenth century, the Portuguese held a monopoly on Japanese trade carrying goods back to Europe.

European Traders Infiltrate the Monopoly

When privateer Thomas Cavendish returned to England (see Chapter 4) after circumnavigating the globe, he caused quite a stir. On his ship's yards flew sails made from colorful silk. The ship's hold bulged with exotic treasures. A frenzied obsession with all things "oriental" soon swept through England. And English and Dutch traders set sail for Chinese waters hoping to trade with or rob Portuguese trading vessels.

They're Not Like Us, So It's Okay

By 1590, English pirates were preying on the Portuguese. They also attacked Chinese ships and settlements. In fact, the English viewed Asian traders as coast dwellers, much like they did those of the Indian Ocean.

It's Called a Junk; It's Anything But

The Chinese junk was a versatile ship. The small fishing junk had a 40-foot length with a 9-foot beam. It had two masts. (Oars were used on windless days or if greater speed was required.) The larger cargo junk was 80 feet in length with an 18-foot beam. It had three masts. Depending on water depth, both ships were used interchangeably. Both had rudders that were raised and lowered by ropes. Their lugsails were set on yards at right angles to the mast. This enabled them to catch light breezes. The typical sails were made of bamboo matting. The more-powerful warlords had sails made of colored silk. With an experienced crew and helmsman, a junk was a fast, highly maneuverable vessel.

Junks were easily outfitted for battle by adding swivel guns, called lantaka, along the bow and railing. The powder magazine was a room located in the middle of the hold nestled between the crew's quarters.

The junk was the permanent home to not only the crew but also their families. The captain, his wife or wives, and children had a cabin at the stern of the ship. Crew-members and their families lived in small partitioned rooms in the hold or on deck.

A Piratical Dynasty

Cheng-Chi-Lung (a.k.a. Ching-Chih-Lung, a.k.a. Gaspar Nicholas) converted to Christianity and worked as an interpreter for the Dutch East India Company in 1620. Joining his uncle who owned several junks, he participated in small raids. Because he knew the sailing schedules of the Dutch traders, he was quite successful.

Accused of murder in 1626, Cheng turned to piracy. Within a year, his fleet was terrorizing entire villages and towns and disrupting coastal shipping. The pirates demanded protection money (tribute). In exchange they assured villagers that no pirates from any fleet would raid their homes or junks. So large was Cheng-Chi-Lung's fleet by 1627 that the Dutch governor of Batavia (now Jakarta) in charge of the shipping trade reported, "Commercial navigation has totally ceased." The governor was instructed by the home office to pay the tribute. The Dutch ships were again able to sail.

International Crew

During his 20-year reign, Cheng traveled between the Yangtze and Canton rivers with a fleet of more than 1,000 junks. He had a body of personal guards consisting of former Dutch soldiers and 300 Black Africans freed from Macao (Macau) in southern China.

Visions of Grandeur

The imperial Chinese navy could not stop him. Thus, the emperor offered him a navy commission. Cheng accepted. He then became even more ambitious when the Manchus (Tartars) invaded China and he realized the end of the Ming dynasty was near.

In 1646, Cheng made a deal with the Manchu rulers in Beijing. Cheng offered the fleeing Ming Emperor and his court sanctuary in his pirate province of Fukien. When the emperor and his court arrived, Cheng handed over the entire province to the Manchus and with it the last Ming emperor.

In 1648, Cheng entered the Manchu court at Beijing to receive his new imperial title and other rewards. It was a trap. Fearing his influence and large fleet, the Manchus had Cheng arrested. He was executed in 1661.

A Son's Revenge

With the arrest, torture, and eventual execution of his father, Koxinga (Cheng-C'eng-Kung, a.k.a. Kuo-Hsing Yeh) mounted a savage campaign of revenge.

When his father handed the Fukien providence to the Manchus, the 22-year-old Koxinga relocated the pirate fleet to Taiwan and the Formosa Straits. He welcomed all dissidents to join his crew. He proceeded to cut off the city of Nanking from 1649 to 1650 from all trade by successfully blockading the Yangtze River for nearly a year. He then set his sights on regaining the providence of Fukien: a feat he accomplished within one year. So savage were his attacks, the Manchurian navy left the South China Sea under his control for the next 10 years.

The Mix of Politics and Revenge

He hated the European encroachment into Chinese territory as much as he hated the Manchurians. By 1661, Koxinga successfully drove the Dutch out of Taiwan. His wave of terror was so great in 1662 that the Emperor ordered all individuals living near the coastline of China to evacuate 12 miles inland in an attempt to prevent further killings. Koxinga's fleet continued raiding until his death in 1683. In death, he became a national hero who fought for the Ming cultural dynasty and civilization. He was also immortalized as one of the great pirate warlords.

Scramble for Control

After the death of Koxinga, his great fleet splintered into smaller groups ruled by various warlords. In the face of crumbling dynasties and the scramble for regime control, piracy and open rebellion became entwined. In many ways, pirates and revolutionaries were one and the same.

To the Chinese, piracy (fighting Europeans and corrupt government officials) was considered patriotic, not criminal. This ideology was passed on to generations. Of course, as is always the case, there were the cutthroats sailing for pure gain. It wasn't until the 1800s that another pirate leader as great as Cheng would arise.

The Largest Confederation

Cheng I (a.k.a. Ching Yih) was born in 1765 to a piratical Chinese family fighting a political rebellion in what today is known as Vietnam. Departing in 1802 with his own fleet of 200 junks, he sailed to the province of Kwangtung, and from his base controlled the entire Chinese coast from Korea to the Vietnamese or Indo-Chinese Peninsula.

Cheng's Great Fleet

By 1807, Cheng I's fleet was so large he divided it into six squadrons. The commanders each signed a written constitution of rules regarding their conduct and that of their crews. They became a confederation. To ensure no rivalry would break out between his squadrons, Cheng I assigned each squadron their own territory and independent base of operation.

> ### Treasure Chest
>
> Each squadron was assigned a color. The flagship squadron of Cheng I was red. The other squadrons were yellow, green, blue, black, and white. With each ship of the squadron flying its own colors, there was little confusion during battle. The flag bearers led all boarding parties. Aboard each ship would also be the flag of the empress of heaven, Tien Hou. She was "the calmer of storms and protector of merchant ships."

Cheng I's Red Squadron numbered 600 war junks and more than 30,000 pirates. His entire confederation numbered 150,000, with people continually joining. His larger war junks carried rowboats with 12 swivel guns and room for 20 people. They were used to board captured ships or sail to shore.

The semi-independence of his squadrons ensured cooperation within the confederation. If one squadron was overwhelmed, another large force of compatriots moved to turn the tide of battle. They were so powerful they did not even consider the Qing dynasty navy a threat.

By 1807, the British navy began patrolling the waters from Hong Kong to Macao, but they did not have enough ships to be effective.

Joining to Expel the Invaders

As the power of the Qing dynasty waned in the 1800s and the European power base grew stronger, an increasing number of Chinese villagers joined the fleet. But as pirates they were not simply fighting the Europeans. As in the Chinese piratical tradition, the confederation of Cheng I demanded tribute from villages and cities. By 1808, he began to demand tribute from ship owners.

Passes, Peaceful Surrender, or No Quarter

Ever the entrepreneur, Cheng I issued safety passes to paying vessels. The passes guaranteed none of his squadrons would harass the ship, nor should any other warlord in the area.

Operating similarly to the buccaneers in the Spanish Main, Cheng I had his own rules of surrender. Once hailed, if a ship offered no resistance, the pirates would only take the cargo. If they dared fight, the crew would be in mortal danger. Taking the cargo, the crew would be held for ransom, or tortured and killed. If the pirates did not need the ship, it was burned. But Cheng I was ruthless against any member of the Chinese navy.

Cheng I was washed overboard during a typhoon in 1807. His wife Cheng I Sao became commander.

A Shrewd Fighter and Businesswoman

As a Cantonese prostitute named Shih Yang, Cheng I Sao worked the many *flower boats* in the numerous harbors of China.

Cheng I Sao, which literally translates to "wife of Cheng" (a.k.a. Ching Shih Sao, a.k.a. Cheng Yih Sao), married Cheng I in 1801. As was the custom, Cheng I Sao had fought side by side with her husband during the Vietnamese rebellion. She was able to easily take command of the Red Squadron because of the long-held custom of women fighting alongside their men. This was helped by the Chinese folklore that attributed great mystical powers to women, especially during times of war.

> **Knowing the Ropes**
>
> **Flower boats** were huge floating brothels. They were two or three stories high, ornately carved and decorated on the outside as well as the inside. Flower boats were decorated to reflect the social level of the clientele they wished to attract.

Cheng I Sao was an exceptional leader and businesswoman. She kept detailed records of all her squadrons' "purchases" (thieveries) and profits from the stolen goods, or "trans-shipping of goods," as she preferred.

Too Powerful for Her Own Good

At the height of her reign, Cheng I Sao commanded a confederation consisting of 800 war junks and 1,000 smaller junks and boats, with a total population of 7,000 to 8,000 men and women. The confederation became so powerful there were few commercial vessels to attack. With shipping at a near standstill, large forces mobilized to crush the confederation.

Brutality Mixed with Intelligence

In 1808, Cheng I Sao began ravaging the villages west of Bocca Tigris (an estuary of the Canton River). Aboard her flagship were Richard Glasspoole, a British officer captured off the East Indian ship *Marquis of Ely*, and some of his sailors. They were aboard waiting ransom. During the five months aboard, he and his men were forced to participate in the attacks or risk torture and death. Noticing the Englishmen were not attacking enthusiastically, Cheng I Sao added an incentive: the equivalent of $20 for each head each man brought back aboard.

> **Pirate Yarns** _____
>
> History states Cheng I Sao went into battle with the heads of her enemies tied casually around her neck, hanging by their pigtails. Although this might be true, she was not the one who invented the practice of wearing enemy heads. According to Glasspoole, the English sailors who were offered money for each man they killed were the first to board her flagship with the heads slung over their necks and shoulders. Some men had as many as six heads tied together by their pigtails.

The Dynasty Collapses

Cheng I Sao's downfall came not from outside forces, but from dissension within her ranks. She had taken as her lover and second in command Chang Paou, her late husband's lieutenant.

Kwo Po Tai, the commander of the Black Squadron, was jealous of Chang's position of command and his relationship with Cheng I Sao. The next time Chang called for assistance in battle, Kwo ignored him. Chang managed to survive.

The Battle Between Chang and Kwo

Chang and his Red Squadron sailed to meet Kwo in battle. A savage engagement between former compatriots began. Ships were blown up or burned. Boarding parties slaughtered crews. Thousands of men died before Chang withdrew.

An astute warrior, Kwo realized the battle marked the end of the powerful pirate federation. He surrendered to Chinese officials and was offered a position of naval mandarin (admiral of a river fleet) if he agreed to hunt down the very men who once sailed with him. Kwo agreed. The Chinese government offered amnesty to all pirates in February 1810. Upon learning of Kwo's desertion and new position, Cheng I Sao persuaded Chang to surrender the remaining confederation and seek pardons. Only the Yellow and Green Squadrons refused to surrender. It must have been a shocking sight to see hundreds of war junks, with colored pennants flying, sailing up the river to Canton.

Coming to Terms

The government's initial terms not to her liking, Cheng I Sao left. She returned to the governor general's house in Canton the following day, this time unarmed and with a company of pirate wives and children. The terms were accepted. Chang was offered the position of naval mandarin, a fleet of 20 junks, and a large sum of money. The men were all offered the choice of returning to their homes with full pardons or joining the imperial navy under Chang's command. Thousands instead decided to join the army and hunt down the pirates of the old Yellow and Green Squadrons. According to the terms, Cheng I Sao was directed to retire. She agreed.

What became of Cheng I Sao? She spent the next 34 years happily running a gambling establishment and brothel in Canton until her death at age 60.

Shap-ng-tsai

One of the great Asian warlords of the 1840s was Shap-ng-tsai (a.k.a Shap-n'-gtzai). With a fleet of 70 war junks, he extorted protection money from Hong Kong to the Vietnamese Peninsula. His activities along the Gulf of Tonkin were ignored until his junks began capturing British opium ships. The East India Company convinced the Royal Navy that they had to deal with this threat as the pirates were also attacking merchant ships along the Pearl River on their way to Canton.

Pirate Junks Running from Paddle Steamers

In October 1849, Commander Dalrymple Hay commanded a force of two steam-driven warships, the paddle steamer *Phlegethon*, and eight junks of the Chinese navy in search of Shap. Hay chased the pirate fleet more than 1,000 miles. Believing they were safe, Shap's pirates anchored in the harbor at Tonkin.

Shap Trapped

When Shap realized he was trapped, there was no time to pull up anchor and escape. Hay entered the harbor over the sandbar at high tide with guns blazing. As the wind shifted and

---

Treasure Chest

The British were the first to ship opium into their country. Control over the opium routes and distribution was the cause of great tension between the Chinese and British, which eventually erupted into the First Opium War (1839–1842). It was a huge financial commodity for British shipping and businesses. In the year 1843 alone, some 40,000 chests of opium were shipped to England.

caught in their sails, the still-anchored junks began to turn with all 240 guns now pointed at each other rather than at the British. A slaughter ensued. Some 1,800 pirates were killed, and 58 junks were sunk. Miraculously, Shap escaped. He was offered the standard pardon and a commission in the Chinese navy.

The *Real* Dragon Lady

China's civil war in the 1920s brought piracy back to her shores. And again, it was a woman who commanded a fleet.

Sailing the waters of the South China seas between 1922 and 1939, Lai Choi San (a.k.a. Lai Sho Sz'en) was born into a pirate family. Her father owned seven fully armed and armored junks. The officials in Macao had made him an "inspector," essentially pardoning one pirate to then catch or restrain others. After his death, Lai took over and increased the size of her fleet to 12 ships.

Known in China as "the queen of the Macao pirates," Lao made her fortune through thievery, ransoming, and demanding tribute. Her notoriety was established in 1930 when Aleko Lilius, an American journalist, investigated the sudden increase in attacks upon Western ships. In an article, Lilius stated that he paid Lao for the privilege of going on raids with her. He states he was able to take one photograph of her, but it is not known if it still exists.

> **Treasure Chest**
>
> Aleko Lilius's article on Lai Choi San fired the imaginations of many readers when it first appeared. One man in particular was fascinated with her story. Milton Caniff, the author and artist of the famous 1930s comic strip "Terry and the Pirates." He created his famous main female villain, the Dragon Lady, as a glamorized homage to Lai Choi San.

(As of this writing no reputable pirate historian has been able to verify Lilius's claims. Though his son adamantly defends his father's story as true, with no "hard" evidence Lao's story needs to be classified as fiction.)

Just When You Thought It Was Safe

Piracy has never been—and will probably never be—wiped out. Following the end of World War II—and the subsequent downsizing of world navies—piracy worldwide again began to rise. Such activities increased throughout the second half of the twentieth century. Pirate attacks spiked dramatically in the 1980s and 1990s with the advent of modern seaborne technologies, including handheld GPS (global positioning system) devices, high-powered telescopes, and super-fast speedboats, as well as an increase in the accessibility of automatic weapons, hand and rocket-propelled grenades, and other weapons.

The primary reason for modern-day pirates is no different from what it has ever been: a chance for easy money.

Attacks on merchant ships have occurred along the old pirate haunts of Brazil, the Caribbean, the Mediterranean, the Western and Eastern coasts of Africa, and the Far East. Fishermen in the Philippines augment their meager incomes by attacking local seafarers. In the Malacca Strait, the shortest route between India and China, the heaviest concentration of modern merchant shipping is also the prime target of modern pirates. And raids against both cargo and luxury vessels off Somalia have become a serious international concern.

Chasing Oil

Large cargo ships and oil tankers are targets. Using converted fishing boats with modern engines, modern-day pirates are able to maneuver alongside large ships beneath radar. Then using rope ladders, grappling hooks, or thick bamboo poles, they climb aboard and surprise the crew. Modern crews are no match for heavily armed pirates. Taking what they can find—supplies, money, personal belongings, and electronic equipment—they disappear as quickly as they strike.

Over the past several years, pirates have been known to seize oil tankers. They change the ships' registration numbers, names, logs, and then sail them to remote ports and sell them.

Coming Full Circle

The West Indies and Caribbean islands, as well as the Indian Ocean, are again pirate hot spots. Drug smugglers attack ships they suspect might reveal their identities. Pleasure yachts are also prime targets. The boats are worth millions, as are the passengers and their jewels. Spotting a potential victim, pirates often "hang back" until nightfall. When the boat anchors after dark, they strike, killing the inhabitants and speeding off with their treasure.

Seas Still Deadly

The ICC International Maritime Bureau tracks every registered pirate attack committed around the world. Pirate attacks in 2005 included the following:

- **February 28, 2005.** A tug towing a barge of coal was attacked off the port of Penang (Malay Peninsula). The pirates abducted the captain and chief officer and held them for ransom.

- **March 12, 2005.** An oil tanker sailing Indonesian waters was attacked by 35 heavily armed pirates. The captain and chief officer were kidnapped.

- **March 14, 2005.** A Japanese tug towing a construction barge was attacked. Armed pirates in three motorized fishing boats abducted the captain, chief engineer, and a crewman.

- **June 6, 2005.** Three gunmen in a white speedboat opened fire on a bulk carrier near the capital of Somalia. The U.S.S. *Gonzalez* responded to their distress call, firing flares and .50 machine guns.

- **June 30, 2005.** A UN–charted ship carrying aid to tsunami victims in Somalia (North Africa) was hijacked by pirates. The 10-person crew and vessel are still missing.

- **October 19, 2005.** A Maltese-registered freighter carrying iron ore from South Africa to Europe was seized by pirates off Somalia. A ransom for the ship and crew has since been demanded.

- **November 5, 2005.** A Bahamian-registered luxury cruise liner was attacked by heavily armed pirates in two speedboats. The pirates fired automatic weapons and rocket-propelled grenades into the ship. Fortunately for the passengers and crew, the pirates were unable to pursue and seize the liner after the ship's crew took evasive action and headed out to deeper waters.

The International Maritime Bureau reported (as late as November 11, 2005) that pirates operating off Somalia were holding seven ships seized in 2005. The attack on the cruise liner was the nineteenth such attack that year.

As Cruel as Ever

Not much has changed since the beginning of time. We tend to view pirates throughout history as romantic characters. A few may have been, most were not. Whatever their motivations, most were and are nothing more than seaborne brigands. These modern cutthroats shun the notoriety of pirates of the past, preferring to strike and disappear before anyone can identify them.

In fact, we view all pirates in the twenty-first century as being nothing more than murderers and thieves. Those persons traveling the oceans and living along the coastlines during the golden age of piracy had similar perceptions of their own pirates in their own era.

That in mind, 200 years hence, what will be the perception of pirates operating in the first decade of the twenty-first century? Will they be elevated to the mythic, romantic heights to which we've raised the likes of Blackbeard, Captain Morgan, and Bartholomew Roberts? Or will they be seen for who and what they really were?

The Least You Need to Know

- ◆ The Portuguese were the first to trade in the Far East. Their attempts at a monopoly failed when England and Holland were able to establish their own trading settlements.

- ◆ The Chinese junk was a versatile ship that easily converted from a fishing vessel to a warship. The crew's entire family lived aboard.

- ◆ Cheng-Chi-Lung created the first large pirate fleet that dared to regularly attack European ships. After his arrest and execution, his son, Koxinga, went on a quest for revenge.

- ◆ The invention of the steam-powered ship enabled the Royal Navy to destroy the last sizeable organized pirate fleet.

- ◆ Lai Choi Shan emerged in the 1920s and continued her family's tradition of piracy.

- ◆ Piracy has seen a resurgence in the twenty-first century. This is due to modern seaborne technologies and the ever-present motivation of greed.

Appendix A

Glossary

aft The sternward part of a ship.

asafetida A vile-smelling spice that was used in cooking and stinkpot bombs.

backstaff A navigational tool invented in 1595 that measures latitude.

baldric A broad strip of leather worn diagonally across the right or left shoulder that held a sword and sheath at waist or hip level.

barca-longa A two or three-masted Mediterranean ship with a single lugsail on each mast.

billet An appointment, post, or berth on a ship. The term is also used to denote how many people an area can accommodate.

black gold trade The term used to describe the African slave trade.

blunt Slang for money or coin.

booty Treasure, loot.

bowsprit Long spar running from the bow of the ship from which the jibs (and sprit, in older ships) are set.

broadside Firing all the artillery on one side of the ship simultaneously.

broadsides Single-sheet paper printed on one side.

buccaneer   A French or English game-hunter living on the island of Hispaniola in the seventeenth century. In time, the buccaneers became pirates, thus "buccaneer" became synonymous with "pirate."

careen   To lean a ship on its side to clean or repair.

carrack   A large heavily built ship for travel and cargo with a castlelike superstructure at the bow and stern.

cat-o'-nine tails   A nine-strand whip used by European navies to mete out punishment. If the crime was theft, the end of each strand was knotted. It is no longer in use.

cob   A silver piece-of-eight roughly minted in the Spanish Main.

cochineal   Natural red powder dye made from crushed female cochineal (Dactylopius coccus) bugs found on some cactus species in Mexico.

corsair   The Anglicized French term for "privateer," loosely applied to those privateers and pirates who hailed from the Barbary Coast of North Africa.

ditty bag   Seaman's personal bag made from canvas.

doubloon   A Spanish gold coin worth four silver pieces-of-eight.

fire-ship   Ship loaded with incendiary material that is ignited and steered toward enemy ships.

flintlock   Firing mechanism used in pistols and rifles. Also used to refer to the flintlock pistol.

fore   The forward section (bow) of a ship.

fore-and-aft sails   Sails set in line with the length of the ship, such as the jibs and staysails.

fore-and-aft rigged   Ship with all her sails placed in line with the length of the ship.

forecastle (fo'c'sle)   A short raised deck at the fore end of a vessel, originally a stand for archers, now the place where seamen are berthed.

foremast   The foremost mast on a ship.

frigate   A fast, 3-masted, fully rigged ship carrying 20 to 50 guns on the main deck, with a raised quarterdeck and forecastle.

furl   Rolling up and securing a sail on a yard; also, rolling up a flag as in "furling the colors."

gibbet   A metal cage on a wooden gallows that held a corpse upright for viewing.

Golden Age of piracy   The period from 1692 to 1725 during which piracy flourished.

gunport   Square winged opening in the hull to aim and shoot the cannon.

gunwales   The upper edge of the side of a ship.

hard tack   A large round biscuit that was made with flour, water, and salt.

head   The ship's toilet area for the seamen, found in the "head" or fore part of the ship. Of a sail, the upper part.

hull   The body of a ship.

islet   A land mass off shore or a small island. Also references an area that becomes an island at high tide accessible only by a boat.

jib   Triangular-shaped sail that is attached to the bowsprit.

Jolly Roger   The somewhat affectionate albeit infamous moniker applied to the pirate flag, originally emblazoned with the skull and crossbones.

junk   The Chinese trading and fishing vessel. The term is a bastardization of the word *junco*, Portuguese for "vessel."

keel   The principal piece of wood that determines the length of a ship. The backbone of the timbers that make up the hull.

lateen sail   A triangular sail on a yard attached at a 45-degree angle to the mast.

letter of marque   Commission from a government official, legally allowing a person to seize goods and ships of that government's enemy.

lugsail   A four-sided sail that is secured to a yard just two thirds the length of the sail, so that the sail hangs obliquely.

Mestizo   A child of European and Amerindian parents who has a 50-50 ratio of mixed heritage.

mizzenmast   The sternward mast of a three-masted ship.

muster book   The record of everyone who is sailing on a ship.

nautical knot   The sea equivalent of 1.15 miles.

nimcha   An Algerian sword hilt with squared hook pommel.

no quarter   No mercy given to captives; surrender not accepted. Defeated opponents would be killed rather than captured. This was often the policy if opponents resisted after being invited to lay down their arms.

"on the account"   A term meaning that a voyage was being mounted where no money would be paid to a pirate until treasure was captured. The expression "no prey, no pay" stems from this arrangement.

passes   Issued by warring countries to evade their enemy's navy and privateers. They used neutral countries to secretly ship cargo and weapons.

piece-of-eight   Silver Spanish coin used as currency of the time. It was worth approximately $1. It would be broken into sections to make change.

pink   A small narrow-sterned square-rigged ship used primarily for fishing or transporting merchandise.

pinnace   A small eight-oared boat sometimes carried on larger vessels for shallow water excursions.

Pirate Round   Pirate hunting route from North America to New Providence on to Madagascar and back to North America.

portage   The transporting of a canoe or small boat overland.

powder monkey   Generally, a young boy who carried gunpowder from below deck to the upper-deck cannon.

press gang   Men authorized by the Navy to seize able-bodied men by force to crew ships.

privateer   A state-sanctioned "civilian" sailor (or vessel) that was commissioned to attack enemy cities and ships. During war, privateers became adjuncts to their state's navy.

prize   A captured ship.

quarterdeck   The section where the ship's wheel is situated, and from where the captain, master, or officer of the watch issues orders to the men.

ratlines   The rope rungs attached to the shrouds forming steps to climb.

rigging   The term for all the rope lines used on a ship.

running rigging   Lines that move and control all the sails.

ship's articles (letters of agreement)   Detailed obligations that each crew member promised to observe while at sea.

shipwright   One who designs and builds ships.

shrouds   The ropes that support the masts and are part of the standing rigging of the ship. The ratlines are attached to these, making a "rope ladder" to the mastheads.

sloop   A small, single-masted sailing ship. The name applied to any of a number of small warships prior to the 1760s.

Spanish Main   The geographical area encompassing the sea and all of the islands bordering the Caribbean Sea and the Gulf of Mexico (Trinidad to Cuba and the Straits of Florida) and consisting of Mexico and Central and South America.

spar   General term for wood poles used to secure rigging and sails.

square–rigged   Term for a ship with yards and sails that were set horizontally across the masts.

standing rigging   The unmoving lines that support the masts and yards.

swag   Any amount of goods or treasure.

sweet trade   Term for going pirating.

Teach's Hole   Blackbeard's favorite anchorage spot on Ocracoke Inlet, North Carolina.

tin   Slang for money or coins.

tricorn   A three-cornered cocked hat.

unfurl   Loosen a sail or free a flag.

wracking trade   The business of diving for sunken treasure.

yard   The long wooden spar centered on a mast that supports the sail.

yardarm   Both ends of a yard.

Appendix B

Resources

Books

Abbott, John, S. C. *Captain William Kidd, and Others of the Pirates or Buccaneers Who Ravaged the Seas, the Islands, and the Continents of America Two Hundred Years Ago*. New York: Dodd, Mead & Co., 1874.

Bolster, W. Jeffrey. *Black Jacks: African American Seaman in the Age of Sail*. Cambridge: Harvard University Press, 1998.

Brenner, Robert. *London's Overseas Traders 1550–1653*. Cambridge: Cambridge University Press, 1993.

Burg, B. R. *Sodomy and the Pirate Tradition: English Sea Rovers in the Seventeenth-Century Caribbean*. New York: New York University Press, 1984.

Carse, Robert. *The Age of Piracy*. New York: Grosset & Dunlop, Inc., 1965.

Casson, Lionel. *The Ancient Mariners: Seafarers and Sea Fighters of the Mediterranean in Ancient Times*. New York: Minerva, 1959.

Chambers, Anne. *Granuaile, the Life and Times of Grace O'Malley c. 1530–1603*. Dublin: Wolfhound Press, 1979.

Cordingly, David. *Under the Black Flag, the Romance and the Reality of Life Among the Pirates*. New York: Random House, 1995.

Cordingly, David (ed.). *Pirates, Terror on the High Seas from the Caribbean to the South China Sea*. North Dighton, MA: JG Press, 1998.

Creighton, Margaret S., and Lisa Norling. *Iron Men, Wooden Women, Gender and Seafaring in the Atlantic World, 1700–1920*. Baltimore: John Hopkins University Press, 1996.

Currey, E. Hamilton, R.N. *Sea Wolves of the Mediterranean*. London: John Murray, 1910.

Davis, William C. *The Pirates Laffite: The Treacherous World of the Corsairs of the Gulf*. Orlando: Harcourt, Inc., 2005.

Defoe, Daniel. *A General History of Pyrates*. New York: Dover Publications, Inc., 1999.

Dow, George Francis, and John Henry Edmonds. *The Pirates of the New England Coast, 1630–1730*. New York: Dover Publications, Inc., 1996.

Druett, Joan. *Hen Frigates. Passion and Peril, Nineteenth-Century Women at Sea*. New York: Simon & Schuster, 1998.

———. *Rough Medicine, Surgeons at Sea in the Age of Sail*. New York: Routledge, 2000.

———. *She Captains, Heroines and Hellions of the Sea*. New York: Simon & Schuster, 2000.

Dudszus, Alfred, and Ernest Henriot. *Dictionary of Ship Types. Ships, Boats and Rafts Under Oar or Sail*. London: Conway Maritime Press, Ltd., 1986.

Earle, Peter. *The Sack of Panama, Sir Henry Morgan's Adventures on the Spanish Main*. New York: The Viking Press, 1981.

————. *The Pirate Wars: Pirates Vs. the Legitimate Navies of the New World.* London: Methuen Books, 2004.

Eastman, Tamara, and Constance Bond. *The Pirate Trial of Anne Bonney and Mary Read.* Cambria by the Sea, CA: Fern Canyon Press, 2000.

Ellms, Charles. *The Pirates' Own Book, or Authentic Narratives of the Lives, Exploits, and Executions of the Most Celebrated Sea Robbers.* New York: Dover Publications Inc., 1993.

Esquemelin, Alexander Olivier. *The Buccaneers of America.* Glorieta: The Rio Grande Press, Inc. 1992.

Gosse, Philip. *The History of Piracy, Famous Adventures & Daring Deeds of Certain Notorious Freebooters of the Spanish Main.* Glorieta: The Rio Grande Press, Inc. 1988.

————. *The Pirates' Who's Who, Giving Particulars of the Lives & Deaths of the Pirates & Buccaneers.* Glorieta: The Rio Grande Press, Inc., 1988.

Grossman, Anne Chotzinoff, and Lisa Grossman Thomas. *Lobscouse & Spotted Dog.* New York: W. W. Norton & Company, Inc., 1997.

Harland, John. *Seamanship in the Age of Sail.* Annapolis: Naval Institute Press, 1996.

Hayward, Arthur L. *The Book of Pirates.* London: Cassell & Company, Ltd., 1957.

Honychurch, Penelope N. *Caribbean Wild Plants and Their Uses.* London: Macmillan Publishers Ltd., 1980.

Jameson, J. F. (ed.). *Privateering and Piracy in the Colonial Period.* New York: MacMillan Company, 1923.

Kemp, Peter (ed.). *The Oxford Companion to Ships and the Sea.* Oxford: Oxford University Press, 1988.

King, Dean, with John B. Hattendorf and J. Worth Estes. *A Sea of Words, A Lexicon and Companion for Patrick O'Brian's Seafaring Tales.* New York: Henry Holt and Co., 1995.

Konstam, Angus. *The History of Pirates.* Guilford: The Lyons Press, 2002.

Lampe, Christine Markel (ed.). *No Quarter Given Magazine.* Vol. 1 through Vol. 12, 1993–2005.

Lee, Robert E. *Blackbeard the Pirate, A Reappraisal of His Life and Times.* North Carolina: John F. Blair Publishing, 1974.

Lind, Lew. *Sea Jargon. A Dictionary of the Unwritten Language of the Sea.* Cambridge: Patrick Stephens Ltd., 1982.

Marx, Jenifer. *Pirates and Privateers of the Caribbean.* Malabar: Krieger Publishing Co., 1992.

Marx, Robert. *Pirate Port, The Story of the Sunken City of Port Royal.* Cleveland: The World Publishing Co., 1967.

McCarthy, Kevin M. *Twenty Florida Pirates.* Sarasota: Pineapple Press, Inc., 1994.

Mitchell, David. *Pirates, An Illustrated History.* New York: The Dial Press, 1976.

Ormerod, H. A. *Piracy in the Ancient World.* New York: Dorset Press, 1987.

Partridge, Eric, abridged by Jacqueline Simpson. *Dictionary of Historical Slang.* London: Penguin Books, 1972.

Pennell, C. R. (ed.). *Bandits at Sea: A Pirates Reader.* New York: New York University Press, 2001.

Pickford, Nigel. *The Atlas of Ship Wrecks & Treasure, The History, Location, and Treasure of Ships Lost at Sea.* New York: D. K. Publishing, 1994.

Reinhardt, David. *Pirates and Piracy.* New York: Konecky & Konecky, 1997.

Ritchie, Robert C. *Captain Kidd and the War Against the Pirates.* Cambridge: Harvard University Press, 1986.

Rogozinski, Jan. *Honor Among Thieves, Captain Kidd, Henry Every, and the Pirate Democracy in the Indian Ocean.* Mechanicsburg: Stackpole Books, 2000.

Stanley, Jo. *Bold in Her Breeches, Women Pirates Across the Ages.* London: Pandora Press, 1995.

Stark, Suzanne J. *Female Tars, Women Aboard Ship in the Age of Sail.* Annapolis: Naval Institute Press, 1996.

Seitz, Don Carlos (ed.). *The Tryal of Capt. William Kidd For Murther & Piracy Upon Six Several Indictments.* New York: Rufus Rockwell Wilson, Inc., 1936.

———. *Under the Black Flag, Exploits of the Most Notorious Pirates.* New York: Dover Publications, Inc., 2002.

Stephens, John Richard (ed.). *Captured by Pirates.* Cambria by the Sea, CA: Fern Canyon Press, 1996.

Takakjian, Portia. *The 32-Gun Frigate Essex, Anatomy of the Ship.* Cedarburg: Phoenix Publications, Inc., 1990.

Verrill, A. Hyatt. *The Real Story of Pirates.* Glorieta: The Rio Grande Press, 1989.

Ward, Ralph T. *Pirates in History.* Baltimore: York Press, 1974.

Wilbur, C. Keith, M.D. *Pirates & Patriots of the Revolution, An Illustrated Encyclopedia of Colonial Seamanship.* Chester, CT: The Globe Pequot Press, 1984.

———. *Revolutionary Medicine, 1700–1800.* Chester, CT: The Globe Pequot Press, 1997.

Williams, Robert. *Memoirs of a Buccaneer.* London: Mills & Boon, Ltd., 1900.

Woodbury, George. *The Great Days of Piracy in the West Indies.* New York: W. W. Norton & Company, Inc., 1951.

Websites

The following are just a few of the websites providing piratical information one can find on the Internet. All of the URLs are valid as of this printing.

www.noquartergiven.net   *No Quarter Given* quarterly pirate magazine.

www.deadmentellnotales.com/library.shtml   Online bookstore for fiction and nonfiction books about pirates.

www.cindyvallar.com/piratearticles.html   Website for Cindy Valler, author of *Pirates and Privateers: The History of Maritime Piracy.*

www.whydah.com   The treasure of the Expedition *Whydah* (ongoing archaeological underwater dig).

www.qaronline.org   *Queen Anne's Revenge* (ongoing archaeological underwater dig of Blackbeard's ship salvage site).

http://nautarch.tamu.edu/portroyal/   Archaeological site for Port Royal, Jamaica.

www.geocities.com/Tokyo/Garden/5213/   Isle of Tortuga and general pirate information site.

www.nmm.ac.uk   National Maritime Museum.

www.royalnavalmuseum.org/   British Royal Naval Museum.

www.du.edu/~jcalvert/tech/cannon.htm   History of cannons and gunpowder.

www.coinsite.com/content/Articles/Spanish.asp   Spanish-American colonial coinage.

www.geocities.com/cdelegas/PIRACYWEBSITE_legal.html   International Maritime Bureau and site concerning modern piracy.

www.pirateinfo.com/main.php   General pirate information site.

www.privateerdragons.org/pirates_famous.html#A   General pirate biography information site.

www.kipar.org/piratical-resources   General pirate information site.

http://blindkat.hedgewisch.net/pirates/pirates.html   General pirate information site.

Reenactment Groups

Each pirate reenactment group has its own unique style. Some are more authentic in portrayal than others. The bottom line is they enjoy the camaraderie of the brotherhood as did pirates of old, and members share their historical knowledge with one another. Fun is a must. Depending on the group, reenactors attend renaissance fairs and sailing festivals. They speak at museums and schools. Often, to attend an event, groups travel much farther than their bases of operation. Those listed in this appendix are open to new members. For an extensive list of pirate groups to join, refer to *No Quarter Given* magazine (their website is listed in Appendix B).

Australia

The Pirates of the Morningstar (www.piratesofthemorningstar.com). Based in Brisbane, Queensland, this group re-creates pirates from 1650 to 1770. Biggest reenactment group in the southern hemisphere. Maria Symes, Captain: omegastar@optusnet.com.au.

United Kingdom

Seathieves Pirate Association (seathieves@yahoo.com). Based in the Midlands, but travels the world. Authentic reconstruction of life as a member of a pirate crew during the Golden Age. Dave Underhill, Quartermaster: dave@selab.co.uk.

United States

In the Mid-Atlantic and Midwest:

Blackbeard's Crew. The group organizes a pirate festival in Hampton, Virginia, which is now in its sixth year. Pernell Taylor, Captain: capnpern@pyracy.com.

Revered Order of Pirates and Rogues (www.reveredorderofpiratesandrogues. com). A new group formed in the Tidewater, Virginia area, they portray pirates as a social group of freebooters, rogues, and scallywags. Sam Nailbauer, Captain: naibs2000@yahoo.com.

The Pirate Brethren (www.piratebrethren.com). Based in Maryland, Pennsylvania, Virginia, and Delaware, this group is interested in historically accurate portrayals of pirates while still having fun. John Macek, Captain: jbmacek@yahoo.com.

The Church of the Jolly Roger (www.jamesjessup.com/CJR). Based in Pittsburgh, Pennsylvania, the group travels to events throughout the United States and Canada. James Jessup, Captain: amergin@jamesjessup.com.

The Scurvvy Dawgs (www.scurvvydawgs.com). Based in Waukesha, Wisconsin, the group is strong on swashbuckling humor with a flair for history. Christopher Reeves, Captain: lightningjack@scurvvydawgs.com.

In the Southeast:

Devil Men of Cape Fear (pyratenc@yahoo.com). Based in Wilmington, North Carolina, the group mans a 24-foot, eighteenth-century rigged sailboat with guns, striving for authenticity, hard sailing, and fun.

The Crew of the Devil's Shadow (Johnnyreb6@aol.com). Based in Irmo, South Carolina, the group operates in the Carolinas and Georgia. Interested in portraying pirates from the 1700s to the 1800s.

Thee Bleeding Rose (www.theebleedingrose.com). Based in Palm Bay, Florida, this group portrays the Barbary corsairs as crew, merchants, and tavern owners. They welcome all races and nationalities, as did corsairs. Diversity and varying experience levels are welcome. Steven Rosbury, Captain: captain@theebleedingrose.com.

In the Pacific Northwest and Southwest:

The Pirates of Treasure Island (piratestreasisland@yahoo.com). Based in Mountlake Terrace, Washington, they entertain at fundraisers, charity events, renaissance fairs, and parades throughout the state.

The Lion's Share (lionsharepirates@yahoo.com). Based in Chandler, Arizona, this pirate performance group combines improvisational comedy, historic reenactment, and music.

Port Royal Privateers (www.portroyalprivateers.org). Based in Southern California, the group has been in existence for more than 12 years. Members share a passion for the history, adventure, and romance of the years 1600 through 1800. Varied interests and keen interaction with people at various nautical events and Renaissance fairs keeps everyone entertained.

Clan Darksail (www.geocities.com/LaVillaABroka). Based in Southern California, this is a historic group as well as a pirates-for-hire group. They have appeared in movies and television, and they play at renaissance fairs. Richard Rasner, Quartermaster: mn_detective@yahoo.com.

House Deterioatta (www.deterioatta.com). Based in Southern California, the group is a long-running true heavy-fighting pirate group with weekly practices. Michael Gonzales, First Mate: kanazuchi@earthlink.net.

The Pirates of Rogues Cove (www.roguescove.org). Based in Las Vegas, this is a nonprofit educational and theatrical re-creation group. Rakaiah McSherry, Scribe: Rakaiah@roguescove.org.

The Texican Privateers (www.texicanprivateers.com). Based in Houston, Texas, the crew portrays the years 1550 through 1865.

Index

C

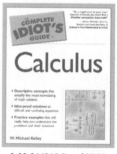

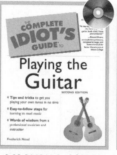